Thinking Ethically

A Handbook for Making Moral Choices

Scott Gelfand, Ph.D., J.D.

DETROIT

About the Author

Scott Gelfand, Ph.D., J.D., is a certified philosophical counselor and a tenured associate professor in the Department of Philosophy at Oklahoma State University. He received his Ph.D. in philosophy from the University of Maryland and his J.D. from Georgetown University Law Center. He's devoted the last decade of his career to trying to better understand moral and political division in the United States as well as ways to heal or alleviate this division. His academic publications focus on a variety of issues in ethics, including theoretical ethics, biomedical ethics, and research ethics. Scott spends most of his time in Tulsa, Oklahoma; Chicago, Illinois; and Barcelona, Spain.

Thinking Ethically

A Handbook for Making Moral Choices

Scott Gelfand, Ph.D., J.D.

Thinking Ethically: A Handbook for Making Moral Choices

Visible Ink Press®
43311 Joy Rd., #414
Canton, MI 48187-2075

Visible Ink Press® is a registered trademark of Visible Ink Press LLC.

Managing Editor: Kevin S. Hile
Cover Design: John Gouin, Graphikitchen, LLC
Page Design and Typesetting: Kevin S. Hile
Proofreaders: Larry Baker and Suzanne Goraj

Cover image: Shutterstock.

ISBNs
Paperback: 978-1-57859-843-4
Hardcover: 978-1-57859-879-3
eBook: 978-1-57859-880-9

Cataloging-in-Publication data is on file at the Library of Congress.

Printed in the United States of America.

10 9 8 7 6 5 4 3 2 1

Contents

Also from Visible Ink Press

Censoring God: The History of the Lost Books (and Other Excluded Scriptures)
By Jim Willis
ISBN: 978-1-57859-732-1

Conspiracies and Secret Societies: The Complete Dossier of Hidden Plots and Schemes, 3rd edition
By Brad Steiger and Sherry Hansen Steiger
ISBN: 978-1-57859-767-3

The Constitution Explained: A Guide for Every American
By David L. Hudson, Jr., J.D.
ISBN: 978-1-57859-750-5

Control: MKUltra, Chemtrails, and the Conspiracy to Suppress the Masses
By Nick Redfern
ISBN: 978-1-57859-638-6

Cover-Ups & Secrets: The Complete Guide to Government Conspiracies, Manipulations & Deceptions
By Nick Redfern
ISBN: 978-1-57859-679-9

Disinformation and You: Identify Propaganda and Manipulation
By Marie D. Jones
ISBN: 978-1-57859-740-6

Earth Magic: Your Complete Guide to Natural Spells, Potions, Plants, Herbs, Witchcraft, and More
By Marie D. Jones
ISBN: 978-1-57859-697-3

Everyday Magic: How to Live a Mindful, Meaningful, Magical Life
By Marie D. Jones and Denise A. Agnew
ISBN: 978-1-57859-721-5

Grifters, Frauds, and Crooks: True Stories of American Corruption
By Richard Estep
ISBN: 978-1-57859-796-3

The Handy American Government Answer Book: How Washington, Politics, and Elections Work
By Gina Misiroglu
ISBN: 978-1-57859-639-3

The Handy Bible Answer Book
By Jennifer R. Prince
ISBN: 978-1-57859-478-8

The Handy Christianity Answer Book
By Stephen A. Werner, Ph.D.
ISBN: 978-1-57859-686-7

The Handy Civics Answer Book: How to Be a Good Citizen
By David L. Hudson, Jr., J.D.
ISBN: 978-1-57859-811-3

The Handy Islam Answer Book
By John Renard, Ph.D.
ISBN: 978-1-57859-510-5

The Handy Law Answer Book, 2nd edition
By David L. Hudson, Jr., J.D.
ISBN: 978-1-57859-592-1

The Handy Philosophy Answer Book
By Naomi Zack, Ph.D.
ISBN: 978-1-57859-226-5

The Handy Psychology Answer Book, 2nd edition
By Lisa J. Cohen, Ph.D.
ISBN: 978-1-57859-508-2

The Handy Religion Answer Book, 2nd edition
By John Renard, Ph.D.
ISBN: 978-1-57859-379-8

The Handy Supreme Court Answer Book: The History and Issues Explained, 2nd edition
By David L. Hudson Jr., J.D.
ISBN: 978-1-57859-782-6

The Handy Western Philosophy Answer Book: The Ancient Greek Influence on Modern Understanding
By Ed D'Angelo, Ph.D.
ISBN: 978-1-57859-556-3

The Religion Book: Places, Prophets, Saints, and Seers
By Jim Willis
ISBN: 978-1-57859-151-0

Photo Sources

BootBearWDC (Flickr): p. 135.
California Department of Corrections and Rehabilitation: p. 42.
Deror avi (Wikicommons): p. 143.
Egghead06 (Wikicommons): p. 182.
Robert J. Fisch: p. 25.
Scott Gelfand: pp. 50, 51.
Getty Images: p. 266.
Justin Hoch: p. 88.
Library of Congress: p. 38.
Metropolitan Museum of Art: p. 264.
National Portrait Gallery, London: pp. 36, 100.
Nature.com: p. 240.
Paul Arthur Schilpp: p. 92.
Shutterstock: pp. 2, 4, 6, 8, 12, 14, 15, 17, 24, 27, 29, 31, 35, 39, 43, 48, 55, 59, 62, 63, 65, 66, 70, 74, 75, 90, 93, 95, 97, 98, 103, 105, 110, 111, 112, 115, 116, 122, 126, 127, 130, 131, 137, 139, 142, 145, 148, 149, 151, 153, 156, 160, 163, 164, 167, 171, 172, 176, 177, 180, 188, 190, 198, 200, 201, 205, 207, 211, 217, 218, 222, 224, 228, 231, 235, 236, 241, 246, 252, 253, 258, 259, 261, 270, 272, 275, 277, 280, 282, 284, 286.
SupremeCourt.gov: p. 245.
Ula Zarosa (Wikicommons): 165.
U.S. Marshals Service: p. 283.
Public domain: pp. 57, 71, 183, 247.

Introduction

As a philosophy professor and certified philosophical counselor who specializes in ethics and relationships, I'm often approached by friends, students, and family members wrestling with moral questions. Is it okay to lie to spare someone's feelings or to protect confidential information? Is it wrong to read my child's text messages? What about lying about my age on a dating app? What if everyone does it? What should I do if I hear someone say something hateful or a use a slur? When, if ever, is it right to withdraw life-sustaining treatment from a terminally ill loved one?

My usual response: "It depends."

Some questions focus on social policy and politics. Should the government recognize the right to abortions? Is the death penalty a just punishment? Should colleges and universities admit only the most qualified applicants? Has political correctness gone too far?

Again, my usual response is: "It depends." I like to follow up with: "What do you think?"

In this book, we'll explore a wide range of moral questions. You'll notice that I rarely share my own opinions, and I'll *never* tell you what to believe. Instead, as we explore these questions, we'll focus on how people make moral and political decisions and how we might improve this process. My goal isn't to convince you of any viewpoint. Rather, I hope to help you clarify your own.

That said, when I mention I rarely offer my own opinions, I'm not suggesting that I believe "anything goes." I'm certainly not defending behaviors like lying to swindle money that can be used to pay for a dinner in a fancy restaurant, stealing candy just to satisfy a sweet tooth, cheating on a partner to fulfill a sexual fantasy, or breaking a promise to drive a friend to a doctor's appointment because I'd prefer to be at the mall or the beach.

I'm confident you agree that these behaviors are wrong in most instances. In fact, I'm confident that you, I, and most other Americans embrace a remarkably

similar set of basic moral of "rules of thumb"—general principles like "It's wrong to steal," "It's wrong to lie," "It's wrong to break promises," and "It's right or praiseworthy to donate to charity."

Morality gets interesting when we encounter situations that seem to be exceptions to these rules of thumb. Sure, it's wrong to lie or break a promise, but is it *always* wrong?

Imagine you received this book as a gift. But before you opened it, you came across a disturbing story about me. A few months ago, I was at home when I heard a noise come from my living room. When I investigated, I found an intruder pointing a gun at me. "I'm here to kill your best friend, Joseph," he said. "I know he lives here. Is he home right now?"

Let's further imagine you learned I answered truthfully: "Yes. He's asleep in his bedroom." Seconds later, I heard the gunshot that ended Joseph's life.

Shocked, you decide to dig a little deeper and find a news article about the incident. When the journalist asked me why I didn't lie, I responded: "Seriously? Isn't it obvious? Everyone knows it's wrong to lie. Joseph was a good friend, and I miss him deeply. But I wasn't going to lie, even if that was the only way to prevent him from being murdered. At least I can sleep at night knowing I did the right thing. Telling the truth in this situation proves that I'm a morally good person."

After reading the article, would you still want to read this book? Would you want to take my class or schedule a philosophical counseling appointment to explore an important relationship? Probably not.

The intruder scenario highlights several ideas or questions I'd like to explore with you. First and foremost, although we often rely on moral rules—like "It's wrong to lie" or "It's wrong to steal"—most of us understand that these rules are just rules of thumb and not absolute principles. That is, we believe these rules should generally be followed, but we also recognize that there are exceptions.

If our moral rules of thumb have exceptions, how do we know when to follow them and when to set them aside? If lying to an armed intruder is morally permissible (or even obligatory), what other situations might justify bending or breaking the rules of thumb we typically uphold?

Is it permissible to lie to a friend about liking their new haircut if the truth would crush their confidence and they have a job interview in less than an hour? What about stealing life-saving medicine you can't afford in order to save your sick child or even a stranger? Is it wrong to break a promise you made to a dying parent to never reconnect with an estranged sibling if doing so would bring about a reconciliation?

These are hard questions. And they lead to other hard questions like: "Are there any moral rules that should never be broken?" "If it's okay to lie/steal/break a promise in some cases, what makes those cases special or different?" "Do good intentions make a morally wrong act acceptable or even right?" Much of this book will explore these questions.

Rather than tell you what you should do in difficult moral situations—because frankly, I probably don't know—I aim to help you develop the tools to think through these questions yourself.

Along the way, I hope you'll come to see something that changed my life: Living a moral life and thinking about morality isn't just complex or complicated. It's also rich, deeply human, and beautiful. When I say it's complex or complicated, I don't mean it's complicated like calculus or physics. Rather, it's complicated in the sense that many moral questions have many possible answers and frequently more than one plausible or reasonable answer. And often, our initial judgments shift as we learn more.

Take a simple question: "Is lying wrong?" Most of us would answer, "Yes." But what if lying is the only way to keep a surprise party secret or to save a close friend's life? When we learn those details, we might reassess our answer or discover we're no longer sure what's right.

The same thing happens when asked whether we support a social policy or a new law. At first, we might believe the answer is obvious. But as we learn more about the details and real-world consequences, we often realize that it isn't as simple as we thought.

Consider the death penalty. Suppose a recently enacted law mandates execution for anyone who intentionally kills another person. At first, we might support it, believing that justice demands such a punishment.

But now imagine you learn that a similar law in a neighboring state led to the wrongful execution of 10

innocent people. That knowledge might motivate you to reconsider.

Now imagine you also learn that the law has deterred 50 potential murders. That is, 50 innocent lives were saved because the would-be murderers were afraid of being executed. Does that mean it must be a good and just law? Should we support it?

Regardless of what you believe, can you understand how or why a rational, moral individual might disagree with you? Can you see why I claim it's not so easy to determine whether a law is moral or just?

Each chapter in this book begins with a moral question. As we explore these questions, I'll introduce key concepts from moral philosophy that help us think more clearly and deeply about morality. While each chapter can stand on its own, reading them in order will provide a richer and more cohesive experience, as later discussions build on earlier ones.

As you progress, you won't just gain insights into moral philosophy; you'll also gain a deeper understanding of your own core values. This in turn will help you make moral and political decisions that are consistent with these values.

Many psychologists, philosophers, and ethicists believe that most people have a deep, natural desire to be aligned with the good. That is, we want to live with moral integrity and do what's right. Discovering what are our true core values and understanding how we make moral decisions—and how we might make them better—helps us live more intentionally and morally.

One of the most powerful outcomes of exploring our own moral beliefs is gaining a deeper understanding of others. When we understand *why* our family members, friends, and even strangers agree or disagree with us, we get more than just intellectual clarity. We get insight into who they are and what matters to them. That kind of understanding fosters deeper, more meaningful relationships. We feel closer to others when we truly grasp not just *what* they believe, but *why*.

What may be even more powerful is what we learn about each other in the process. As we reflect on our own values and better understand the values of others, we often come to realize that our moral disagreements aren't as deep or irreconcilable as they first appear.

We all know that we live in a time of deep political and cultural division. We've been told this division is deeper than at any time in recent history. Some politicians and influencers go further, claiming that those whose political beliefs are different from our own—those on "the other side"—aren't just wrong, but immoral, ignorant, dangerous, or even un-American. They want us to believe that if those on the other side gain power, they'll destroy everything we care about.

When we see others this way, maintaining friendships or respectful relationships, even with family members, can seem to be impossible. We stop seeing one another as fellow citizens and begin to see one another as enemies. I find this to be heartbreaking, and I'm not alone.

In a 2018 public opinion poll, 83% of Americans said they believed that division between Americans was a serious problem. Even more, 90%, said we should try to find common ground with those who see things differently. But is this really possible?

After more than two decades of teaching and writing about morality, I believe it is. In fact, I'm convinced that we Americans (and those in the rest of the world) share a much wider and deeper set of moral values than we've been led to believe. And we'll see, when we explore the different questions posed in this book, that at a foundational level, we agree much more often than we disagree.

This shared foundation makes real, meaningful, and productive moral dialogue possible, even with those whose moral and political views are different from our own. Not only that, but rather than pushing us apart, these conversations can actually strengthen our relationships and bring us closer together. If nothing else, I hope this book helps make your next Thanksgiving dinner something to anticipate with optimism rather than dread.

Most of all, I hope this book inspires you to engage more deeply with the beautiful and fascinating world of morality. Share the questions you encounter here with family, friends, and anyone else willing to think out loud with you. Talking about morality and social issues can be challenging, but also meaningful, eye-opening, and even fun. And if these conversations deepen and strengthen our relationships along the way, well, that's just icing on the cake.

Dedication

To Avi, Leah, and Boas —
For your support, love, and patience — you made this labor of love possible.

To my mother, Shirley —
Who taught me to hear between the words and keep going when life gets difficult.

To my sister, Joanne —
A constant supporter of my path and a quiet force behind my life as an ethicist and professor.

And to my brother, Michael, and sister-in-law, Mary —
Steady and always there when it counts.

1: Breaking Promises

The Issue: Can you only be a moral person if you keep your promises in every circumstance imaginable, or are there exceptions to the rule?

Imagine walking past a hospital and suddenly hearing someone sobbing behind you. Turning around, you see a stranger rushing toward you, tears streaming down her face. She hugs you and cries, "I don't want to kill my husband. I promised him I'd do everything I could to keep him alive, but now I know that will only prolong his suffering."

You try to think of words to calm her, but before anything comes to mind, she steps back, looks directly into your eyes, and says: "I don't know what to do. What would you do if you were me?"

What would you do if you were in a similar situation? Would you keep your promise and consent to aggressive medical treatment, even if this would mean your loved one might suffer intensely for another week before inevitably passing away? Or would you choose to stop the treatment, allowing your loved one to die more peacefully, even though this means breaking your promise?

As a member of a hospital ethics committee, I wrestled with moral questions like these. The committee's job was to help physicians, nurses, social workers, patients, and their families navigate morally challenging situations. Frequently, there were no easy answers, and our discussions lingered with me for days or even weeks.

The most agonizing cases involved decisions about withdrawing life-sustaining treatment—stopping ar-

tificial nutrition or hydration or removing a ventilator—knowing that doing so would hasten a patient's death.

One case I can't forget involved Mary, a loving wife, who faced the same dilemma described above. She had promised her husband she would do everything possible to keep him alive. The medical team's prognosis was clear: There was no chance of recovery. Continuing treatment might extend his life for another week or 10 days, but in that time, he would likely endure significant pain. The alternative was to withdraw life-sustaining treatment, allowing him a peaceful, less painful death.

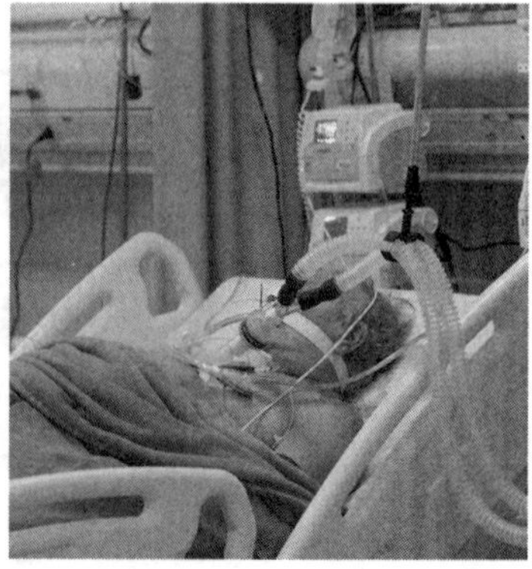

Mary made a promise to her husband to do everything she could to keep him alive in a desperate medical situation, but then she found out the doctors could only extend his life for a few painful days. What would you do if you were her?

Mary understood all of this, and she believed stopping treatment was the most compassionate choice. Yet she couldn't forget her promise. Time and again, she reminded the committee (and perhaps herself) that she had vowed to do everything in her power to keep her husband alive.

If you were a member of the ethics committee and Mary asked you for advice, what would you say? Should she break her promise and choose what she believed was the most compassionate option? Or should she uphold her promise, even if it meant prolonging her husband's suffering? More importantly, how would you justify your advice?

Are Promises, Like Pie Crusts, Made to Be Broken?

As our committee discussed Mary's case, I found myself thinking about Immanuel Kant, one of the great Western philosophers (discussed in Chapter 5). For Kant, breaking promises is always morally wrong, no exceptions. Alexander Hamilton echoed this idea, stating simply: "A promise should never be broken."

Who was I to argue with them?

Fortunately, I didn't have to. Others had done so already. John Stuart Mill, another one of the greats, believed that doing the right thing involved bringing about the best consequences: If breaking a promise leads to better consequences than keeping it, then breaking it is the right thing to do. On a lighter note, self-help author Soul Dancer, in a book entitled *Pay Me What I'm Worth: Say It. Mean It. Get It.*, once wrote: "Promises, like gardens, need weeding from time to time to produce healthy results."

Perhaps one of my students said it best: "Surely, if in a fit of anger, I promise to break someone's legs or take their life, I shouldn't keep my promise."

I wondered whether to share these insights with Mary. Would it help to tell her about Kant, Mill, or Soul Dancer? Would my student's words offer an important insight? Or would all of this only complicate an already difficult decision?

Discussion

How Do We Make Ethical Decisions or Judgments?

As I mentioned in the Introduction, when making moral decisions or judgments, we often start by looking for a "rule of thumb" that seems to fit the case. Rules of thumb are simple, commonsense, rather than formal principles, that we can use when making decisions. When discussing lying, we might appeal to the rule of thumb "It's morally wrong to lie," "We should tell the truth," or something similar. I'm confident that when reading about Mary's case, many of you initially thought about the rule of thumb "It's morally wrong to break promises." This may have led you to tentatively conclude that Mary shouldn't break her promise and should do everything possible to save her husband's life.

However, we also know that rules of thumb have exceptions. When confronting complex or confusing choices, we may acknowledge that a rule of thumb applies, but after thinking about it for a little while or learning more details, we may discover or have a hunch

Is it okay to borrow money from a family member under false pretenses as long as you pay it back?

that the situation we're confronting might, in fact, be an exception to the rule.

Sometimes these exceptions arise when more than one rule of thumb applies to a situation and these rules conflict with each other. One of the applicable rules tells us we should do X, while a different rule tells us we should do something other than X.

Imagine I promise to take a close friend to dinner at a nice restaurant, but I later discover I don't have enough money. The only way I can think of to get the money is to ask my brother to lend it to me, but I know he wouldn't lend it to me if I told him the truth, that I wanted the money to pay for a meal at a nice restaurant. But if I lie and tell him I need the money to pay my electric bill, he'd probably lend me the money. Should I break my promise to my friend, which would eliminate the need to lie to my brother? Or should I lie to my brother in order to get the money to keep my promise?

Two rules of thumb are at work in this situation, and they're in conflict: (1) It's wrong to break promises and (2) It's wrong to lie. In this situation, no matter what I do, I'll break one of the rules. I can break the rule "It's wrong to lie," which will result in me obtaining the money to take my friend to dinner and thereby abide by the rule "It's wrong to break promises." Or I can break the rule "It's wrong to break promises" and not take my friend to dinner, and this will allow me not to violate the rule "It's wrong to lie."

Beyond conflicting principles, there are a variety of other reasons or factors that might lead us to conclude or at least question whether we should break a rule of thumb. These include situational, circumstantial, and historical factors.

Two rules of thumb are at work in this situation, and they're in conflict: (1) It's wrong to break promises and (2) It's wrong to lie.

Kirsten's Promise: A Lesson in Moral Complexity

I once read a short novel, *Kirsten's Promise,* to my daughter and son. This novel illustrates the idea that details matter and sometimes there are exceptions to rules of thumb, such as "It's wrong to break promises."

In this historical novel for young teens, Kirsten is walking to school with her dog, Caro. Suddenly Caro runs down a tree-covered hill. Kirsten hears another dog growl and runs after Caro, fearing the growling dog will attack her own dog. In a clearing at the bottom of the hill, Kirsten sees a boy aiming a rifle at Caro. Then she sees a big, black, growling dog sitting on a pile of stones and nearby a covered wagon on its side.

After restraining Caro, Kirsten asks the boy what happened.

At first he tells her to leave him alone, but after some coaxing he tells her his name is Ezra and explains that he and his mother were traveling to California to meet his father and then they had an accident.

Kirsten offers to get help, but Ezra rejects her offer and asks her to promise not to tell anyone about him.

Kirsten makes the promise.

The next morning, Kirsten leaves for school, but leaves Caro at home. She returns to the clearing and is again met by the growling dog that's still standing on the pile of rocks. She sees Ezra, who seems thin and weak, and offers him and his dog some food.

Kirsten notices traces of tears on Ezra's cheeks, and she invites him to her house. She explains he can stay with her family until his mother returns. She even offers to start a search party for his mother, who might be lost or hurt.

Ezra finally admits that his mother was killed when a tree fell on her after the accident, and he buried his mother under the pile of rocks that the big dog won't leave. He explains that he promised his mother before she died that he'd stay with the wagon and reminds Kirsten she promised not to tell anyone about him.

Kirsten now faces a choice. She can keep her promise and not tell anyone about Ezra, or she can return home and tell her parents everything.

She chooses the latter. When she and her father return to the clearing, her father tells Ezra how much courage

he has. He says that even though Ezra promised to stay with the wagon, his mother would have wanted him to leave if staying wouldn't make anything better.

The novel ends with Kirsten's father telling her she did the right thing when she broke her promise and told him about Ezra. Her actions saved Ezra's life.

When I read this novel to my children, I especially liked it because it was meant to teach teen readers about the complexity of morality. Young children are taught to obey simple rules, like "Lying is wrong" or "Breaking promises is wrong," but the main point of this book was that the rules we learn as children are really rules of thumb. If abiding by the rule of thumb "It's wrong to break promises" will lead to horrible consequences, breaking the rule might be the right thing to do. If I remember correctly, I told my children this applies to other rules as well, like keeping secrets or not lying.

The Nature of Promise-Keeping

Sometimes understanding what underlies or motivates a rule of thumb helps us better understand when it's permissible or even right to violate it. Let's explore what underlies the rule of thumb "It's wrong to break promises."

It might be helpful to begin this exploration by getting a better understanding of the nature of promises. Philosophers and ethicists have constructed numerous complex analyses of what constitutes a promise, but let's keep it simple. A promise is essentially a declaration of intent. The promisor (the one who makes the promise) is saying that they're committed to do something (or refrain from doing something) in the future. Thus, we see that promises are understood as being relational and can be conceived of as a deal or agreement between the promisor and the promisee (the one who receives or accepts the promise).

Pinky swears are not required when making a promise (though they are a fun addition!). Basically, a promise can be understood as any declaration of intent between two parties.

Promises only work or make sense if the promisee trusts the promisor. If I ask a friend to lend me some money and promise to repay her in three weeks, she'll be disinclined to accept my promise and lend me the money if I've repeatedly broken promises in the past. Put simply, promises depend on trust.

Some have suggested that promises only make sense within a broader social "institution of promise-keeping." If we generally trust people to honor their promises, we're more likely to accept them, and this is the case even if we don't know the promisor well. If, however, promises are routinely broken, the system or institution collapses. The words "I promise" lose their meaning, and the social benefits of the institution are lost.

Consider a scenario in which you recently moved into a new apartment. Your new neighbor knocks on the door and asks if he can borrow $20 to buy medicine for his child, promising to repay you at the end of the week when he gets paid. If you believe most people keep their promises (and you have the money), you're likely to accept his promise and lend the money or at the very least consider doing so. If, on the other hand, you believe most people don't keep their promises, you're less likely to even consider accepting his promise and lending the money. (That's not to say that you won't just *give* him the money, but that's a different matter.)

Why Is It Usually Wrong to Break Promises?

So, why do we embrace the rule of thumb "It's morally wrong to break a promise"? I suggest it's more than simply being nice.

First, and perhaps foremost, breaking a promise is usually unfair to both the promisor and the promisee. If I promise to help you move next week in exchange for your help with my move this week and then I break the promise even though you helped me, you suffer an injustice. You don't get the benefit (help with moving) you deserved. Not only that, but I received a benefit (help with moving) I didn't deserve. I repeat, that's unfair.

Second, breaking promises erodes trust in relationships. Trust is essential in friendships and other relationships. These relationships are valuable, and break-

Breaking a promise damages relationships by eroding trust between two or more people. Worse, if you never intended to keep a promise, you're just wasting the other person's time when they could have looked to others for help.

ing promises diminishes trust and thereby harms these relationships. Thus, breaking promises is wrong.

Third, and closely related to the first, not keeping promises frequently harms others who don't deserve to be harmed. Most of us believe we shouldn't intentionally harm others, or we embrace a rule of thumb like "It's morally wrong to intentionally harm others." If intentionally breaking promises harms others, and it's wrong to intentionally harm others, it follows that it's wrong to intentionally break promises.

Staying with the moving example, if you hadn't relied on me to keep my promise to help you move, you might have tried to find someone else to help. But you counted on me to keep my promise and didn't even try to find others to help. When I don't show up, you're in a worse position than you would have been in if you hadn't relied on me. I harmed you. Not only that, but the time you spent helping me move could have been spent doing something that benefitted you or was more enjoyable. You could have cleaned your house, spent time with a friend, or taken a walk in the woods. You lost this opportunity, and this harmed you.

Fourth, some say we have control over very little in life, but one thing we can control is our own behavior and whether we live with integrity. If we promise to do something and then break the promise, our integrity is damaged.

Finally, as suggested above, if promise-keeping is indeed a social institution, breaking promises harms or weakens this institution. As trust erodes, fewer people will agree to promises, and the social benefits associated with promises will be decreased or even lost.

It may now be clearer why we believe that Kirsten's decision to break her promise to Ezra wasn't wrong. Unlike many cases where breaking a promise is unfair, Kirsten's behavior didn't involve any unfairness to Ezra, and Kirsten didn't receive any unearned benefits. Nor did she harm Ezra. In addition, she didn't sully her reputation or injure her relationships with others. In fact, breaking the promise strengthened her relationship with her father (and maybe others, even Ezra), who believed she demonstrated maturity and good sense.

Unlike many cases where breaking a promise is unfair, Kirsten's behavior didn't involve any unfairness to Ezra, and Kirsten didn't receive any unearned benefits.

Let's look at some other scenarios.

Breaking a Promise for Self-Gain

Imagine I was job hunting and asked you, my friend, if the company you worked for was hiring.

"I'm going to be completely honest with you," you replied. "We're trying to hire someone to work in my office, but I'm worried that if they hire you, I'll look bad. You're more qualified than me. I think I'll be up for promotion in a few months, but if you're working in the same office, they might offer the promotion to you."

In response, I said, "If you help me get the job, I promise I won't apply for a promotion until you are promoted or quit your job."

You accepted my promise and recommended me, and I was hired. Several months later, a promotion opens up and I'm considering applying, even though I promised you I wouldn't.

In this case, breaking the promise seems to be unfair and might harm you. With your assistance, I obtained a job that I couldn't get without your assistance. Fairness dictates I should keep my part of the bargain and not break my promise. I received a benefit as a result of you accepting my promise, and if I break the promise, you'll be susceptible to harm that you wouldn't have been susceptible to if you didn't accept my promise. It would be unfair to put you in this position. I'll leave the rest of this analysis to you, but it appears that breaking this promise would be wrong.

Prisoner's Dilemma and Promise Keeping

The Prisoner's Dilemma, a classic thought experiment, involves two burglars, creatively named A and B, who are arrested and interrogated separately. Each faces a choice:

- If both refuse to testify against each the other, they'll each serve one year for a lesser crime.
- If one testifies and the other doesn't, the testifier walks free, and the other gets a five-year sentence.
- If both testify, they each serve three years.

Notice that the best combined outcome for both will be realized if both refuse to testify. Conversely, if both testify, the worst combined outcome will be realized.

Number Testifying	*Total Years Incarcerated*
0	2 (1-year sentence for each)
1	5 (no sentence for testifier and 5-year sentence for non-testifier)
2	6 (three-year sentence for each)

Imagine you and I are the burglars, and before we were separated and interrogated, we promised each other that we would remain loyal and refuse to testify, resulting in us receiving the best combined sentence.

Now we are separated and interrogated, and each of us must decide whether to testify against the other or refuse to do so. Should I keep my promise? Can I trust you to keep your promise? Doubt begins to set in. I realize that no matter what I choose to do, you'll be better off breaking the promise.

(*cont. p. 11*)

(*cont. from p. 10*)

If I keep my promise not to testify and you keep yours, we'll each be sentenced to one year in prison. But if I keep my promise and you break yours and testify against me, you'll be set free. Thus, if I keep my promise, you're better off breaking yours.

If I break my promise and you keep yours, you'll be sentenced to five years. If I break my promise and you do the same, you'll be sentenced to three years. Thus, if I break my promise, you'll be better off breaking yours.

Thus, regardless of what I do, if you are motivated by self-interest, you will break your promise. It's actually worse than this because I know you may be thinking this, and you know that I know this. Thus, you know that I may be thinking of breaking my promise, and you're not going to be a fool and spend five years behind bars while I'm set free. So, you're even more likely to break your promise. Of course, I realize this and am even more fearful that you'll break your promise.

What would you do?

What is the way out of the Prisoner's Dilemma? How can we increase the likelihood we'll both keep our promise, which will result in the best combined sentence—a combined two years in prison? Introduce external consequences.

If we give someone on the outside the power to punish us if we break our promise and believe this person will administer the punishment, assuming it's severe enough, we'll both have a reason to believe the other will keep their promise. For example, if we know that if we break our promise, someone on the outside will break both of our legs, we'll each have a reason to keep our promise and to believe the other will keep their promise. This will result in us getting the best combined sentence.

Perhaps social pressure is enough to ensure people keep promises when it comes to normal cases of promise keeping. After all, we don't want to be pariahs. This is an example of peer pressure leading to good results!

Breaking a Promise to Prevent Harm

Let's consider another scenario involving the prevention of harm. Imagine you're in the grocery store with Jason, a friend of yours. You reach for your wallet (or phone) only to discover you left it at home, and Jason offers to pay for the groceries as long as you promise to pay him back as soon as you get home. You agree and make the promise.

After putting away the groceries, Jason reminds you of your promise.

Would it be morally right to break your promise and not repay Jason? Why or why not?

Your initial response might be: "Of course I should repay Jason. I promised him I'd do so, and breaking promises is wrong—that's a rule of thumb."

If you asked me whether it was right to repay Jason, I'd probably begin by saying, "It depends. It's usually wrong to break a promise—that is, you and I embrace the rule of thumb 'It's wrong to break a promise'—therefore repaying Jason is *probably* the right thing to do. Before committing to a final answer, however, I want to learn more about the situation. Details matter."

What if, on the drive home, you learned Jason was a recovering heroin addict and intends to use the money to buy heroin? Suddenly, it's not at all clear breaking your promise would be wrong. In fact, it might be wrong to keep your promise.

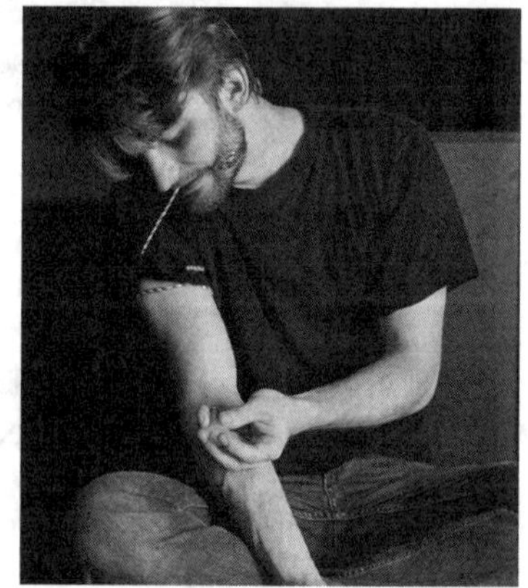

Is it wrong to renege on a promise to pay back money if you knew for certain that money would be spent for something harmful such as illicit drugs?

What if, on the drive home, you learned Jason was on a diet and intends to use the money to buy a pie and a quart of chocolate milk?

Should you break your promise? Before answering, you might want more details.

Suppose Jason told you, "You know I'm always on a diet, but I never told you I'm borderline diabetic and have some other health problems. I'm so tired of always watching what I eat. My doctors told me I must stay on this diet for at least two years,

and maybe the rest of my life. If I eat the pie and drink the chocolate milk, I might end up in the hospital, but I don't care. Right now, all I want is to forget about my diet, relax, and eat some pie. And maybe, if I am hospitalized, my ex will feel guilty and want to get back together."

What's the right thing to do knowing this?

Ultimately, as I said in the Introduction, morality is complex or complicated, but it's not complicated like calculus or physics. Rather, morality is complicated because it's frequently not clear what is the right thing to do. We might believe we should do something like break a promise or lie, but at the same time we believe we shouldn't break a promise or lie. It's as though we're being pulled in two different directions.

Ethicists, and with practice all of us, can think of numerous ways of changing and complicating hypothetical situations, thereby making it difficult to determine what's the right thing to do and revealing the complexity of the moral life.

Suppose you're in the grocery store line and discover you don't have your wallet and phone. You tell the cashier you can't buy the groceries now, but you'll come back later. The person behind you is a stranger, and she taps you on the shoulder.

"I overheard what you said to the cashier. I'm always forgetting my wallet, and several times in the past someone in line paid for my groceries. I can't do that, but if you promise to repay me as soon as you arrive at your house, I'll pay for your groceries."

You agree. Perhaps, because she doesn't know you well and isn't confident you'll repay her, she suggests she'll drive you home and you can repay her when you get there.

While driving to your house, she tells you she has diabetes.

"I've been on a special diet for over six months. As soon as you repay me, I'm going to my favorite bakery where I'll use the money to buy a cherry pie and a quart of milk. I may end up in the hospital after eating the pie, but I'll risk it."

This situation introduces new factors and seems to be murkier. It might be right or even praiseworthy not to repay a friend if she's going to use the money in a way that will possibly result in her being hospitalized, but

Making ethical decisions is almost never a black-versus-white choice. Often, the answer is: "It depends!"

in this new case the person you promised to repay isn't a friend. It's a stranger. Might it be wrong to be so intrusive in the life of a stranger and break your promise?

At least for me, it's less obvious that breaking the promise is the right thing to do in this situation. That said, I'm confident others disagree. (In Chapter 8, we'll explore why it might be permissible or even obligatory to prioritize the well-being of friends and family.)

It Depends

As a certified philosophical counselor and an ethics professor, I'm often asked by friends, students, family members, and others what is the right thing to do in a given situation. My favorite answer is: "It depends." That might sound evasive, but if you think about it, you may begin to do the same. When we make moral decisions or judgments, we typically begin by appealing to rules of thumb. However, we frequently find exceptions to these rules. We might remember a short story, television show, or personal story where breaking the rule of thumb was the right thing to do. Simply put, details matter. Before we determine what's morally right and wrong, we need to understand the context. And even then, we may be uncertain.

Sometimes I think that trying to make the right moral decision is much like creating a piece of art. If you asked a great painter whether you should put a little blue dot in the corner of a canvas, they'll likely respond: "I don't know" or "It depends. I need to see the whole painting and understand what you're trying to achieve." Similarly, when it comes to morality, there frequently aren't simple answers. Details matter. Context matters. History matters. Intentions matter.

Back to Mary

Let's return to Mary and her end-of-life decision. The health care providers wanted to discontinue treatment because continuing it would likely unnecessarily prolong Mary's husband's suffering. Mary, however, had promised her husband that she'd do everything to keep him alive. At the same time, Mary didn't want her husband to suffer unnecessarily. Put differently, Mary embraced two rules of thumb that couldn't be reconciled. She could abide by the rule "It's wrong to break promises" or the rule "It's wrong to act in ways that cause others to suffer unnecessarily," but she couldn't abide by both rules. This is known as an *ethical dilemma*—a situation in which it appears that there's no right answer or no way to meet your moral obligations.

After consulting with the ethics committee and medical team, Mary met with a social worker. Hospital social workers are like saints with excellent communication skills. I wasn't present during any of their conversations, but within 24 hours, Mary agreed to terminate aggressive treatment, even though this meant her husband would die sooner than he would die with these treatments.

Perhaps, during the course of several meetings, the social worker helped Mary realize that although she embraced the rule of thumb "It's wrong to break promises," she embraced other rules of thumb as well. Like almost all of us, Mary most likely embraced the rule of thumb "We should try to eliminate the unnecessary pain others are experiencing, especially if the pain is great and eliminating it doesn't cost us very much."

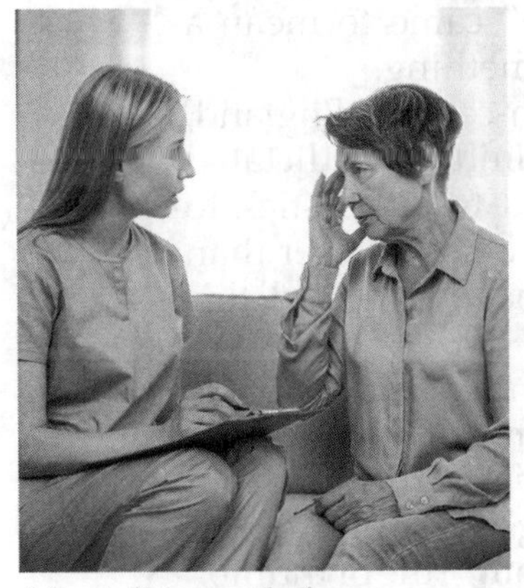

After talking with the professionals, including a social worker, Mary decided it made more sense to forgo her promise in order to prevent her husband from further suffering.

Again, I'm just speculating, but I wouldn't be surprised if at some point the social worker asked Mary to think about whether she believed it was more important to keep her promise or to do what she could to alleviate the pain of someone she loved deeply. Assuming this is

what happened, presumably Mary concluded that even though at first it seemed wrong to break a promise she made to her husband, it wouldn't be wrong if doing so would alleviate his suffering.

How do *you* arrive at answers when a rule of thumb doesn't seem to apply, or two rules of thumb give conflicting answers? Do *you* believe it's ever acceptable—or even obligatory—to break a promise to prevent harm to someone you love? Do our obligations change depending on the relationship we have with the person affected?

These are complex questions with no easy answers. But by exploring them, we gain deeper insight into how we make moral judgments and whether there might be ways to improve our decision-making processes.

Rule of Thumb

There is disagreement concerning the etymology of the idiom "rule of thumb," but the different accounts share some similarities. Some claim that builders, cooks, and others used their thumbs to obtain a quick measurement. A builder could use their thumb, which was approximately one inch wide, instead of a measuring stick to quickly measure a piece of wood or a stone. Cooks or chefs could roll dough between their thumb and forefinger to determine whether dough had the right consistency. Thus, the idiom "rule of thumb" came to mean a quick, rough measurement of something.

Some claim that in seventeenth-century England, there was an actual "rule of thumb" that dictated that a man was legally permitted to use a stick to beat his wife, but the stick could be no thicker than his thumb. Some etymologists have criticized this explanation.

The Wordsworth Dictionary of Phrase and Fable defines "rule of thumb" as: "A rough, guesswork measure; practice or experience, as distinguished from theory, as a guide for doing things."

Regardless of its origin, the idiom "rule of thumb" has come to be used by many to refer to a quick or rough rule that has exceptions. It is distinguished from "principle" in that principles are carefully articulated and don't obviously admit exceptions.

Are We Really So Divided?

Open a news website, listen to a current events podcast, or scroll through social media and you'll quickly encounter someone saying Americans are deeply divided, engaged in culture war, or more polarized than ever.

Our divisions are often framed in terms of moral and political beliefs. We see or hear those on the political left—Democrats, liberals, and progressives—criticizing the morality or political viewpoints of those on the right—Republicans or conservatives. Those who consider themselves to be religious might criticize those they believe are irreligious or not religious enough. Rural Americans often see urban dwellers as out of touch with their values, while those with higher education might criticize those without it. Of course, this is a two-way street. The right criticizes the left; the less religious criticize the more religious; urban dwellers criticize those living in rural areas; and those without higher education criticize those with it.

And yet, ironically, as mentioned in the Introduction, there is broad agreement among Americans that divi-

In the United States, especially, it seems as if differences in politics and social issues have created a deep schism that nobody can cross. But perhaps if we consider the fundamental humanity in both sides, we can see we aren't so different after all.

sion itself is a serious problem. A recent public opinion poll reveals 83% of Americans believe this.

Maybe We Aren't So Divided after All

Despite the constant rhetoric about division, I believe Americans aren't, in fact, as divided as we're made out to be. Throughout this book, I express confidence in predicting how most readers would answer many of the moral questions I pose. I say: "I'm confident that most readers ..." and "I imagine most of you ...." Why? Because, in my experience, Americans embrace a remarkably similar set of moral principles or rules of thumb.

Most of us agree that keeping promises is generally the right thing to do. Most of us agree that lying and stealing are usually wrong and that we shouldn't unnecessarily hurt others. We believe in fairness and helping those in need. These are not partisan or controversial ideological claims; rather, they're widely shared core moral beliefs.

We Embrace the Same Rules of Thumb

Perhaps the primary differences between Americans become apparent when we confront the hard cases or situations that can't be easily understood by appeal to one rule of thumb or a simple moral principle. Returning to Mary's case, just about all of us embrace the same two relevant rules of thumb:—"It's wrong to break promises" and "We should try to prevent unnecessary suffering." But in this case, we can't abide by or follow both rules.

Some may conclude Mary should keep her promise, while others may believe she should prioritize alleviating her husband's suffering. Thus, it seems there is significant disagreement concerning what's the right thing for Mary to do. But notice this: even if you and I disagree about what's the right thing to do, the disagreement isn't over the moral principles themselves. Both of us embrace the same rules of thumb. Our disagreement is over which of the two rules carries more weight. You might put more weight on the "wrong to break promis-

es" rule, while I might put more weight on the "prevent unnecessary suffering" rule.

Politicians, media personalities, and influencers seeking "clicks" benefit from amplifying division because it drives engagement and profits. But the truth is, most of us operate within a shared moral framework.

This is an important insight. Many of the moral disagreements (and as we'll see later, political disagreements as well) that seem to divide us are, at their core, not so deep. They often stem from shared moral commitments that are weighed differently.

Throughout this book, I'll continue to challenge the notion that Americans are hopelessly divided. Political and moral disagreements are tearing the United States apart and breaking up friendships, families, and other relationships. It doesn't have to be this way.

We should remember that politicians, media personalities, and influencers seeking "clicks" benefit from amplifying division because it drives engagement and profits. But the truth is that most of us operate within a shared moral framework. Recognizing that others embrace the same moral principles or rules of thumb that we embrace reminds us that we're all humans struggling to do what's best. This recognition makes it easier to respect, like, and care for those whose political and moral views are different from our own. Surely, this is a beautiful outcome.

Final Thoughts

The primary goal of this chapter was to explore the nature of promises and why we embrace the rule of thumb "It's wrong to break promises."

We've seen that promises can be understood as a declaration by the promisor to do or refrain from doing something in the future, and there are a variety of reasons why we should keep promises, including fairness, not harming others, developing a reputation for being trustworthy, and maintaining our integrity. However, we've also examined cases where breaking a promise might be the right thing to do, especially when doing so prevents significant harm.

A second goal was to begin exploring how we make moral decisions. When we're confronted with a moral decision, we usually begin by appealing to a moral rule of thumb like, "It's wrong to break promises," "It's wrong to lie," or "We should try to help people in need of assistance." In most situations, these rules of thumb do the job. They tell us what to do. But sometimes rules of thumb aren't enough or don't apply. When we say we embrace the rule of thumb "It's wrong to break promises," what we mean is that in most instances breaking promises is wrong, but there are some exceptions to this rule.

Frequently, exceptions to rules of thumb are present when following the rule of thumb will bring about bad or horrible consequences. Most of us agree, I imagine, that it's wrong to follow the rule "It's wrong to break promises" if keeping a promise will result in great suffering or someone's death, as in the story *Kirsten's Promise*.

Breaking a rule of thumb may also be right, or even unavoidable, when two different rules of thumb are relevant but the two are in conflict. When that happens, we must look deeper, weigh competing values, and make judgments based on the particulars of the situation.

The final goal of this chapter was to begin considering the issue of moral and political division in the United States. I suggested that claims concerning a divided America are largely exaggerated. If you were asked to list the moral rules of thumb that you embrace, I'm confident that most of those "on the other side" would say they embrace almost all the same rules. Republicans and Democrats, people from the city and rural areas, and religious and nonreligious people embrace the rules of thumb "It's wrong to lie," "It's wrong to steal," "It's wrong to break promises," "It's right to repay our debts," "It's right to give to charity or help people in need," and many others.

If we embrace the same basic rules of thumb, then perhaps our differences aren't as vast as we've been led to believe. Sure, we may disagree about which rules should take priority in difficult cases—cases in which the rules come into conflict—but even then, we're still working with the same rules.

In future chapters, we'll continue to explore how we make moral decisions when rules of thumb don't apply

and further examine the moral and political divisions in contemporary America.

2: Killing One to Save Many

The Issue: Is It Wrong to Kill One Innocent Person to Save 1,000,000? To Save 100? To Save Five?

Imagine you're a contestant on a new TV show called *Do the Right Thing*. The show challenges contestants to explain what they'd do in various hypothetical scenarios. For your first challenge, the host asks you to step into the role of a U.S. senator.

"There's a proposed bill in Congress that would allow the military to shoot down passenger airplanes hijacked by terrorists. Proponents argue it's essential to prevent terrorists from crashing hijacked planes into occupied office and apartment buildings, power plants, bridges, and other structures."

"Opponents," the host explains, "argue that shooting down passenger planes amounts to deliberately executing innocent people. Innocent passengers aboard planes will almost certainly die, as will people on the ground if falling parts of the plane hit them, their homes, or their places of work."

The host continues, "As you may know, the U.S. Senate will vote on a bill like this next week. If you were a senator, would you support it? Why or why not?"

Just 10 days after the show was aired, the senate and house voted in support of the bill, and 24 hours later the president signed it into law. Three months later, something you could never imagine happens. Your doorbell rings, and when you open it, you see the president of the United States, flanked by advisors and Secret Service agents.

"Hello," the president says, "I saw your appearance on *Do the Right Thing*, and I'd like to talk with you for a few minutes. May I come in?"

The American president calls you on the phone and begs you to help make a decision that will affect thousands of people. What do you do?

"Of course," you reply, wondering what's going on as you invite the president into your home.

The president wastes no time. "About an hour ago, four commercial airplanes were hijacked by terrorists. Our intelligence suggests that each plane is targeted to crash into a different nuclear reactor in the U.S. It's too late to evacuate the surrounding areas. If the reactors are hit, it's likely at least two of them will explode, spewing deadly radiation into the air. We estimate a minimum of 50,000 immediate deaths from the explosions, and in the following decade, up to 10 times that number will die prematurely from radiation exposure.

"As commander in chief, it's my responsibility to decide whether to shoot down these planes. The law you discussed on *Do the Right Thing* grants me the legal authority to take action, but my advisors and I are conflicted. Shooting down the planes will result in the deaths of hundreds of innocent people—both passengers onboard and people on the ground."

The president pauses for a few seconds, and then continues, "When I ran for office, I promised Americans I wouldn't rely solely on the so-called experts for every decision. One of my aides was particularly impressed by your appearance on *Do the Right Thing*, and after showing me the video, I thought it would be a good idea to hear your perspective on this situation."

You ask the president how many lives will be lost if the planes are shot down, and one of the president's advisors responds: "There are 648 people on the four planes, and we're confident they'll all die. In addition, we estimate 50 to 100 people will die as the wreckage falls onto homes or businesses. And as the president told you, if the reactors are struck, we expect 50,000 immediate fatalities from the explosions, followed by up to 500,000 more from radiation exposure."

The president leans forward, and with urgency in his voice says, "We don't have much time, maybe 10, 15

minutes. What do you think would be the right course of action?"

What would you advise the president? Should the planes be shot down? Why or why not?

Real and Not-So-Real Scenarios

As you'll see throughout this book, philosophers love hypothetical scenarios and cases. Some are absurd or far-fetched, while others closely resemble real life situations. Regardless, they serve an important purpose: They help us uncover what we really think about morality or what our true moral beliefs or commitments are.

The scenario above isn't as removed from real life as it might seem. On September 11, 2001, after terrorists crashed two commercial aircraft into the Twin Towers in New York and one into the Pentagon in Arlington, County, Virginia, the military identified a fourth plane heading toward Washington, D.C. Vice President Dick Cheney faced a similar moral question: Should he order the plane to be shot down or allow it to hit the terrorists' intended target, most likely resulting in much greater loss of life and property?

Cheney gave the order to shoot down the plane. However, before the military could act, as you may know, passengers stormed the plane's cockpit, forcing the plane to crash in a remote area of Pennsylvania. While all aboard perished, no one on the ground was killed.

Now let's look at a more extreme hypothetical case.

When the terrorist attacks of September 11, 2001, began, it became known ahead of time that one of the planes was heading toward Washington, D.C., and there was an opportunity to shoot it down before it crashed. Vice President Dick Cheney gave the order, but passengers on the plane took action first.

A Not-So-Real Scenario

Imagine waking up in a strange room. You're disoriented and confused. When you look around, you discover the room has no windows,

but there's a door. You try to open it, but it's locked. Panic sets in, and you start screaming and banging on the door, trying to get help. Suddenly a video screen in the corner of the room comes to life.

To your surprise, your closest friend appears on the screen. Before you can say anything, he says: "Hi. I imagine you're scared and confused. There's something I never told you: I work with the CIA. We recently uncovered a terrorist plot to destroy the United States. Twenty nuclear weapons have been placed in the country's 20 largest cities. If these weapons detonate, millions of people will die, and these cities will be uninhabitable for decades."

You try to interrupt and ask where you are and what this has to do with you, but your friend cuts you off. "Listen, we don't have much time. We captured the leader of the terrorist organization that placed the weapons, and under truth serum, he revealed the bombs are set to detonate at noon today. It's currently 11:50 a.m. We also learned there's one way to stop the detonation of the bombs, but to do this we need to get the password to the terrorist's cellphone. Without it, there's no way to prevent the attack. There's no doubt the terrorist is a mentally ill genius, and there's no way we'll be able to break into the phone in time. But the terrorist gave us an option: He'll give us the password if I kill an innocent person."

Confused and horrified, you ask what this has to do with you and why you're locked in the room.

"Let me explain what's going on and your role in this," your friend begins. "We know the terrorist designed the room you occupy. They arranged for you to be drugged, kidnapped, and locked in the room. If you look below the video screen, you'll see two buttons. The terrorist told us, if you push the button on the left, the red one, I have the option to go outside with a rifle and kill the first person I see. If I do so, he'll give us the password.

You're coerced into choosing between two buttons: pressing one will result in the death of one innocent person; pressing the other will kill millions.

I'm in a truck parked next to a public park. Most likely, the person I kill will be innocent, maybe even a child. But we're absolutely sure if you push the red button and I kill someone, we'll get the password for the phone and prevent a catastrophe. You may think we can't trust the terrorist, but just trust me. If you push the red button and I kill an innocent person, we'll be able to stop the bombs from exploding."

He pauses, then continues: "If you push the second button, the black one, I'll do nothing. The twenty nuclear weapons will detonate, killing millions."

Then he adds, "Just so you understand the situation, we don't know where you are. The terrorist told us, while under the influence of the truth serum, that regardless of which button you push, you'll be released unharmed from the room you currently occupy. If you don't push any button, however, the nuclear bombs will be detonated and you won't be released from the room until we find you, if we find you. We might not, and if that happens, you'll probably die from lack of hydration. It's that simple. It's now 11:55. Push a button or do nothing."

The television goes dark.

The clock is ticking.

What are you going to do? What should you do? Perhaps more interesting, how would you justify your choice?

I imagine if I were in this situation, I'd wish I could do nothing. Like many of you, I firmly embrace the rule of thumb "It's wrong to kill innocent people." At the same time, I'd be thinking that this might be one of those situations when following a rule of thumb is wrong. Perhaps, this is an exception. Since doing nothing would result in death of millions of innocent people and maybe the end of my own life, I'd reluctantly push the red button. Maybe not so reluctantly.

If I had to justify this decision after being released, I'd probably say that if I didn't push the button, millions of innocent people would have been killed. By pushing the red button, I ensured only one innocent person was killed. Certainly, one innocent person getting killed is better than millions being killed. I'm fairly certain most of you would make the same choice and provide the same justification.

Discussion

Rules of Thumb Revisited

As I explained in the previous chapter, when trying to justify our own moral decisions or judgments, we usually appeal to general moral rules or what are called rules of thumb.

For example, imagine our friend Polly lies to a cashier to get extra change—say Polly tells the cashier she gave him a $20 bill even though she really gave him a ten. We'd likely think to ourselves (or even tell Polly) that what she did was morally wrong. If pressed to justify this belief, we might say: "It's simple. Lying is wrong"—a rule of thumb—"and Polly lied; therefore, what she did was wrong."

In most situations, this type of simple argument—referring to a rule of thumb to justify our belief concerning the morality of an action—does a good job of

You made a promise to help a friend move to new digs, but what you really want to do is stay home and watch TV. In this case, the "breaking promises is wrong" rule is more likely to be compelling because your excuse not to keep your promise is rather weak and selfish.

explaining why we judge an act as right or wrong. If we learned Polly recently walked into a drug store and stole a candy bar, we'd likely conclude Polly did something wrong because we believe "Stealing is wrong"—a rule of thumb—"and Polly stole a candy bar; therefore, she did something wrong." Similarly, if we promised a friend we'd help him move to a new apartment but are now contemplating breaking the promise because we want to stay home and watch the latest episode of *The Bachelor*, we'd think: "Breaking promises is wrong"—a rule of thumb—"and I promised my friend I'd help him move; therefore, watching *The Bachelor* and breaking the promise to help my friend move would be wrong."

Exceptions to Rules of Thumb

But, as we already know, morality is complex or complicated, and sometimes we believe these rules of thumb don't work or apply, or there are exceptions to them. That is, occasionally we decide to violate a rule of thumb and at the same time believe our action was morally right.

Consider this scenario: Polly's surprise birthday party is next Friday. On Wednesday, you bump into her, and after a quick chat, Polly asks, "What are you doing on Friday night? Let's go out dancing."

How would you respond to Polly? Presumably, you don't want to spoil the surprise, but you also embrace the rule of thumb "Lying is morally wrong." Would you lie?

I imagine most of you would try to avoid lying outright (me too). But let's imagine you're caught off guard and can't think of an evasive answer. You're left with two choices: lie and keep the party a surprise or tell the truth and ruin the surprise.

Chances are, many of us would choose to lie in an effort not to spoil the surprise. Maybe, we'd say we were working late. If later in the day we think about the lie, we might tell ourselves it was a harmless white lie. Essentially, we're trying to convince ourselves we didn't act immorally or do something wrong. That is, we'd try to justify breaking the rule of thumb "Lying is wrong."

Now, imagine the party is a success. Polly walks through her front door and her friends yell "Surprise." It's obvious to everyone that Polly is ecstatically happy

Is keeping a secret about a surprise party a "lie"? Technically, yes, but most people would likely agree a little white lie like this is not a terrible thing because it didn't hurt anyone.

and moved by her friends' efforts to celebrate her birthday. She feels cared for or even loved.

During the party, Polly approaches you and says, "Last weekend, when I lied to the cashier, you told me lying was wrong. Yet a few days later, on Wednesday, you lied and told me you were working tonight. It seems like you believe lying is right for you but wrong for me. What's up with that?"

How might you respond to Polly?

If you're like me, you'd probably try to explain why the rule of thumb "Lying is wrong" applied to Polly when she lied to the cashier but not to you when you lied to keep the surprise party a secret.

Perhaps you'd say, "When you lied, you hurt someone. For all we know, the cashier was disciplined or even fired at the end of her shift. At the very least, she might have had to replace the missing $10 out of her own money. But no one was hurt as a result of my white lie. Therefore, your lying was wrong and mine wasn't." Or you might focus on motives or intentions and explain that you lied in an effort to increase Polly's

well-being or happiness. You were motivated by care or concern for your friend. These are good or praiseworthy motives. Polly's lie was different. It was motivated by selfishness or a desire to improve her own well-being. Since care and concern for others are praiseworthy motives, and selfishness and callous disregard for the well-being of others are blameworthy or morally bad motives, your lie was morally permissible, and Polly's was wrong.

Introduction to Ethical Theory

Knowing that "rules of thumb" have exceptions can make it difficult to identify what we truly believe is right or wrong. If it's acceptable to lie to keep a surprise party under wraps, then what about lying to avoid hurting someone's feelings? What about lying to get a better job or save money? Is it really wrong to lie about your age on a dating app? What if lots of people do the same thing?

Philosophers and ethicists have been aware of this difficulty for centuries. In response, some have attempted to develop a principle or a set of principles that explain when breaking a rule of thumb is permissible and why it's permissible. This principle or set of principles is called an *ethical theory*.

You might think of an ethical theory in the same way you think of a scientific theory. Scientific theories are supposed to explain or help us understand the physical world. For example, Newton's first law states that an object at rest stays at rest and a moving object moves in a straight line, unless some force compels it to change. This law helps us understand and predict the movement of objects.

Whereas scientific theories help us understand the physical world, ethical theories aim at helping us understand the moral world. Ideally, an ethical theory can tell us what actions are moral or immoral in every situation, and this includes helping us understand when rules of thumb should be followed and when there are exceptions to these rules. In addition, ethical theories usually tell us why an act is right or wrong. I think an example will clarify what an ethical theory is and how we use ethical theories.

Utilitarianism: Our First Ethical Theory

One of the most prominent ethical theories is *utilitarianism*. According to utilitarianism, an action is morally right if it brings about the greatest overall happiness or best consequences. This applies to all actions. Thus, according to utilitarianism, if lying to Polly is the action that would bring about the most happiness or best consequences, then not following the rule of thumb "Lying is wrong" would be the right thing to do. Similarly, if breaking a promise or shoplifting will bring about the most happiness or best consequences, breaking a promise and shoplifting are the right things to do.

I want to make clear that utilitarianism isn't about maximizing happiness for yourself. Rather, according to utilitarianism, right actions bring about the best overall consequences or most happiness for everyone affected by the action. (Some utilitarians include the happiness experienced by animals in their calculation of what action will bring about the most happiness.)

According to utilitarianism, an action is morally right if it brings about the greatest overall happiness or best consequences.

Another point of clarity: When utilitarians say the right action maximizes happiness, they really mean the greatest amount of net happiness. Suppose Action 1 will bring about 20 units of happiness and 18 units of pain or unhappiness; the net amount of happiness is positive 2. If Action 2 will bring about 10 units of happiness and only 1 unit of unhappiness, the result will be a net of 9 units of happiness. Thus Action 2 is the best or right action. If all of our options will result in net unhappiness or pain, the one that brings about the least net pain or unhappiness is the right action. If one action will result in the suffering of 10 people and the only other option will result in the suffering of 14 people, assuming each person suffers the same, the former is the right action.

Utilitarianism in Everyday Life

Years of talking with people about ethics has taught me that all of us utilize utilitarianism at one time or an-

The Trolley Problem

In 1967, English philosopher Philippa Foot introduced a thought experiment or hypothetical case known as the "Trolley Problem," which has become one of the most famous moral dilemmas discussed today.

The scenario is straightforward yet challenging: Imagine a runaway trolley barreling down the tracks. Up ahead five innocent people are tied to the tracks and face certain death. However, you happen to be next to a lever that can divert the trolley to a side track. Do you pull the lever? Well, there's a catch: There's a person tied to the side track, and they will be killed if you pull the lever. What should you do? Pull the lever, which will save the five people but result in the death of one person? Or do nothing, which will result in the death of the five people tied to the track?

Surveys reveal that 80% to 90% of respondents say they would pull the lever. Many interpret these results as evidence that most of us are utilitarians or use utilitarian thinking at times. But morality is seldom that simple or straightforward.

Philosophers and psychologists have designed numerous variations on the Trolley Problem, and in many of these, far fewer people make the utilitarian choice. For instance, imagine a scenario in which the only way to stop the trolley from killing the five people tied to the tracks is to physically push a large person over the bridge and onto the track. Although the outcome is similar to the outcome in the original Trolley Problem—one life lost and five saved—in this variation, about 50% of respondents claim they would perform the action that leads to fewer deaths. Why? Many claim that actively pushing a person to their death is morally different, or at least it feels different, than pulling a lever.

For decades, many saw the Trolley Problem as another example of academics spending time—maybe wasting time—on non-real-world dilemmas. But

(cont. p. 34)

(*cont. from p. 33*)

with the advent of self-driving cars, this dilemma has gained practical, real-world urgency. Should automakers program autonomous cars to swerve onto a sidewalk, possibly killing a pedestrian, if that action could prevent a greater loss of life—say, a collision that would kill multiple passengers or numerous people in a parade ahead?

other when trying to justify a moral judgment. We may not realize we use this theory, and we might never have heard of utilitarianism, but nevertheless, we in fact use it.

For example, when trying to justify pushing the red button in the hypothetical scenario from earlier in this chapter, most of us would say, "Sure, it resulted in one death, and that's not a good thing. But it saved millions of innocent lives. Pushing the black button or doing nothing would have resulted in the death of millions of innocent people." In essence, we believe pushing the red button was right because it brought about the best overall consequences or most happiness. Whether we realize it or not, we're thinking like a utilitarian.

As suggested above, many of us would appeal to utilitarianism to justify lying to keep Polly's surprise party under wraps. You might explain that your lie resulted in Polly not learning about the party, and this resulted in Polly and her family and friends having a fun night or many people experiencing happiness. If you told Polly the truth and spoiled the surprise, this happiness would have been lost. Therefore, you believed lying was the right thing to do or it was right not to follow the rule of thumb "Lying is wrong" because lying maximized happiness.

Batman and Utilitarianism

In a movie entitled *The Dark Night,* Batman must choose between saving the life of Harvey Dent or Rachel. Dent was Gotham's district attorney, and Batman believed he was an honest crime-fighter. Batman wanted to save him, because he believed Dent would continue to fight crime and in doing so increase the happiness

Batman is an ethically complex superhero who often makes choices based on utilitarianism rather than on laws or societal norms.

or well-being of those living in Gotham. But he loved Rachel and wanted to save her life as well.

Batman seemed to believe, at some level, that saving Rachel would be selfish and wrong because it wouldn't bring about the most happiness or best overall consequences for everyone who would be affected by his action. He therefore chose to save Dent, and his choice was based on utilitarianism. (Of course, things don't always go as planned, and this is a problem with utilitarianism. Dent became a villain, and saving his life didn't bring about the good consequences predicted by Batman. Sometimes we may believe an action will bring about the best consequences, but we are incorrect. In these situations, if another act would have brought about more happiness, according to utilitarianism the act we performed was wrong.)

Understanding Ourselves and Others

One of the goals of this book is to help you gain a better understanding of your own moral beliefs and commitments and where they come from. Additionally, I hope that after reading this book you'll be better able to understand the moral beliefs and commitments of others. As we proceed, we'll explore three other ethical theories. I decided to write about utilitarianism first because, as I stated above, whether we realize it or not, all of us sometimes utilize utilitarianism when trying to determine what's the right thing to do in ethically challenging or confusing situations, or in situations in which we question whether we should follow a rule of thumb.

Can you think of some situations in which you used utilitarianism to justify something you did, something that was inconsistent with a rule of thumb you embrace?

Not only might we use utilitarianism to justify not abiding by the rule of thumb "Lying is wrong" in order not to spoil a surprise party or "It's wrong to kill

innocent people" to prevent the detonation of multiple nuclear bombs, but we might also appeal to it to justify actions that violate any of the other rules of thumb we embrace. Consider the rule of thumb "Stealing is wrong." If stealing a bottle of medicine from a pharmacy was the only way we could save the life of a loved one, our best friend, or a stranger, many of us would believe stealing the medicine was the right thing to do. Why? Because saving the life of a human being brings about more overall happiness or better overall consequences than not stealing the medicine.

We'd likely reason or tell ourselves that if we steal the medicine, it won't significantly harm the owner of the pharmacy—she'd lose some money—but not stealing it would lead to much pain for the person who was dying and this person's family and friends. This reasoning would lead us to believe stealing brings about better overall consequences or more happiness and is the right thing to do.

Utilitarianism in Public Policy

The theory of utilitarianism was originally proposed by a philosopher named Jeremy Bentham in the late eighteenth century. Bentham believed he found the key to morality: the morality of all actions depended on the consequences of the actions. Bentham famously wrote: "It is the greatest happiness of the greatest number that is the measure of right and wrong." Acts that bring about (the greatest) total happiness (the combined happiness of everyone affected) are correct or morally right.

English philosopher, social reformer, and jurist Jeremy Bentham (1748–1832) is considered the founder of utilitarianism.

Bentham correctly observed that in addition to using utilitarianism to justify our actions, we also use it to justify public policies and laws. We frequently assess whether a public policy or

Jeremy Bentham's Body

Jeremy Bentham left detailed instructions as to what should be done with his body after he died. He wanted it to be preserved as an auto-icon, a term that he invented. The Bentham auto-icon consists of his skeleton dressed in his own clothes. Due to poor preservation, his actual body was replaced with a wax replica.

The Bentham auto-icon is displayed in a glass enclosure in the public atrium of the Student Center at University College London (UCL). Seated with a cane and hat, Bentham's figure is among the most visited attractions on campus.

Bentham's connection to UCL is foundational, even though he wasn't directly involved in establishing the university. Many of his followers helped establish UCL, driven by Bentham's vision of a university accessible to all. At a time when higher education was typically limited to the elite, Bentham believed that universities should welcome students from all social classes, genders, and religious backgrounds.

It might seem as though Bentham's desire to be displayed on UCL's campus was self-centered, but his supporters claim he wanted to challenge social norms about death and hoped his auto-icon would motivate people to think about his moral philosophy: utilitarianism. He even suggested that others should follow his lead and leave directions for their auto-icons to be placed in strategic, thought-provoking locations.

law is just or morally good by attempting to determine whether the policy or law will bring about the most happiness or best consequences. Bentham claimed that a piece of legislation or a public policy, just like an action, is morally just or right if it brings about "the greatest happiness for the greatest number."

For example, consider construction projects. We all know that large-scale infrastructure projects, like building skyscrapers, bridges, tunnels, and stadiums, is dangerous and frequently results in the deaths of

A 1907 photo of the Panama Canal under construction gives one an idea of the enormity of the project. More than 25,000 people died making the canal a reality, mostly through accidents and tropical diseases. The canal was a huge boon to trade, but was it worth the loss of so many lives?

construction workers. Thirty construction workers died building the Brooklyn Bridge, and 11 died building the Golden Gate Bridge. Five workers died building the Empire State Building, 60 died building the Twin Towers (which were destroyed by terrorists in 2001), and more than 25,000 died building the Panama Canal. Most of the latter were deaths from tropical diseases. Estimates suggest that more than 1,000 workers (possibly many more than that) died building the stadiums and infrastructure for the 2022 World Cup soccer competition in Qatar. And we know building or repaving an interstate highway may result in deaths.

Despite this, Americans (and others) will continue to construct buildings, bridges, and roads, and most of the time you and I believe this is the right thing to do. Knowing these projects will potentially lead to the deaths of innocent people may give us pause, but this doesn't mean we oppose them.

I assume we agree life is valuable and it's morally right or good to protect the lives of others. Put differently, we embrace the rule of thumb "We have an obligation to protect the lives of others (assuming doing so doesn't cost us too much)." If this is the case, how can we justify construction projects that will likely result in the deaths of innocent people?

What do you think?

A Collapsing Bridge

Let's imagine an important bridge—say, the Bay Bridge, which connects San Francisco on the west side and Oakland and Berkeley on the east—is in disrepair and may collapse unless it's rebuilt. We have three options: (1) Do nothing and wait for it to collapse, which we predict will result in the deaths of 50 people who

The Bay Bridge connects Oakland and San Francisco, California, providing a shortcut for 260,000 vehicles per day. If it required significant repair or renovation, at least a few construction workers would likely be injured or lose their lives. How does one weigh costs and benefits when it comes to human lives?

happen be on the bridge during the collapse; (2) Rebuild the bridge before it collapses, which we predict will result in the deaths of five construction workers; or (3) Close the bridge and do nothing else, which means no one will die as a result of the bridge collapsing, and since we're not rebuilding it, no construction workers will die.

What should we do? Why?

First, I want to point out that when we're faced with this hypothetical case, most of us immediately focus on the consequences associated with the different options. That is, without even thinking about it, we appeal to utilitarianism to determine what's the best choice. At first glance, it appears that Option 1 is the worst choice and should be rejected.

What now? Should we choose Option 2 or 3?

Again, most of us will continue to focus on consequences. Option 2, closing the bridge before it collapses and rebuilding it, will result in the deaths of five people, while Option 3, closing the bridge before it collapses and not rebuilding it, will result in zero deaths.

Should we select Option 3?

Initially, Option 3 may seem to be the best choice since it results in zero deaths, while Option 2 results in five deaths. That said, we'll likely want to take a closer look at the two options.

I suggest that, after thinking about it for a little while, most of us would select Option 2, closing the bridge before it collapses and rebuilding the bridge. We'd conclude that even though this option might result in five deaths during the construction of the bridge, while Option 3 would result in no deaths since there wouldn't be any construction, we believe Option 2 would bring about more overall happiness or better consequences in the long run.

The Bay Bridge is one of the busiest bridges in the United States, carrying over 250,000 vehicles—cars, trucks, and buses—a day, and it significantly decreases the time it takes to get from San Francisco to Oakland, Berkeley, and other East Bay cities. In 2009, the bridge was closed over Labor Day weekend for seismic retrofitting, and the result was a traffic nightmare. Vehicles were diverted to the San Mateo and Richmond–San Rafael bridges, and traffic at times almost seized up. This diversion added about 30 miles to the commute between San Francisco and Oakland, which amounted to more than an hour extra travel-time.

Given what happened in 2009, we can predict that if we rebuild the bridge, it will save hundreds of thousands of people every week an hour or more time in a vehicle. That's time they can spend doing things that actually bring them happiness, whether working, relaxing, seeing family, or just getting home sooner.

Not only that, but if people spend less time in vehicles, it's reasonable to assume there will be fewer accidents, perhaps even fewer deaths as a result of accidents. Finally, we can reasonably conclude that if people spend less time in cars and trucks, it will result in fewer exhaust fumes. Regardless of whether you believe human activity contributes to climate change, it's uncontroversial that exhaust fumes are unhealthy for humans and other animals. Thus, spending less time in our cars will likely result in better societal health. These are good things we weigh against the deaths of the five construction workers.

In the end, I imagine most of us will agree Option 2,

Crucially, regardless of whether we believe Option 2 or 3 is the best or right option, we agree that we should use utilitarianism when attempting to determine what is the right thing to do when thinking about building bridges, roads, airports, and buildings.

rebuilding the bridge, is the right option because it brings about the most happiness or best overall consequences. Crucially, regardless of whether we believe Option 2 or 3 is the best or right option, we agree that we should use utilitarianism when attempting to determine what is the right thing to do when thinking about building bridges, roads, airports, and buildings. (I'm not saying that there aren't other considerations, which we'll discuss later. All I'm trying to demonstrate is we frequently focus on the consequences of the different options when thinking about public policies like whether we should build a bridge or road. That is, we all, at some point or another, appeal to utilitarianism.)

Returning to the Big Question

So, is it morally permissible to kill one person to save 1,000,000? If we appeal to utilitarianism, the answer is simple: If killing one person to save 1,000,000 brings about the best overall consequences or the greatest amount of happiness, it's permissible or even obligatory to kill the one person. The same reasoning would justify the killing of one innocent person to save 100.

But what about killing one person to save five people or just three people? Let's imagine we can kill one person and harvest their organs to save five people. If doing this would maximize overall happiness, utilitarianism would tell us killing the one person was the right thing to do. Yet, this is something most of us believe is wrong. This is a problem for utilitarianism, because it seems to give us the wrong answer. In later chapters we'll look at other ethical theories that might not share this problem.

Are We Really So Divided?

I want to point out that it may be easy to conclude killing one person will bring about more happiness or

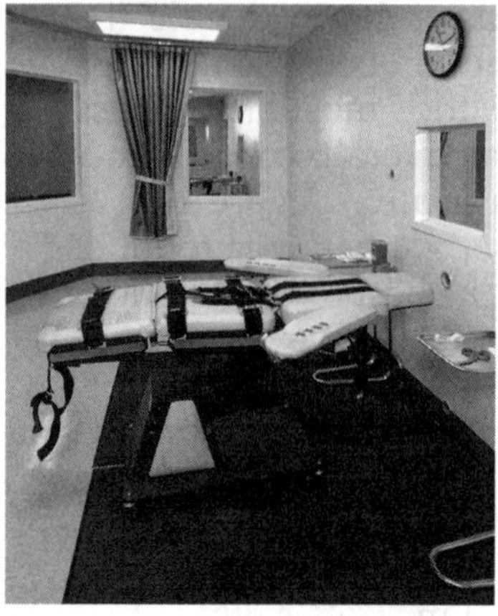

An execution room at San Quentin State Prison, where convicted murderers are given lethal injections. Some argue that the death penalty deters people from commiting murder; others feel that capital punishment does nothing to reduce killings.

better consequences than letting 1,000,000 people die. However, determining which action truly leads to the best consequences is frequently difficult. Determining what social policies or laws will maximize happiness is even more complicated, and this complexity often lies at the heart of political disagreements.

Take, for example, the debate over the death penalty for murder. A Republican senator might support it because she believes it has a deterrent effect. Some potential murderers, knowing they might be executed if they are caught, will decide not to murder someone because they fear execution or don't want to die. This results in less murder and presumably more overall happiness.

A Democrat senator might oppose the death penalty because he believes it doesn't deter potential murderers. After all, murderers believe they won't get caught, or maybe they kill in the heat of passion without even considering the possible legal consequences. In either case, the death penalty won't deter them from committing murder.

Those who want to fan the flames of division might claim that this disagreement is another example of the culture war—it's another policy that Democrats and Republicans can't agree upon.

I suggest this claim—that this is another example of the culture war—isn't well-founded.

Notice that despite their opposing views, their disagreement isn't about morality itself and isn't as deep as it might seem. Both the Republican and the Democrat appeal to the same ethical theory or framework—utilitarianism—to justify their positions on the issue of the death penalty. The Republican believes it will deter murder (and maybe other criminal activity) and therefore results in the best consequences, and the Democrat

At its base, the arguments for and against capital punishment aren't so much about moral choice but about utilitarian choice. Will executing murderers result in fewer killings (a good outcome) or not? And, if not, then is there really no benefit to the practice and should it be discontinued?

believes it won't deter murder (or other criminal activity) and won't, therefore, bring about the best consequences.

Their disagreement, at a foundational level, isn't about morality or justice. Rather, they disagree over the issue of whether the death penalty will deter murder or bring about the best consequences. That is, their disagreement is over an empirical claim, not a moral claim, as they both embrace utilitarianism. It's important to recognize this distinction, as it may help us better understand our disagreements with others. Frequently, we aren't debating over *values* but rather outcomes.

The Surprise Party Revisited

Let's return to the surprise birthday party example. Suppose I believe I should lie to Polly because no one will be harmed, and the party will bring joy to 20 people. You, however, disagree. While you acknowledge the party will be enjoyable, you worry my willingness to lie might harm or undermine important relationships in the long run. Perhaps you believe that my close friends, after they learn about my lie, will start doubting my honesty. Maybe they'll question whether I can be trusted to keep promises or not disclose confidential information they share with me. As a result, you believe the relationships between my friends and me will be harmed and this loss outweighs the happiness that will result from the party. Accordingly, you believe it would be wrong for me to lie.

Again, notice our disagreement isn't about whether we should act to bring about the most happiness or best consequences. We agree on this principle. Our disagreement concerns which action will in fact bring about the most happiness or best consequences. This, like the

senators' disagreement over the death penalty, is a disagreement over outcomes rather than values.

Final Thoughts

In this chapter, we explored the question: Is it morally permissible to kill one innocent person to save 1,000,000?

To answer this question, we explored how we might justify violating a rule of thumb we all embrace: "It's wrong to kill an innocent person."

This exploration began with the introduction of what's known as an ethical theory. Ethical theories are similar to scientific laws or theories, but whereas scientific laws or theories help us understand the physical or scientific world, ethical theories help us understand the moral world. Ethical theories usually consist of one or a small number of principles, and we can and do use these theories when trying to determine whether an action is morally right, even if it violates a rule of thumb we embrace.

Although utilitarianism, when first proposed by Bentham, claimed that right actions must maximize happiness, some later utilitarians suggested that we don't always have to maximize happiness to do the right thing.

We then explored utilitarianism, the first of four ethical theories we'll be looking at in this book. According to utilitarianism, an act is morally right if it brings about the most happiness or best overall consequences. We might appeal to utilitarianism if asked to justify why we believe it's morally right to kill one innocent person to save 1 million. Most of us would say: "Certainly, one death is better than a million deaths." We use the same reasoning to justify building a road or bridge, even though we know that building the road or bridge will lead to the death of a number of construction workers.

We also examined how we use utilitarianism in our private lives, such as justifying lying to keep a surprise party secret. Even though we believe lying is usually wrong (we embrace the rule of thumb "It's wrong to lie"), we believe lying isn't necessarily wrong if it's the only way to keep the party secret. We argue that lying

in this situation is permissible because it leads to greater overall happiness than not lying.

Before concluding this chapter, I want to clarify how I'll approach or understand utilitarianism throughout the rest of this book. Although utilitarianism, when first proposed by Bentham, claimed that right actions must *maximize* happiness, some later utilitarians suggested that we don't always have to *maximize* happiness to do the right thing. Rather, actions that bring about enough happiness (whatever *enough* means) are morally right. Thus, if donating $100 to a charity that provides food to malnourished children would bring happiness to 40 children and donating $90 would bring happiness to 36 children, Bentham would say the former is right and the latter wrong because bringing about happiness to 36 children doesn't *maximize* happiness. I imagine that most readers would conclude the former may be better than the latter, but both actions are morally right or even praiseworthy. This second formulation of utilitarianism—acts that bring about enough happiness are morally right—would say just that.

I'll be using both formulations as we proceed. Sometimes I may say an action is right if it brings about enough happiness, while other times I may say an action is right if it maximizes happiness. You may be wondering how much happiness we need to produce in order for an action to bring about enough happiness. That's something that's open for debate or discussion. I won't address that question in this book. It would take too long to answer, if I could in fact find an answer.

In future chapters, we'll explore three other ethical theories. But before we dive into those, let's explore a more fundamental question: Are there moral truths?

3: Are There Moral Truths?

The Issue: Is morality one of the greatest conspiracies of all time, something foisted on us by a powerful minority so they can control us? Or are there absolute moral truths that exist independent of cultural beliefs and personal opinions?

As a teenager and into my early 20s, I believed (or at least I thought I believed) it was wrong to judge the morality of others whose moral beliefs were different from my own. If you thought drinking alcohol was morally wrong, and I thought it was morally right or permissible, then it was wrong for you and right for me. Who was I to question or judge your beliefs?

I was even more convinced (or so I thought) that it was wrong to judge or criticize people from different cultures. "If people in another country believe it's morally permissible to eat cats and belch at the dinner table," I once declared at my grandparents' house, "Let them eat cats and belch." Back then, I could usually belch at will, and I wanted to belch at that moment to make my point, but I chickened out. Looking back, I'm glad my lack of courage (or maybe it was good sense or a combination of the two) prevented me from offending everyone present.

Later that evening, my father and grandfather, speaking as if I weren't there, agreed I was a relativist. I wasn't entirely sure of what they meant, but I knew they didn't intend it as a compliment. I took it as one anyway. I assumed older, close-minded people used the term to describe younger, open-minded individuals like myself. If being a relativist meant having an open mind, it sounded good to me.

Cows, Culture, and Moral Relativism

I imagine many of you know that in India eating beef is widely considered to be morally wrong, and most states ban the slaughter of cows. In contrast, in the United States (and most other countries) eating beef isn't just permissible; it's a way of life.

Do you believe there's an absolute truth with respect to the claim "It's morally wrong to eat cows?" That is, do you believe it's possible that people in India who believe eating cows is immoral might be incorrect or that people in the United States who believe eating cows is morally right might be incorrect?

Put differently and more generally, do you believe that the truth or falsity of moral claims depends on what the majority in a culture believe? Or is the truth or falsity independent from what the majority believe? Can the majority be wrong?

If you believe the morality of eating cows depends on cultural consensus or the beliefs of the majority in a culture, you lean towards *cultural moral relativism.*

If, instead, you believe the morality of eating cows is determined by the beliefs of the individual, then you lean toward a more radical theory called *individualist moral relativism*. An individualist moral relativist would say that even though there's a consensus in India that eating cows is morally wrong, if someone living there believes it's right, then it's right for that person. We might say that individualist relativists believe morality is entirely personal. That is, regardless of where you live or your culture's beliefs, if you believe something is morally right, it's right for you. If you believe it's morally right to belch at the dinner table and morally wrong to wash your hands after using the toilet,

In India, cows are considered sacred, so it is immoral to slaughter, cook, and eat them. In many other countries, however, eating beef is a big part of people's diets. This would seem to indicate that some matters of morality lack an absolute truth.

Cows in India

Why is it wrong to eat cows in India?

The most straightforward answer is that cows are considered sacred in Hinduism, India's predominant religion, as well as in Jainism and some sects of Buddhism. But this doesn't tell the whole story, as practical concerns, such as nutrition and economics, probably also play significant roles.

In Hinduism, which permeates India's culture, the cow symbolizes purity, nonviolence, and maternal care. Krishna, one of the most beloved of Hindu deities, is often portrayed as a cowherd, playing his flute amidst cows and humans. Krishna is also known as Govinda, which means "protector of cows." This, of course, reinforces the idea that caring for cows is a divine duty. In addition, the deity Shiva is associated with his sacred bull, Nandi, which is a symbol of strength and devotion. And Kamadhenu, a mythical wish-fulfilling cow, is believed to be the source of prosperity and abundance.

Beyond religious symbolism, cows have historically played a practical role in India's predominantly agrarian society. Cows provide milk, which is an important part of the Indian diet, as it is used to make ghee (clarified butter), yogurt, cheese, and other staples. In addition, cow dung has long been used as fuel and fertilizer, while bulls have been used for transportation and plowing fields. Thus, cows were practically important as they contributed to nutrition and economic well-being.

Ancient kings and nobles revered cows and demonstrated their wealth by donating them to Brahmins and temples. And Mahatma Ghandi, the famous Indian independence leader, elevated cow protection to a moral duty. He saw the cow as a symbol of nonviolence and human compassion. He famously stated: "The cow is a poem of pity.... Protection of the cow means protection of all that lives and is helpless and weak in the world."

Which came first, practical value or religious value? This is still an open question, but each reinforces the other, making cows integral to India's culture and social fabric.

then belching at dinner and not washing your hands after using the toilet are morally right actions for *you*. Of course, if I believe these behaviors are wrong, they're wrong for *me*.

The Alternative: Moral Absolutism

If you reject both forms of moral relativism and believe the truth or falsity of moral claims isn't determined by the beliefs of individuals or the majority of those in a culture, you're not a moral relativist. Most likely, you're a *moral absolutist*.

Moral absolutists believe the truth or falsity of moral claims has nothing to do with people's beliefs. A moral absolutist might say that in the same way the truth or falsity of the claim "The earth is a sphere" is independent of what people believe, the truth or falsity of moral claims (such as that eating cows is morally permissible) is independent of what people believe.

A moral absolutist would claim that in the same way a majority can be wrong about claims concerning the shape of the earth, they can also be wrong about moral claims. That is, a majority of those in a culture may believe that the earth is flat, but just because they believe this, it doesn't follow that they are correct. Similarly, a majority of those in a culture may believe that it's wrong to eat beef or that slavery is permissible, but according to moral absolutism, just because they believe this doesn't mean they're correct. Like those who believe the earth is flat, they can be wrong.

Relativism, Absolutism, and Art

Let's take a look at the sketch below:

At first glance, most of you probably see a sketch of a group of people (maybe a family) and a dog in a room with a window positioned above a woman's head. But some of you, especially if you didn't grow up in the United States or the West, might see something different. Perhaps you see a sketch of a group of people outdoors. You might believe that what to most of us looks like the corner of a room is, in fact, a tree, and what looks like a window *above* a woman's head is a box *on* a woman's head.

I imagine that after learning that there are two interpretations, many of you, regardless of your initial thoughts, took a second look at the sketch and considered whether your initial interpretation was the only valid one. At the very least, although you might lean towards one interpretation, if a friend or even a stranger explains why they disagree, you'd conclude we can't be certain who's right.

Crucially, even if we'll never know for sure which interpretation is correct, it doesn't follow that there's no truth about whether it's a sketch of an indoor or an outdoor scene. The artist likely had one or the other in mind when he made the sketch.

Let's take a look at a different picture.

This famous image, Rubin's vase, is an optical illusion. If you glance at it and then look away quickly, some of you will believe you saw a vase, while others will believe they saw two faces. Significantly, regardless of whether you saw a vase or two faces, you were correct. And when you learned some people saw two faces while others saw a vase, regardless of what you initially saw, you wanted to look at the picture again in an effort to see what others saw. You recognized that you might be missing something, but this recognition wasn't threatening.

The Dress That Became a Social Media Phenomenon

In 2015, Cecilia Bleasdale sent her daughter Grace, a soon-to-be bride in Scotland, a photograph of the dress she planned to wear at Grace's wedding. Cecilia saw the dress as blue and black, but Grace saw it as white and gold. To settle their disagreement, Grace posted the photo on Facebook. However, this only deepened dispute as some of her friends agreed with her mother, while others agreed with her.

Shortly after the wedding, a friend posted the photo on her Tumblr account, where it quickly went viral, gaining hundreds of thousands of views each day. People worldwide debated about whether the dress was blue and black or white and gold.

Enter Rosa Lafer-Sousa, Katherine L. Hermann, and Bevil R. Conway, three MIT professors specializing in cognitive science. The professors conducted a survey, asking 1,400 participants to complete the statement "this is a _______ and _______ dress"—not limiting the choice to white/gold and blue/black. Fifty-seven percent described the dress as blue/black, 30% as white/gold, and, surprisingly, 11% as blue/brown. The remaining 2% provided other combinations.

So, what was the actual color of the dress? According to the dressmaker, it was definitely blue and black. This was based on looking at the actual material rather than a photograph.

Regardless of the true color of the dress, why was there so much disagreement over the colors in the photograph? Several explanations have been proposed. The first suggests that the human brain automatically corrects for varying lighting conditions in order to increase the likelihood we perceive the true color of things, even if the lighting changes. Given this capacity, some viewers assumed (not consciously) that the background light was warm (indoor light), and they perceived a blue and black dress. Others assumed daylight, which is bluish, and they perceived white and gold.

(cont. p. 53)

(cont. from p. 52)

Related to this explanation, one study discovered that early risers were more likely to see the dress as being white and gold, while late risers were more likely to see blue and black. The study posited that maybe early risers were exposed to more natural daylight, thus they were more likely to see white and gold.

A different explanation focuses on cones, the cells in our eyes that perceive color. It suggests that individuals whose cones are biased toward seeing warmer tones tend to see white and gold, while those whose cones are more sensitive to cool colors tend to see blue and black.

Regardless of the correct scientific explanation, this phenomenon illustrates the subjective nature of human perception. Even something seemingly straightforward, like identifying colors, is far more complex than it initially appears. Surely, the way we think about, feel, or see moral issues must be even more complex.

So, what do these pictures have to do with morality? They offer a useful analogy for understanding moral relativism and absolutism.

Rubin's vase can represent relativism. Just as no viewer is wrong in seeing either two faces or a vase, individualist relativists argue that no individual is wrong about their moral beliefs. If I believe it's morally permissible to eat cows, then the claim "It's morally permissible to eat cows" is true for me. If you believe it's morally wrong to eat cows, the claim "It's morally permissible to eat cows" is false for you.

The sketch illustrates absolutism. Despite disagreement concerning whether it's a sketch of an indoor scene or outdoor scene, there's an absolute truth regarding what is being depicted in the sketch. Similarly, moral absolutists hold that individuals or entire cultures can be mistaken about moral issues. Just because most people in a society believe an act is morally right, this doesn't make it morally right. It may in fact be wrong.

Two hundred years ago, a majority of those living in the southern United States believed slavery was morally right or permissible. A cultural relativist would say the claim "Slavery is morally right" was true for those living in the southern United States during that time period. A moral absolutist would disagree and assert that what people believed is irrelevant. Regardless of whether they believed slavery was right or wrong, it was in fact wrong.

So, I ask you once again: Do you lean more towards moral relativism (cultural or individualist) or moral absolutism? Do you believe moral truth is determined by the beliefs of an individual or a culture? Or do you believe certain moral principles are true (or false), regardless of what people believe?

Discussion

In today's world, it's trendy to claim we live in a *post-truth* society. But if we think about it for a little while and are honest with ourselves, we'll admit that we still believe there are absolute truths with respect to many things.

We can confidently say there's an absolute truth regarding how many stars are on the flag of the United States, whether it snowed in Miami yesterday, whether the sun's diameter is greater than the diameter of the moon, or whether a Model T Ford can fly.

Similarly, when it comes to the sketch we looked at earlier, I imagine most of us believe it's a sketch of either an indoor scene or an outdoor scene, even if we never learn which it is for sure. Our beliefs don't determine the reality behind the sketch. Rubin's vase differs significantly. There is no absolute truth as to whether it depicts faces or a vase. Both interpretations can coexist validly.

Are Moral and Political Disagreements More Like the Sketch or the Vase?

Let's imagine I believe we have a moral obligation to save a drowning child if it only requires reaching into a shallow fountain, but you disagree. You believe we don't have this obligation. Is our disagreement more

If you saw a child drowning in a shallow fountain and that it would be a simple matter to rescue her, are you morally obligated to do so?

like our disagreement over our interpretations of the sketch or our interpretations of Rubin's vase?

Or take a political issue like the death penalty. If I believe the death penalty is morally wrong or unjust and you believe the opposite, can we both be right, as we can when interpreting Rubin's vase? Or is one of us wrong, as when we're interpreting the sketch?

If moral and political disagreements are more like disagreements concerning interpretations of the sketch, then absolute truths exist, and they are independent of what we believe. We might *believe* we have no moral obligation to save the drowning child or the death penalty is unjust, but just because we believe these things or see them in this way, it doesn't follow we're correct. We could be mistaken.

If moral and political disagreements are more like disagreements concerning our interpretations of Rubin's vase, then absolute moral truths don't exist. If I believe we don't have an obligation to save a drowning child and you believe we do, neither of us is incorrect. It might be more accurate to say that if individualist moral relativism is true, the claim "People don't have an ob-

ligation to save drowning children" is true for me and false for you. The same is true with respect to political disagreements, like whether the death penalty is just. If you believe the death penalty is unjust and I believe it's just, then the claim "The death penalty is unjust" is true for you and false for me.

Similarly, if we are cultural relativists and believe cultures determine whether the sketch is a picture of an indoor or outdoor scene—there is no absolute truth—we might also believe that cultures determine whether a moral or political claim is true or false. Claims can be true for one culture and at the same time false for another.

The Allure of Cultural Moral Relativism

At times, many of us find cultural moral relativism to be attractive or appealing. When we learn some cultures don't eat beef and other cultures don't eat pork, most of us don't respond critically or question these practices. Instead, we adopt a cultural relativist stance and say something like: "If they believe eating beef or pork is wrong, it's wrong for them. But that doesn't apply to my culture or to me. It's right or permissible to eat beef and pork where I live."

But how deep does this attraction to relativism really go? Even though we're inclined to respect cultural differences, I'm convinced most of us do not, in fact, embrace cultural or individualist moral relativism. That is, despite what we might believe about ourselves, most of us reject cultural and individualist moral relativism and embrace the idea that there are absolute moral truths and cultures and individuals can be wrong about their moral and political beliefs.

Put differently, we believe moral and political truths exist, and they are independent of what cultures and individuals might believe.

Shirley Jackson's "The Lottery"

Many of us read Shirley Jackson's short story "The Lottery" in school. Set in a small town on a sunny June morning, the story begins innocently enough. "The

flowers were blossoming profusely and the grass was richly green." The town's children were the first to arrive at the town square. The boys were busy gathering stones, while the girls were talking amongst themselves. The adults arrived shortly thereafter, the men arriving first. Although we know some sort of lottery will take place, we don't yet know the nature of the lottery or what will happen next. That said, there's a sense of foreboding. The men's "jokes were quiet and they smiled rather than laughed."

Mr. Summers, the owner of a coal business, is in charge. He arrives carrying "the black box" and places it on a three-legged stool. The box has been in use since before "the oldest man in town was born." A father and son hold the box steady as Mr. Summers mixes up the slips of paper in the box. Mr. Summers instructs the heads of families to draw a slip of paper for their families, but they're instructed not to look at it.

When all the heads of family are holding a slip, Mr. Summers tells them to open the slips.

"'It's Hutchinson. It's Bill,' 'Bill Hutchinson's got it.'"

Bill's wife, Tessie, shouts that the drawing wasn't fair because Bill was rushed. We now believe "winning" the lottery is likely a bad thing.

Public stonings are a tradition in many cultures for punishing those who have transgressed against a society's laws or religions (the illustration shows an adulteress being punished in a nineteenth-century publication of *1001 Knights*). In fact, stoning is still practiced in some places today. When Jackson's story came out, South Africa banned it because stonings still occurred there.

Five new slips of paper are put into the black box, one for Bill, Tessie, and each of their three children. A second drawing takes place and Tessie draws the slip of paper with a dot in the middle.

"It isn't fair," Tessie screams as the first stone hits her on the side of the head. "'It isn't fair, it isn't right' . . . and they were upon her." We now know that since Tessie "won," the townspeople will stone her to death.

Although Jackson never explicitly states the point of the story, many pages of criticism and interpretation have focused on it. One interpretation is that the story explores the issue of cultural relativism. As the slips are being drawn, Mrs. Adams states some towns are discontinuing the lottery. Upon hearing this, Old Man Warner exclaims: "'Pack of crazy fools. Listening to the young folks, nothing's good enough for them.'" He then tries to justify the lottery: "'Used to be a saying about Lottery in June, corn be heavy soon.... There's always been a lottery.'"

"The Lottery" prompts us to think about whether we ought to question current societal practices or blindly follow them. If, like Old Man Warner, you believe societal practices are right or good just because they've been around for years and a majority of those in the society embrace or follow the practices, you're likely attracted to cultural moral relativism. If, as "The Lottery" seems to suggest, you believe societal practices may be wrong or bad, even if a majority of those in a society embrace or follow the practices, you probably reject cultural moral relativism and believe there are absolute truths when it comes to moral or political questions.

Are We Absolutists without Realizing It?

I understand many find relativism attractive and believe they're relativists in the same way that I believed I was a relativist. I don't know how many times I said, "To each their own." As stated above, I now believe almost all of us are, in fact, absolutists, even though many of us don't realize this is the case. That is, we believe many of our moral and political disagreements—e.g., whether we have an obligation to help people in need (charity) or whether women ought to have a right to abortion—

Young John finds sprinkles on donuts disgusting, but you absolutely love them! Just because you have different tastes doesn't mean one of you is right and the other is wrong. This concept might also be applied to something such as social conventions, including what is or is not considered rude behavior.

are more like disagreements over interpretations of the sketch than disagreements over interpretations of Rubin's vase. We believe there's an absolute truth concerning these issues.

Why do I think most of us are absolutists? Our behavior and words betray our true beliefs. Even though we try to be tolerant of moral differences, deep down we believe there's an absolute truth with respect to moral and political claims. Let me explain.

Think about how you might respond to those who disagree with you about Rubin's vase. If you saw two faces and someone said she saw a vase, would you start a debate with her and claim she was mistaken? I doubt it. Instead, you'd likely believe that for her it was correct to say it was a picture of two faces and for you it was correct to say it was a picture of a vase. This response—not even *thinking* she was incorrect—reveals you're probably an individualist relativist when it comes to claims about Rubin's vase.

I suspect you'd react in the same way to disagreements about taste. If you heard me say "Chocolate ice cream tastes good" and you believe it tastes bad, you wouldn't argue with me. You might say something like: "If you're being honest and chocolate ice cream really tastes good to you, then it's true that chocolate ice cream tastes good to you." You might continue, "It tastes bad to me. But even though we disagree, neither of us is wrong."

I'm suggesting most of us believe taste claims, like claims about Rubin's vase, are true if the person making the claim believes they're true. We don't respond to these claims by thinking or saying the speaker is wrong. We're individualist relativists when it comes to these claims.

When it comes to moral (and political) disagreements, our reactions are quite different.

Imagine you're at the 90th birthday party of your best friend's grandmother. As the cake is brought out and everyone begins singing "Happy Birthday," your friend's sister opens her cellphone and starts talking about the upcoming Super Bowl.

After the party, you overhear your friend telling his sister, "Kathy, you owe Mom and Grandma an apology. You know talking on the phone while everyone was singing was wrong."

Kathy responds, "It might be wrong for you, but it wasn't wrong for me."

How would you react?

I suspect most of you wouldn't automatically accept Kathy's view as valid. That is, you'd react differently from the way you'd react to disagreements about interpretations of Rubin's vase or taste claims. Instead of simply agreeing that it's right for Kathy and wrong for your friend, you'd be thinking (even if you didn't say it aloud) something like: "My friend's right. Kathy's behavior was wrong, even if she believes it was right. It was disrespectful and probably hurt her mother and grandmother's feelings."

Not only would you reject the claim "It's right for me and wrong for you," but you'd probably be able to provide reasons why you believe Kathy's behavior was wrong. Maybe you'd think it was disrespectful, and you embrace the rule of thumb "We should respect others, especially those older than us." The fact that you believe what Kathy did was wrong because we should respect others, especially those older than us, reveals that deep down you believe there is, in fact, a truth when it comes to moral claims. And, importantly, this truth is based on reason, not just someone's unreasoned opinion.

Similarly, when someone makes a political claim—say, that capital punishment is morally wrong—and you disagree, you don't think: "Capital punishment is wrong for them but right for me." Instead, you might want to understand his reasons for believing capital punishment is wrong. You'd expect a rationale and wouldn't be satisfied if he said, "I just think it's wrong, so it's wrong for me." Many of us might want to avoid a discussion or argument and say nothing, but internally we'd be thinking: "I think they're wrong, but I won't say anything."

In both moral and political discussions, we reject

the adage "To each their own." When someone utters a moral or political claim, most of us almost automatically think about what they said and decide whether we think the claim is true or false. We don't react in this way when one makes a taste claim or tells us their interpretation of Rubin's vase. The different ways we react to these different types of claims suggests we reject individualist relativism when it comes to moral and political claims and embrace individualist relativism when it comes to claims about taste and Rubin's vase.

In both moral and political discussions, we reject the adage "To each their own." When someone utters a moral or political claim, most of us almost automatically think about what they said and decide whether we think the claim is true or false.

Our behavior also reveals we don't embrace *cultural* moral relativism. Remember, cultural moral relativism dictates that the truth or falsity of moral claims is determined by the beliefs of the majority. If you were a cultural moral relativist and someone asked you whether it's true that abortion is morally permissible, you'd respond by saying "I just looked at a bunch of public opinion polls, and they all said a majority of Americans believe abortion is morally permissible. Since a majority believe it's permissible, it is." Most of us wouldn't respond in this way because most of us aren't cultural moral relativists. That is, we don't believe the truth or falsity of moral and political claims is determined by the beliefs of the majority.

I haven't answered the question posed in the title of this chapter: Are there moral truths? You might not appreciate this, even though you might expect it, but I can't answer this question with any confidence. What I can say with confidence is that most of us (dare I say 95% of readers) believe absolute moral and political truths exist. And if we believe this, it has an important implication.

The Implications of Moral Absolutism

If we reject cultural or individualist moral relativism and instead hold that moral and political truths exist,

perhaps we should recognize that our moral and political judgments are similar to our judgments concerning the sketch. Continuing with the analogy, just as it can be challenging or even impossible to determine conclusively whether the artist was sketching an indoor scene or an outdoor scene, it can be equally challenging to ascertain the correctness of our moral or political judgments. Yet this difficulty doesn't imply that there's no absolute truth with respect to these judgments. Rather, it suggests that discerning this truth is complicated.

Acknowledging this complexity should encourage us to approach our own moral and political judgments with caution. Just as we might recognize our fallibility in interpreting the sketch, we should recognize our fallibility in making moral and political claims.

The Role of Tolerance and Humility

If most of us embrace moral absolutism, why do so many of us *believe* we embrace moral relativism? One reason might be that regardless of our political affiliation, religious beliefs, or where we live, most of us believe tolerance (up to a certain point) and humility are virtues. When encountering moral disagreement, these virtues are activated, prompting us toward respectful statements like "If that's what they believe, it's right for them." At first glance, this appears to indicate relativism, but a closer look reveals a different motivation entirely.

For instance, when confronted with India's general consensus that eating beef is morally wrong, our instinctive reaction might be: "If that's what they believe, it's right for them." We might further think: "I don't live there. Far be it for me to criticize them or tell them what's right or what they should eat." Again, while such statements seem relativistic, they primarily reflect tolerance.

Tolerance is an admirable quality in anyone who believes that just because something is not right for you doesn't mean it is not right for other people.

We don't typically admire people who constantly criticize others for their differing

Even though we should be tolerant of other people's beliefs or cultures or politics, there are—and should be—limits. The concentration camps of Nazi Germany and the genocide of Jewish people and others during that time are certainly one case where a line must be drawn about something that is clearly immoral.

beliefs and practices. Thus, when we say, "If that's what people in India believe, it's right for them," we're truly communicating something like "Even if I think my beliefs are correct, I choose to respect and tolerate their practices." Just to be clear, these thoughts reveal that we do believe there's an absolute truth concerning moral questions, but we're tolerant of those whose views or beliefs we believe are incorrect.

In addition to valuing tolerance, most of us value humility. This might make us hesitant to judge or criticize the morality of other individuals or cultures. We might think: "I'm not the expert on morality, and I don't know the history of their culture or their religious practices. And truth be told, I don't know if cows suffer. Who am I to criticize or judge people who live in this culture?" Notice that this disposition to refrain from judging or criticizing those whose moral beliefs are different from our own is not grounded in a commitment to relativism. Rather, it's grounded in a recognition of our own limited perspective and potential ignorance.

However, tolerance and humility have limits. When confronted with practices such as female circumcision

(some call this female genital mutilation) or the infanticide of newborn females, many of us would be compelled to speak out and say, "Enough is enough. Although I value tolerance and humility, some practices are unacceptable. These practices are wrong, period."

When asked how we reconcile tolerating some things we believe are wrong, like India's prohibition on eating beef, and condemning practices like infanticide, we might respond by saying: "Even though I want to be tolerant, even though I strive to be humble and recognize I might not be correct when I make assertions concerning morality, there are times when tolerance and humility go too far. Female circumcision and infanticide can't and shouldn't be tolerated. They cross moral lines that demand condemnation."

Reacting in this way reveals an underlying commitment to moral absolutism. If we are, in fact, absolutists and believe that moral truth is not determined by public opinion, we face the difficult task of critically evaluating our own moral and political beliefs (and the moral and political beliefs of others). This involves evaluating reasons and arguments and attempting to determine which ones hold up best. This may be difficult in the same way that it's difficult to determine the correct interpretation of the sketch, but this difficulty needn't lead us to abandon the pursuit of truth.

Are We Really So Divided?

We're constantly told that Democrats and Republicans, city and rural dwellers, don't embrace the same or similar moral and political values. But is this really true? Evidence suggests this belief is false or at least misleading in some important ways.

When it comes to personal morality, Americans actually embrace a remarkably similar set of values, moral principles, or rules of thumb. Almost all of us agree stealing, lying, cheating, and breaking promises are wrong. We agree it's right or permissible to make charitable donations, attend or not attend religious services, and listen to music. Almost all of us would lend a neighbor a cup of sugar, call for help if we saw someone injured in an accident, and try to save a drowning child (or adult).

The issues that seem to divide us most are political. We're often told Democrats and Republicans distrust, disrespect, and even despise each other or that we're in the middle of a bitter culture war.

The Polls Say We Agree More than We Think

I don't deny that the distrust and disrespect are real. But I do challenge the claim that we don't embrace the same core moral and political values. A 2023 public opinion poll, conducted by the National Opinion Research Center at the University of Chicago, reveals that, across party lines, Americans' moral and political beliefs, commitments, and values are quite similar. Significantly, even though this poll reveals Americans embrace many of the same moral and political values, it also reveals Americans mistakenly believe those "on the other side" don't embrace the same core values that they embrace.

According to this poll, between 86% and 91% of Democrats value respect and compassion, accountable government, rule of law, personal accountability, and representative government. Similarly, between 87% and 90% of Republicans report they embrace the same core values. These numbers clearly suggest a large majority of Americans, regardless of their political affiliations, embrace the same or similar core values.

Yet despite this overwhelming agreement, the perception of division persists. When asked what those "on the other side" believe, only a small percentage of Republicans and Democrats recognized that those on the other side share their values. 30% to 37% of Republicans thought Democrats value respect and compassion, accountable government,

The 2020s in the United States have never seen more division between the two political parties of Democrats and Republicans. But how much of these perceived differences are actually not as important as the morals and ethics we all share?

rule of law, personal accountability, and representative government, and between 27% and 37% of Democrats thought Republicans embraced these same values.

Clearly, there's a disconnect, and this disconnect may explain why many Democrats and Republicans distrust each other or believe those "on the other side" aren't decent people.

Shared Values, Different Policies

Just to be clear, I'm not suggesting Democrats and Republicans support the same policies. Republicans are much more likely than Democrats to be pro-life and oppose a woman's right to abortion than are Democrats. Democrats are more likely than Republicans to oppose the death penalty and laws that expand people's freedom to possess firearms.

The poll discussed above suggests even though many Democrats and Republicans disagree about these and other policies, their *foundational* or basic moral/political commitments are similar. Both sides embrace the same *core* values.

Knowing 80% to 90% of those "on the other side" embrace the same core values can help bridge divides and make it easier to respect and trust those "on the other side." Perhaps we can, in fact, develop cordial relationships or even friendships with those "on the other side."

You might believe strongly in the right of private citizens to own guns while your neighbor does not, but you might also find that both of you believe in more core values such as the importance of the rule of law and of personal accountability.

If I support the death penalty and gun ownership rights and my neighbor opposes both, I might initially assume we're worlds apart morally. Believing this may make it difficult to develop a friendship or respectful relationship with my neighbor.

If I remember my neighbor and I embrace many of the same rules of thumb and core values—compassion, rule of law, and personal accountability—developing a friendship or respectful relationship with

him is easier or more natural. I might think, for example, "Even though we disagree about the morality or justice of the death penalty, it's important for me to remember that like me, he values compassion, accountability, and the rule of law. He is, in fact, a decent person."

What This Means for Moral Absolutists

Knowing and remembering that most of us embrace the same core values is especially important if we're moral absolutists. If we're absolutists and I believe we ought to have a right to possess guns in our houses and you disagree, it follows that one of us is correct and the other incorrect. If I believe you're incorrect about this and other issues, it's easy for me to agree with the pundits and influencers and see you as someone very different from me, someone I can't trust or respect.

But recognizing we share the same rules of thumb and core values allows us to disagree without disrespect. I can think someone is wrong about gun rights and same-sex marriage, for example, but at the same time remember that they likely embrace the same foundational values I embrace. Surely, those who share the same basic values I embrace don't deserve hatred or contempt just because they hold different beliefs or opinions about the right to possess a gun or the right of same-sex couples to marry.

Final Thoughts

In this chapter, we explored the topic of moral relativism. Cultural moral relativists believe the truth or falsity of moral claims isn't set in stone. They hold that if the majority in a culture believe a moral claim is true, then it's true. If the majority believe it's false, then it's false. If, for example, a majority of those living in India believe it's morally wrong to eat cows, the claim "Eating cows is morally wrong" is true in India. Since a majority of Americans believe this claim is false, it's false in the United States.

I tried to demonstrate that despite being initially attracted to relativism, most of us aren't, in fact, relativists. Rather, we're moral absolutists. Simply put, we

believe that even if a majority of those in a culture believe that the claim "Women shouldn't have the right to vote" is true, this doesn't give us reason to believe it's true. Whether this claim is true or false is independent of what a majority of those in a culture believe.

We also explored the issue of whether Americans are, in fact, as divided as we've been told. I provided some evidence from a recent public opinion poll that suggests between 86% and 90% of Americans value respect and compassion, the rule of law, and personal accountability. Even though this is the case, the poll also reveals a large majority of Americans believe that "those on the other side" don't share a commitment to these same values.

Recognizing that almost all of us, regardless of our political identification or affiliation, embrace similar core values can help us foster trust and respect across political divides. Do we really want to live in a world in which we distrust, disrespect, or even hate our neighbors who disagree with us politically? What about family members? I know I don't.

In the upcoming chapters, I'll continue to focus on areas of agreement and disagreement in moral and political life. As we examine different ethical theories, I hope to further demonstrate that most Americans embrace the same fundamental moral principles.

4: What's Wrong with Adultery?

The issue: Adultery involves breaking promises and lying, so does that mean it is always wrong?

I recently had an interesting conversation with a colleague about adultery. We were discussing an article I read years ago, centered around a woman we'll call Susan.

Susan was married to a man suffering from advanced Alzheimer's disease. Though she visited him regularly at his long-term care facility, her husband didn't recognize her and never remembered previous visits. To Susan, visiting her husband was like visiting a stranger, someone entirely different from the man she married.

Seeking emotional support, Susan joined a caregiver group. It was there that she met Quinton, a man in a situation much like her own. For the first time in years, she felt truly seen and understood. What started as a supportive friendship gradually evolved into a full-blown romantic relationship.

Susan believed her relationship with Quinton fulfilled her need for physical and emotional closeness, which gave her the strength and energy to continue visiting and caring for her husband. She was convinced he would never know of the affair or be hurt by it, because his physicians told her there was no hope for him to recover his cognitive abilities.

My colleague and I talked about whether Susan's adultery was morally different from typical cases of adultery.

What do you think? Was Susan's extramarital relationship morally different from typical adulterous relationships? That is, was it less bad, the same, or worse?

Is it possible her adultery wasn't wrong at all?

When I admitted to my colleague that I wasn't sure what to think about this situation, she was clearly surprised and jokingly said, "I'm glad I'm not married to you." She then explained why she believed this case of adultery was the same as most other cases. It involved lying and, more importantly, the breaking of a vow or promise.

Is there ever a valid reason for abandoning one's wedding vows and having an affair with a person who makes you feel valued and worthwhile again after a marriage has broken down?

"When people get married, they usually vow to be faithful," she said. "Unless Susan and her husband had agreed to a non-exclusive marriage, she violated that vow when she began the affair with Quinton. She may have been lonely and exhausted, but this doesn't release her from her vow. Isn't that what 'for better or for worse' means?"

Do you agree with my colleague?

Discussion

A Short Story about Adultery

I think it's fair for me to assume that most of us embrace the rule of thumb "Adultery is morally wrong." But why do we embrace this rule? Are all cases of adultery equally wrong, or are some worse than others? Is there a moral spectrum when it comes to cheating?

Russian author Anton Chekhov explores this idea in his short story, "The Lady with the Dog." At the beginning of the story, Dimitri Gurov, a 40-year-old banker from Moscow, is vacationing in Yalta, far away from his wife and three children. Dimitri, who's unhappily married, regards women as the "lower race," yet he prefers their company to that of men and has had numerous extramarital affairs.

One afternoon, while eating at a restaurant in a park, Dimitri notices a lady with a dog. She sits down at a table next to his, and they strike up a conversation. Dim-

itri learns the lady, whose name is Anna Sergeyevna, is from S, a town near St. Petersburg, and like him, she's on vacation without her spouse.

Their friendship blossoms into romance. Knowing that their time together is limited, they see each other every day. Then, unexpectedly, Anna receives a letter from her husband, informing her that he needs her to return home because something is wrong with his eyes. Dimitri and Anna say goodbye, believing they'll never see each other again.

After returning to Moscow, Dimitri resumes his old habits, going to work during the day and going to clubs and socializing at night. But something's changed. No matter what he does, he can't stop thinking about Anna. He needs to visit her, and he tells his wife he's going to St. Petersburg on business.

When he arrives in S, Dimitri sees a poster advertising the opera *The Geisha*. The first performance is scheduled for that same night, and Dimitri buys a ticket hoping Anna might also attend. Sure enough, he spots Anna and her husband in the audience, and when her husband goes out for a smoke during an intermission, Dimitri approaches her. At first, she runs from him, but eventually they talk. Anna, like Dimitri, hasn't stopped thinking about their affair, and she agrees to meet him in Moscow.

Russian author Anton Chekhov (1860–1904) believed that it was more important for writers to ask questions about the human condition than to answer them. In the case of the short story "The Lady with the Dog," he does just that on the topic of infidelity.

Anna begins making regular trips to see Dmitri, telling her husband she's seeing a doctor specializing in female diseases. As their relationship deepens, Anna and Dimitri come to believe they've found something neither of them has ever known: true love. They believe fate intervened and they're supposed to be together, like husband and wife. They want to stop lying and sneaking around.

The story ends on an uncertain note, with Anna and

Dimitri recognizing "the most complicated and difficult part of their journey was just beginning."

I like this story because, like many of Chekhov's other stories, it portrays the complexity of the human condition and the murky terrain of living a moral life. Dimitri and Anna made a vow of fidelity to their respective spouses, which gives them a moral reason not to begin or continue an affair. And Dimitri is the father of three children, adding another reason as to why his behavior might be wrong.

On the other hand, as we learn late in the story, this is the first time either of them experienced true love, arguably one of the greatest and most profound of human experiences.

Evolution May Reward Women's Infidelity

Most of us have heard the argument that men have an evolutionary inclination towards infidelity or cheating, but it's less common to hear similar arguments made about women. Yet, research suggests that evolution might also favor female infidelity.

There are several arguments claiming that male infidelity is a remnant of evolution. One of the best-known claims is that natural selection favors traits that increase the likelihood one will pass on one's genes or reproductive success. If a man is disposed to have sexual intercourse with many women as opposed to one woman, this argument claims, they will likely have more offspring or pass on their genes more efficiently than if they had sex with only one person. Put differently, evolution favored men who were disposed to have sex with more than one woman.

Just to be clear, even if this evolutionary story is true, it doesn't follow that having an affair in a committed relationship is morally right or praiseworthy. Humans have other predispositions that we don't believe should be praised or acted upon, including aggression and dominance. Some claim that dominant, aggressive individuals had more reproductive success than nonaggressive, passive men, but this doesn't mean that dominant, aggressive behavior—

(cont. p. 73)

Does this somehow justify their behavior or make it less wrong? What do you think? Are all adulterous relationships equally wrong? Or are some cases of adultery different from others? Do circumstances matter? Can true love justify adultery?

Why Is Adultery Wrong?

Before diving deeper into Susan's situation and Dimitri and Anna's affair, let's first explore why we might believe adultery is usually (or almost always) morally wrong. Put differently: Why do we embrace the rule of thumb "Adultery is wrong"?

(cont. from p. 72)

bullying, for example—is something we praise.

Interestingly, some researchers are exploring the possibility that evolution may push women to infidelity. In a recent essay in *Evolution and Human Behavior* (Sept. 2024), Macken Murphy, Caroline A. Phillips, and Khandis R. Blake explore two mechanisms that might result in reproductive success for women. The first, the "good genes" hypothesis, suggests that when women are trying to become pregnant, infidelity might allow women to find a partner with better genes than their primary partner. Thus, infidelity could result in offspring who have a higher likelihood of survival and success.

A second possible evolutionary explanation for women's infidelity is called the "mate-switching" hypothesis. This hypothesis proposes that women would have more reproductive success if they had an affair because this gives them the opportunity to test other potentials mates. Thus, if their partner dies or leaves them, they'll be ready to reproduce with another man. Or perhaps they'll find someone who would be a better father.

These hypotheses help to balance evolutionary perspectives, showings that infidelity isn't necessarily favored only in men. Of course, in the same way that evolutionary arguments don't justify male infidelity, they don't justify female infidelity.

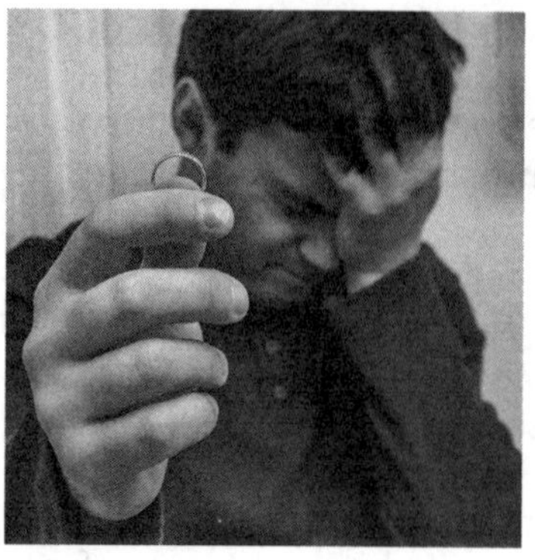

The emotional pain caused by breaking a trust between two married people is perhaps the worst part of infidelity. There is no longer the secure feeling that one can be vulnerable with a partner.

A quick Internet search reveals that my colleague's perspective on Susan's adultery is the most common explanation as to why people believe it's wrong. When people marry, they make a vow or a promise to their partner to remain faithful. Pursuing a sexual or romantic relationship with someone other than their partner breaks that promise. Since we embrace the rule of thumb "Breaking promises is wrong," we conclude infidelity or cheating is wrong.

In a similar vein, most of us embrace the rule of thumb "Lying is morally wrong." And adulterous affairs often involve deception. An adulterer may explicitly lie and tell their partner they aren't pursuing a sexual or romantic relationship with someone else or lie by omission, hiding the truth or manipulating appearances. If lying is wrong and adultery involves lying, then adultery must also be wrong.

Although lying and breaking promises may help explain why adultery is usually wrong, I suspect for most of us there's something deeper at play. After all, we don't react to all lies or broken promises with the same level of moral outrage as we do with adultery.

John, for example, may promise his partner he'll clean the house tomorrow, but when his childhood friend comes into town, John blows off his promise and spends the afternoon with his friend. If we hear this story, we might conclude John shouldn't have broken his promise, but our reaction wouldn't be as strong as if we discovered he broke his vow of fidelity and cheated on his partner.

Likewise, if we learn John lied to his partner and told her he didn't clean the house because he had to go to work, we'd conclude he shouldn't have lied, that lying was wrong. But our reaction would be much stronger if we learned John lied to cover up an affair.

This contrast implies that while adultery may be

wrong because it involves lying and breaking promises, there's likely more to the story. There's something about infidelity that strikes more deeply, something that seems to involve a different kind of violation.

I suggest, and this may be obvious, the deeper reason adultery is wrong lies in the kind of relationship where the lying and promise-breaking take place. These are not just any lies; they occur in a relationship built on trust, mutual care, and emotional safety. Both partners believe, and have reason to believe, that the other wouldn't intentionally do something that would cause them to suffer. Essentially, they believed it would be safe to become vulnerable.

Consider Jan, who says to her partner: "You're ugly and stupid. Not only do I wish I never met you, but I wish you died in a car wreck before we met each other."

Most of us would agree that what Jan said was horrible and morally reprehensible, and this is true even if she didn't lie or break a promise. It was far worse than what John did when he broke his promise to clean the house and lied about it. Why? Because Jan's partner believed,
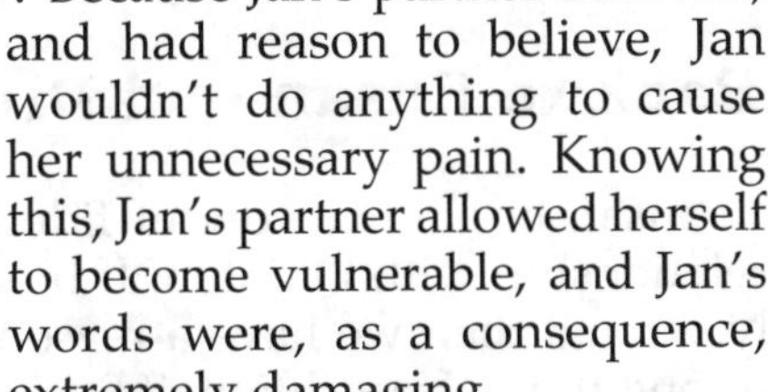
and had reason to believe, Jan wouldn't do anything to cause her unnecessary pain. Knowing this, Jan's partner allowed herself to become vulnerable, and Jan's words were, as a consequence, extremely damaging.

What are we to think of someone saying he wished his partner died in a car crash because he hates her so much? Most of us would agree this is reprehensible behavior not just because it is an awful thing to say, but because the remark is directed at someone who trusted that their emotional vulnerability would never be betrayed by a spouse.

This is what makes love so powerful and so risky. When we're in a loving, exclusive relationship and allow ourselves to become vulnerable, we let our guard down. We put ourselves in a position that gives the one we love the power to hurt us badly. As a result of this vulnerability, we suffer greatly if our partner does things that might not have hurt so much if we weren't in love or didn't allow ourselves to become vulnerable.

If a stranger said they hated us or wished we were dead, it would sting. It would be painful

to hear these things. But if someone we loved said these things, the pain would be devastating, because we allowed ourselves to become vulnerable. We trusted him or her with the most tender parts of ourselves.

If this analysis is correct, we might want to say adultery (and other instances of infidelity) is wrong not just because it involves the breaking of a vow or promise and lying, both of which violate a rule of thumb or principle we embrace. But the more important reason it's wrong is the betrayal of emotional trust. In most cases of adultery, the cheated-on partner gave their loved one the power to deeply hurt or harm them. And the unfaithful partner, fully aware of this power, uses it in a way that they know will potentially cause unnecessary and often intense suffering.

This analysis not only helps us understand *why* we believe adultery is (usually) wrong, but it also sheds light on why we might believe there could be exceptions to the rule of thumb "Adultery is wrong" or why we might believe some cases of adultery are worse than others.

Back to Susan and Dimitri and Anna

Susan broke her vow of fidelity when she began a relationship with Quinton. If breaking a vow is morally wrong, then we have a reason to say Susan did the wrong thing. In addition, if Susan lied to others to conceal her affair, she did something else wrong. But if the morally worst part of adultery is that we hurt someone who's vulnerable, someone who gave us the power to hurt them, then Susan's actions might be less bad or wrong than the typical case of adultery.

Susan believed, based on expert medical advice, that her husband would never regain awareness and would not, therefore, learn about the affair. Thus, he would never suffer from it. In fact, her new relationship might actually increase his well-being because it would potentially give Susan the strength and energy to continue visiting her husband and acting as his caregiver.

I'm not trying to convince you that Susan's behavior was morally right, excusable, or less wrong than normal cases of adultery. That's for you to decide. Rather, I'm explaining that I can understand why someone might believe Susan's behavior wasn't as bad as the behavior

According to a 2022 Gallup poll, 89% of Americans polled said adultery was morally wrong, while only 9% said it was morally acceptable.

of those who engage in typical adulterous affairs. At the same time, I can understand that someone, like my colleague, might reasonably believe breaking the vow of fidelity and lying are the primary behaviors that make adultery wrong, and therefore she believes Susan's adultery was, morally speaking, no different from any other adulterous relationship.

Dimitri and Anna's affair is arguably more troubling than Susan's. Like Susan, they broke their vows of fidelity and lied to keep their relationship a secret. Up to this point, their actions seem to be comparable to Susan's (assuming she did, in fact, lie to keep her affair secret). But their affair risked causing their spouses significant pain.

Although we don't know the details of their marriages, I think we can assume Dimitri and Anna's spouses trusted them and were emotionally vulnerable. Their spouses gave them the power to hurt them, believing it would never be used against them. In addition, Dimitri had three children, and his affair had the potential to cause lasting harm to them as well.

Are We Really So Divided?

Do Americans Disagree about the Morality of Adultery?

You might assume that, just like the hot-button issues of abortion and same-sex marriage, Americans are divided over the issue of adultery. After all, we're supposed to be in the middle of a culture war. But the data tell a different story.

According to a 2022 Gallup Poll, 89% of Americans polled said adultery was morally wrong, while only 9% said it was morally acceptable. Perhaps surprisingly, these numbers have remained steady for years.

Despite this broad consensus, division may arise when we talk about actual cases and fill in the details. In the previous sections, we explored two different cases of adultery that might provoke different responses and moral evaluations.

If you believe the primary or most important reason adultery is wrong is because it involves breaking a vow of fidelity, you're likely to believe almost all cases of adultery are comparably wrong, regardless of the details. My colleague falls into this camp.

If, on the other hand, you believe the wrongness of adultery is primarily a function of the pain the adulterer causes to their spouse, who gave the adulterer the power to hurt them, you might believe some cases are better or less wrong than other cases. You might believe Susan's adultery was less wrong than Dimitri and Anna's adultery or even claim Susan's behavior wasn't morally wrong or criticizable at all.

Introducing the Scale of Morality

With the above in mind, I'd like to introduce a practical tool that can help us better understand moral and political judgments and disagreements. I call this the *Scale of Morality*. It's a tool that can help us visualize how people weigh moral reasons differently. Imagine a classic balance scale, similar to the one Lady Justice holds in statues and paintings.

On one side of the scale, we place blocks representing rules of thumb or other reasons why the action, behavior, or law is morally right or just. On the other side, we place blocks representing reasons why the action, behavior, or law is morally wrong or unjust.

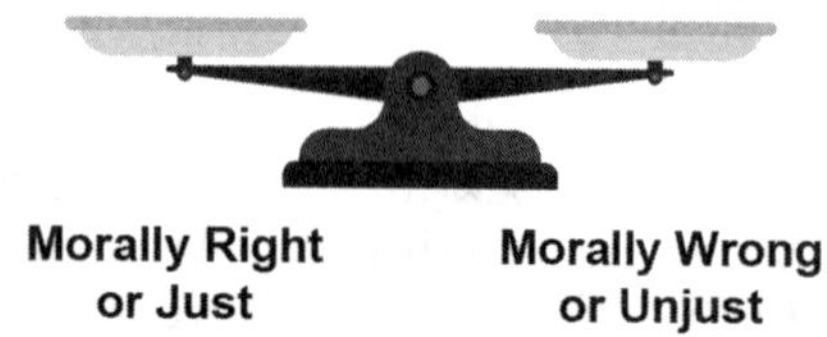

Applying the Scale of Morality to Adultery

The goal isn't to find an exact answer, like "this action weighs seven blocks in favor of the action and four blocks against it." Instead, the scale of morality can help us discover what kinds of reasons matter to us and

others. The scale can help us understand why two people can arrive at different judgments, even if both are thoughtful, caring, and sincere.

Let's see what the Scale of Morality tells us about adultery. On the right side of the scale—the side representing reasons as to why adultery is wrong—we might place the following:

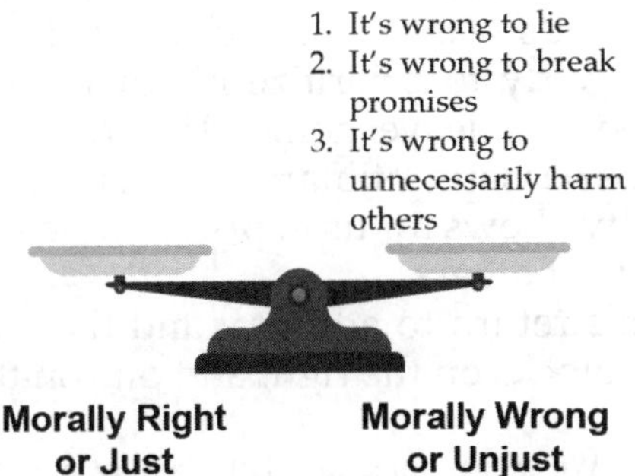

Are there any blocks that might go on the left—reasons as to why adultery might be morally permissible?

I can think of one: People are permitted, within reason, to pursue actions that promote their own well-being.

Certainly, morality allows us to perform actions that make us happy or satisfy our own desires, even if those actions don't maximize overall happiness or bring about the best consequences. Imagine being in a grocery store and putting the last box of Cheerios in your cart. A stranger standing near you says, "If you take those, there won't be any Cheerios for the next person who wants Cheerios."

I'm confident I'd be uncomfortable in this situation, but at the same time I'd be thinking: "I was lucky to find the last box. Even if buying the Cheerios means the next person won't be able to find any Cheerios, buying them isn't wrong." I might think a little deeper and realize I believe it's morally permissible to prioritize my own well-being and buy the Cheerios, and this is true even if a stranger would enjoy the Cheerios more than I would.

An example with more serious consequences might be two people who are in love and want to get married and live together, but the parents of one of them, Andy, would prefer Andy end the relationship and continue living at home. Why? Because Andy is an excellent chef, and his parents, who are quite selfish, love the meals he prepares. Not only that, but they regularly host dinner parties for their numerous friends, and their friends look forward to Andy's meals. Even if not marrying and spending the rest of his life at home would increase the happiness of his parents and their friends, even if the happiness of Andy's parents and friends would outweigh the happiness of Andy and his spouse if they get married, it's reasonable to claim that it wouldn't be wrong for Andy to prioritize his own well-being and get married and leave home. This reveals something important—perhaps, utilitarianism isn't entirely correct and morality allows for us to prioritize self-interest over the interests of others.

Now let's return to adultery and the scale. We now have three blocks on the right and one on the left.

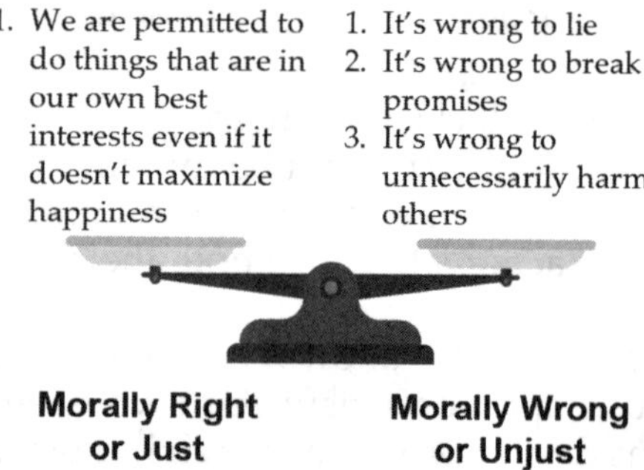

If we believe an act of infidelity is wrong or impermissible, we must believe the combined weight of the three blocks on the right is greater than the weight of the block on the left. Conversely, if we believe the act of infidelity is permissible, we believe the weight of the block on the left is greater than the combined weight of the blocks on the right.

The hard part is determining the size or weight of the different blocks. In fact, I'm convinced we'll never be able to conceive of a formula or algorithm we can use to make this determination. That said, the Scale of Morality can help us understand how much weight we do in fact attach to the different blocks (even if we can't justify this). That is, if we believe a specific case of adultery is wrong, we must believe the combined weight of the blocks on the right is greater than the combined weight of the blocks on the left. In addition, thinking about the

scale and the weight we attach to the different blocks might motivate us to revise our initial judgments.

Evaluating Susan's Case Using the Scale

Let's look at Susan's adulterous behavior. Susan broke a vow of fidelity; thus, the first block on the right should stay on the scale. We don't know if she lied to others about her affair. For the sake of discussion, let's say she did at first and then decided to stop doing so. Perhaps, after thinking about it, she concluded her behavior was morally permissible, and she had no reason to lie. Thus, the block representing the rule of thumb "It's wrong to lie" should remain on the scale as it's relevant to this situation, but it won't be very large or weigh much.

The third block—It's wrong to unnecessarily hurt or harm others, especially those that gave us the power to hurt them—should probably be removed from the scale. If, as Susan and her doctors believe, her husband will never learn about or understand she was engaging in adultery, the adultery will not cause him (or anyone else, let's assume) pain.

What about the left side of the scale? As explained above, most or all of us believe we have a limited permission to do things that make us happy or satisfy our desires, even if doing these things doesn't maximize overall happiness. Thus, the block on the left should remain on the scale.

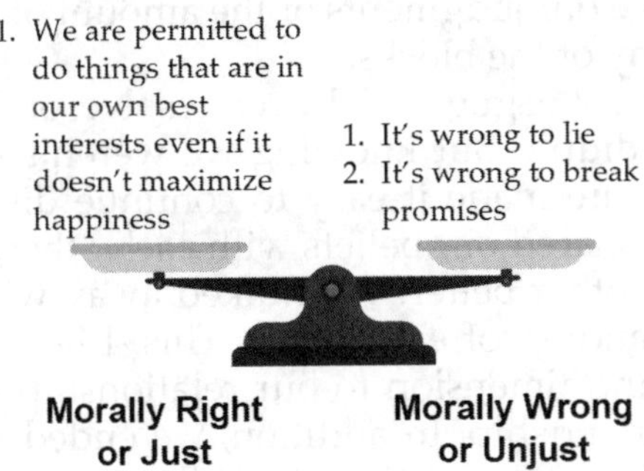

Recall that my colleague believed Susan's behavior was wrong and it wasn't less bad or less wrong than

other adulterous relationships. Looking at the scale, we discover her belief makes sense if she believed the wrongness of lying and breaking promises always outweighs the permission to do what's in our best interest.

I wasn't necessarily convinced by my colleague's reasoning and questioned whether Susan's adultery might have been less bad or less wrong than most other adulterous relationships. The Scale of Morality reveals that my colleague and I embraced both rules of thumb on the right. We disagreed over the issue of whether the block on the left belonged, and even if it did, she believed it could never counteract or weigh more than the blocks representing the wrongness of breaking the vow of fidelity and the wrongness of lying.

Recognizing the primary source of our disagreement helped us realize that even though we disagreed about Susan's adultery, we weren't so far apart. I repeat: We both embraced the rules of thumb on the right side of the scale. Our disagreement primarily concerned the block on the left—whether we have a permission to do things that are in our best interest, even if doing them doesn't maximize overall happiness.

The Scale's Limitations

I want to emphasize the Scale of Morality may not tell us what to do in complicated moral situations. Rather, it helps us understand the complexity of the situation, our own views or beliefs, and the views or beliefs of others. Not only that, but as we think about the weights we and others attach to the different blocks, we may be motivated to change our judgments or the amount of weight we attach to any of the blocks.

Did my colleague and I ever resolve our disagreement? We didn't. But knowing we weren't so divided over this issue made it easy to continue discussing it. And as we shared our beliefs with each other, we got to know each other better. We walked away with a deeper understanding of each other. This, I believe, added an important dimension to our relationship and deepened our friendship. In addition, we ended up having an interesting conversation about the permission to do what's in our own best interest, something we never intended to do.

Evaluating Dimitri and Anna's Case Using the Scale

Let's focus on Dimitri.

Dimitri broke a vow of fidelity, thus the "wrong to break promises" block clearly belongs on the scale. The "wrong to lie" block also belongs because Dimitri repeatedly lied to his wife and, I assume, his children and friends. In addition—and this is the big one—his wife gave him the power to hurt her, trusting he wouldn't abuse this power. But he did abuse it. Presumably the result will be significant emotional pain for her.

His children too, will likely be harmed by the affair. This may explain why many of us are more troubled by adultery and divorce when the couple has children.

We mustn't forget the block on the left. I've tried to establish that most of us believe we can sometimes break a rule of thumb if doing so increases our own well-being or satisfies our own desires. Put differently, we don't have an obligation to always maximize overall happiness. That said, this permission is limited.

Dimitri and Anna's Adultery

1. We are permitted to do things that are in our own best interests even if it doesn't maximize happiness

1. It's wrong to lie
2. It's wrong to break promises
3. It's wrong to unnecessarily harm others

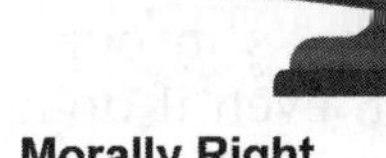

Morally Right or Just

Morally Wrong or Unjust

We can now think about our own views concerning the weight or size of the different blocks. Presumably, if we believe Dimitri's adultery is in no way morally acceptable, we believe the weight of the block representing the permission to do what's in our own interest is small or significantly less than the combined weight of the three blocks on the right.

I'll admit, when I first read this story, I was critical of Dimitri and Anna, but I believed their behavior was somewhat (not completely) redeemed. That said, I wasn't sure why I believed this. Then I thought about the scale. When I considered the different blocks, it became obvious I must be putting a lot of weight on the left side of the scale. I realized I was focusing on the nature of Dimitri and Anna's relationship and how it might affect them (as opposed to how it might affect others). For the first time, they both experienced the profound depth of true love—a feeling that ranks among the most precious or valuable of human experiences, if not the most precious and valuable. What should be the size of the block representing the permission to do what's in our own best interest if it represents the only opportunity we'll ever have to experience true love?

Gaining this understanding of my own thoughts helped me make sense of my ambivalence. I still believed that the affair was morally wrong, but I saw an argument for why it might be less wrong than other cases of adultery.

Not only did the Scale of Morality help me understand my own beliefs or views, but it helped me articulate these beliefs to my colleague later in the day. As we spoke, we realized that her initial thoughts—all instances of adultery are wrong to the same degree—suggested that she didn't even include the block on the left in her evaluations. But after thinking about it for a little while, she realized that she did believe that we do at times have the permission to do what's in our own best interest, even if doing so doesn't maximize overall happiness or involves not following a moral principle we embrace. Thus, we agreed that the block representing this permission, even if it was quite small, belonged on the left side of the scale. I think we were both happy knowing that we both embraced the same principles, even though we didn't agree on the size of the blocks representing these principles.

What should be the size of the block representing the permission to do what's in our own best interest if it represents the only opportunity we'll ever have to experience true love?

As we'll see later in this book, the Scale of Morality is especially helpful when we try to better understand disagreements over political and social issues, like abortion, capital punishment, income taxation, etc.

Final Thoughts

In this chapter, we explored the issue of whether committing adultery or cheating while in an exclusive relationship is seriously morally wrong, and if so, why. While many discussions of infidelity focus on the wrongness of breaking a vow and lying, I suggested there might be another factor that makes adultery wrong: vulnerability.

When we enter a committed, exclusive relationship, we often allow ourselves to become vulnerable. This vulnerability has the potential to deepen and enrich our relationships, but as the word implies, it comes with significant risk. When we allow ourselves to become vulnerable, we give our partner the power to hurt or harm us. BUT we give them this power trusting they won't use it. If they betray us and use this power and hurt us by cheating, they're doing something that's very wrong.

We then looked at whether Americans are divided over the morality of adultery. Polls suggest we aren't divided over this issue. That said, when we discuss specific cases of adultery or infidelity, differences of opinion may arise.

To help us better understand our own beliefs concerning moral or political issues, I introduced what I call the Scale of Morality. Not only does this tool give us insight into why we believe what we believe, but it also helps us better understand why others believe what they believe and what may be the sources of our disagreements with others.

Finally, I explained how using the Scale of Morality can help us recognize that even when we disagree about a specific case of adultery (and this applies to other moral disagreements as well), those disagreements don't necessarily mean we are fundamentally divided over the issue. More often than not, our disagreements stem from assigning different weight to the same set of principles. If we embrace the same principles but assign different weight to these principles, I think it's accurate to say we aren't very divided over the issue. After all, we are appealing to a shared set of moral principles. This recognition—that we share the same moral principles—gives us reason to believe we don't live in different moral universes.

Before we conclude, I invite you, the reader, to reflect on an important question: "What sort of person do I want to be?"

Do you want to be the type of person who engages in behaviors that have the potential to deeply hurt someone you love or care for deeply? If not, you probably don't want to be the type of person who commits adultery or cheats when you're in a committed relationship.

Similarly, you might want to at least question whether you want to be the kind of person who unnecessarily harms others, even strangers. Finally, you might want to ask yourself whether you want to be the type of person who willingly, compassionately, and lovingly helps others, even strangers. Maybe the answers to these questions fall somewhere in the middle.

We'll return to this topic in the final chapter of this book.

5: Are Any Actions Always Wrong?

The issue: Is there some kind of philosophical measuring stick we can use to objectively gauge whether something is inherently wrong?

If you were on a jury, could you ever vote to convict an innocent person?

In the early morning of March 2, 1991, two California Highway Patrol officers observed a 1987 Hyundai speeding on Interstate 210. They pursued the car, driven by Rodney King, a Black man. After a high-speed chase, the officers, with the help of a police helicopter and additional police cars, cornered the vehicle.

King and two other occupants were ordered to exit the vehicle. When King exited the car, he was ordered to lie on the ground. According to some reports, King didn't immediately comply, and Los Angeles Police Department Sergeant Stacey Koon ordered several other officers to subdue and handcuff him.

A local resident, George Holliday, witnessed what was happening and began recording the scene. The footage, viewed by millions of Americans, shows police officers tasering King, repeatedly kicking him, and severely beating him with their batons. While some argued the beating was not an excessive use of force, others believed it was an extreme example of police brutality. (You can see the video online. Be warned: it's disturbing.) Significantly, the chief of the LAPD, Daryl Gates, stated King was hit with batons more than 50 times and the force was excessive.

Initially, King was charged with "felony evading," but those charges were dropped.

Four officers were charged with excessive use of force and assault. Their trial, which was originally scheduled

to take place in Los Angeles, was moved to the predominately White suburb of Simi Valley, California. The jury deliberated, and after receiving the verdicts from the jury, the judge delayed reading them for several hours. He was apparently concerned about public safety and wanted the police and others to be ready for possible unrest.

All four of the officers were acquitted of the assault charges, and three were acquitted of the excessive force charges. Although the fourth wasn't acquitted, he wasn't convicted either, as the jury couldn't agree on whether he was guilty or not.

Rodney King (pictured) was subjected to what many considered excessive force by California Highway Patrol officers in 1991 because he did not comply quickly enough with orders to lie on the ground. King, who was unarmed, was beaten, kicked, and tasered repeatedly.

Significantly, upon hearing the verdict, the mayor of Los Angeles, Tom Bradley, stated: "The jury's verdict will not blind us to what we saw on that videotape. The men who beat Rodney King do not deserve to wear the uniform of the LAPD."

Later that day, the infamous "1992 Los Angeles Riots" began. They lasted six days and resulted in the deaths of more than 60 people, thousands of injuries, and extensive damage to homes and businesses.

Because the original charges had been adjudicated in state court, the officers couldn't be retried as this would violate the Constitution's prohibition against double jeopardy. But they could be tried in federal court. A federal grand jury charged three of the original defendants with using excessive force and the fourth with failing to stop the unlawful assault on King.

Now, imagine you're on the jury in the federal case. Having witnessed the devastation following the first trial, might it cross your mind to convict the officers, even if you weren't sure of their guilt, to prevent another wave of violence and destruction? Wouldn't it be better, or wouldn't there be less overall pain and suffering, to convict and send four innocent police officers to jail for a limited amount of time and avoid another riot or

the civic unrest that might result in the loss of innocent lives, homes, and livelihoods?

While the federal case was being tried, I remember struggling with these very questions and discussing them with my friends. On the one hand, utilitarianism—a theory that says the right action is the action that maximizes happiness—suggests that convicting the officers might be the right thing to do. After all, doing so might prevent more horrific riots or unrest.

On the other hand, like many others, I embraced the rule of thumb that dictates "It's wrong to convict innocent people of crimes and/or send innocent people to jail."

Ultimately, I realized that as much as I was moved by utilitarian considerations, I couldn't support convicting innocent people of a crime or sending innocent people to jail, even if doing so would bring about better, perhaps much better, consequences. If I remember correctly, my friends thought the same thing.

Perhaps some actions are simply wrong, period. Not because they produce bad consequences, but because they violate something deeper. A principle or moral line that should never be crossed.

What do you think?

Discussion

In the novel *Sophie's Choice,* which was later adapted into a critically acclaimed film, Sophie and her two children are forcefully taken to Auschwitz-Birkenau, a concentration camp in Poland during World War II. Upon arrival, a Nazi officer confronts Sophie with a horrific ultimatum: Choose which of your children will be put to death in a gas chamber and which will be allowed to live. If you refuse to choose, they will both be killed.

Sophie chooses to save the life of her son, thereby condemning her daughter to death. This decision tortures Sophie for the rest of her life. She suffers guilt and self-loathing, which, presumably, lead to depression and alcoholism. At the end of the novel, Sophie and her partner die by suicide.

I imagine most of us would agree Sophie shouldn't be criticized for the choice she made. And if she had

In the William Styron novel *Sophie's Choice,* the titular character has to choose whether to send her son or her daughter to slaughter in the Nazi concentration camp Auschwitz.

---

chosen to save her daughter, we wouldn't criticize that choice either. But what if she hadn't chosen at all and allowed both of her children to be put to death? Wouldn't that be the worst result?

At times, I've wondered whether refusing to choose—even knowing this would result in the death of both children—could have been morally praiseworthy. I'm not suggesting that refusing would have reduced Sophie's lifelong suffering. Rather, perhaps refusing to choose would have been *morally* superior, or at least morally comparable, to selecting one child to live while condemning the other to die. Refusing to choose might have demonstrated a depth of love so profound that making a choice was inconceivable or impossible. Maybe refusing to choose could be seen as a tragic act of moral integrity.

At this point, we know what a utilitarian would say: If refusing to choose doesn't maximize overall happiness or fails to bring about enough happiness, refusing would be morally wrong. Hence, at least at first glance, utilitarianism would claim Sophie did the right thing, since choosing allowed one child the chance to experience future happiness (assuming survival within the concentration camp were possible).

But this analysis might feel cold or incomplete.

Buridan's Ass: A Choice That Led to No Choice

Philosophers and others frequently encourage us to be less emotional and make "the rational choice," but the Buridan's Ass paradox, a famous philosophical thought experiment, may suggest otherwise. Imagine that a donkey is positioned exactly midway between two identical piles of hay—they're the same size and have the same shape and smell. If the donkey is deciding which pile of hay it should eat from and is basing this decision on rationality alone, which will it choose?

Given the structure of the setup, the ass has no rational reason to pick or prefer either pile. Unable to choose, it starves to death.

This thought experiment suggests that strictly rational decision-making can lead to paralysis, hinting at the importance of non-rational factors in choices.

Might Buridan's Ass help us understand why some people don't vote? If two candidates seem to be basically the same, a voter might claim that they didn't vote because it didn't matter to them who won. Is it possible that this voter felt "paralyzed" (and maybe didn't realize this was the case) rather than consciously chose not to vote?

Perhaps Buridan's Ass has similar implications for morality. If my choices are based on solely rational considerations and I have two options that seem to be identical (or close enough), I may be paralyzed until I can find a reason to pick one action or another. Of course, if non-rational considerations play a role, this paralysis can be avoided.

Although this thought experiment is named after Jean Buridan, a fourteenth-century French philosopher, most scholars believe that he is not, in fact, the author. Some trace its roots to Aristotle's treatise *De Caelo* ("On the Heavens"), which was written more than 1,500 years before Buridan's birth, and to twelfth-century Islamic philosopher Al-Ghazali, who described a similar paradox.

The Limits of Utilitarianism

Let's return to the earlier example of convicting innocent police officers in order to prevent massive civic unrest.

If sending four innocent people to prison would maximize happiness or bring about more happiness than voting to acquit them, utilitarianism would dictate you should vote to convict them.

While most of us—probably all of us—use utilitarianism at times, I imagine many people can't agree with the utilitarian in this situation. The thought of knowingly punishing innocent people, even if doing so would result in greater overall happiness, doesn't sit well with us.

Introducing Deontology

At this point, it's time to introduce the second ethical theory we'll explore in this book: *deontology*. Derived from the Greek word *deon*, meaning "duty," deontology is an ethical theory that judges actions based on adherence to moral duties or rules, rather than outcomes of those actions. In contrast to utilitarianism, which justifies any action that maximizes happiness, deontology insists we follow certain moral rules or principles, even if following these rules does not lead to the greatest overall happiness.

For example, many deontologists would say: "It's wrong to lie, period end of report." Or, "Breaking promises is wrong, even if doing so would lead to the best overall consequences." They might continue: "These actions are morally wrong because they violate duties or principles that must be respected."

English philosopher and epistemologist C. D. Broad was the first person to use the word "deontological" in its current specialized sense in his book *Five Types of Ethical Theory* (1930).

There are many versions of deontology, and different traditions offer different sets of duties or principles. A familiar example might be the Ten Commandments, which many regard as clearly defining what's morally right and wrong. Crucially, even if violating one of the commandments would maximize happiness, few who embrace them would argue that this justifies violating such fundamental moral rules.

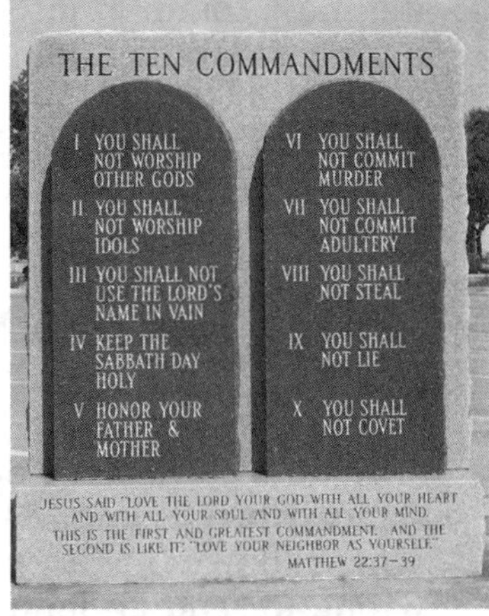

The Bible's Ten Commandments can be considered an example of deontology in which the rules stand by themselves regardless of the consequences.

Regardless of whether we believe that our moral rules are encompassed in the Ten Commandments or some other list of rules, most of us embrace, or sometimes appeal to, some form of deontology. For instance, on the federal jury we might think: "Convicting one or two of the police officers might prevent social unrest or a riot, but it's still wrong. I can't condone convicting an innocent person of a crime they didn't commit in order to make our society calmer, safer, or even more sane."

Similarly, many or most of us would think it's wrong to kill one innocent person to save the lives of three innocent people. Imagine we can kill an innocent person and transplant their organs into three innocent people who will die without the transplanted organs. Even if this maximizes overall happiness, we might believe this behavior is wrong. Why? Because we embrace the principle "It's wrong to kill innocent people."

Rules of Thumb vs. Moral Absolutes

A clarification is in order. It might seem as though I've been appealing to deontology throughout this book as I've frequently discussed "Rules of Thumb." However, rules of thumb are different because when we say "'X is wrong' is a rule of thumb," we explicitly recognize that sometimes X isn't wrong or there are exceptions to the rule. Significantly, as discussed in Chapter 1, one of

the most common justifications for rejecting a rule of thumb is claiming doing so will bring about better consequences.

But deontology is different. It tells us that even if breaking a rule will maximize happiness, it's still wrong to break the rule.

How Do We Determine Moral Absolutes?

If we believe some actions are wrong in all circumstances, then an important question presents itself: How do we know what actions are on the list? If it's always wrong to send an innocent person to jail, is it also always wrong to lie? As I've already suggested, one way to develop this list is to look at our religious texts and see what they say.

But there's another approach, one that comes from a philosophical tradition rather than a religious one. The most influential figure in this tradition is Immanuel Kant, an eighteenth-century philosopher. Kant believed that morality doesn't depend on religion or achieving good outcomes. Instead, he argued moral rules come from reason itself.

Kantian Deontology

Kant's approach is both unique and ingenious. It's also quite complicated. I'll do my best to provide a clear, accessible introduction.

Let's start with an intuitive moral judgment. I think (and hope) we all believe it's morally wrong to buy and sell human beings. Yet, many of us also believe it's morally permissible to buy and sell animals, like cats, dogs, and horses. But why?

After all, cats, dogs, and horses, like human beings, are alive, feel pain, eat, reproduce sexually, and make sounds that come out of their mouths. So, what's the difference? How can we justify not buying and selling humans and buying and selling these other animals?

Kant's answer is that human beings are fundamentally different from other animals because of our capacity to engage in rational thought or make rational decisions. Unlike other animals, humans can think abstractly, plan

for the future, and reflect on the moral and practical dimensions of these choices. And we humans have the capacity to live with *autonomy*. Autonomy refers to the ability to make independent, rational decisions—to legislate for oneself and act according to one's own values and reasoning.

German philosopher Immanuel Kant (1724–1804) has been called the "Father of Modern Ethics."

Kant claimed these capacities give humans intrinsic worth or dignity. This dignity, he argued, isn't based on what we do. Instead, it's based on what we are. Because we have the capacities for rational thinking and autonomy, we're morally special, and we're owed a certain kind of respect. That respect requires that we not be used as mere tools to achieve someone else's goals or ends. This duty of respect—our duty to treat others (and ourselves) as ends in themselves—is, for Kant, the foundation of morality.

In order to discover what are our specific moral obligations and duties, Kant developed a principle he called the *categorical imperative*. (I recognize this is getting complicated, but stick with me and it will all make sense.) We can use the categorical imperative to identify true moral duties—duties that apply always and everywhere, regardless of the situation or outcome.

Unlike utilitarianism, which claims we should break moral rules (or rules of thumb) if doing so produces the most happiness, Kantian ethics tells us that some rules must never be broken, period. For example, if "Lying is wrong" is a true moral principle, then it's wrong to lie even if lying would bring about an abundance of happiness, while not lying would result in widespread pain.

One version of the categorical imperative, known as the "Formula of Humanity," states: "Act in such a way that you always treat humanity, whether in your own person or in the person of any other, never merely as a means, but always at the same time as an end."

The last several words may bring about difficulties. What does it mean to treat someone "merely as a means

to an end"? What is it that we must avoid? There's much scholarship addressing this issue, but for the sake of simplicity, I suggest we understand "treating someone merely as a means to an end" to mean: to deny them the opportunity to make and act on their own rational decisions. It's to deny them the opportunity to be autonomous. We might say treating someone merely as a means to an end is similar to treating them as a tool, like a hammer or wrench, that we can use to satisfy our own desires.

Applying Kant's Ethics

Let's see how this might work in practice. Imagine that a colleague, Barbara, approaches you and says she forgot her wallet at home and needs $20 to buy gas for her car. "If you lend me the money," Barbara says, "I'll pay you back tomorrow." Trusting her, you lend Barbara the money.

The next day, you discover that Barbara quit, and after talking to other colleagues, you learn she told them the same story, and they gave her the money too. You eventually realize Barbara lied. She never intended to pay you back.

Now you ask yourself: What made lying wrong?

Given the attention I've focused on utilitarianism, you might be thinking Barbara's lying was wrong because it didn't maximize happiness. Perhaps Barbara's happiness was increased because she obtained money she could use as she pleased. But the happiness of everyone who gave her money was decreased. Not only that, but her lies might have some longer lasting negative consequences. If in the future another colleague needs to borrow money, you and others will likely be reluctant to lend it to him. Living in a world in which we don't trust others (or working in an office in which we don't trust those we work with) will likely make our lives more difficult or less happy than they'd be if we trusted them. Given that Barbara's lies didn't maximize happiness or bring about enough happiness because the happiness she experienced was outweighed by the unhappiness experienced by her colleagues, utilitarianism would likely claim Barbara's behavior was wrong.

I suggest, however, that before you ever learned about utilitarianism, you would have known Barbara's lie was wrong. Why?

After loaning a colleague named Barbara some cash, you discover the next day that she borrowed from others, too, promising to pay them back, and then promptly disappeared. Clearly, you've all been used and lied to.

According to Kant, it was wrong because it disrespected you as a rational being. By lying, Barbara prevented you from making an informed, rational decision about whether to lend her the money. If she had told you the truth, that she didn't intend to repay you, you probably wouldn't have lent her the money. But she interfered with your ability to make a rational decision. So, she treated you as a tool—merely as a means to an end—rather than as a person worthy of respect. And that's why, according to Kant, her action was wrong.

Importantly, for Kant, lying is *always* wrong because lying *always* treats a person merely as a means to an end. Lying never respects another's dignity or right to make rational decisions. Since lying always treats people merely as a means to an end, we have a duty not to lie to other rational beings. And given that we have this duty, other rational beings have a *right* not to be lied to.

Beyond Lying: Other Violations of Autonomy

Lying isn't the only way we can treat someone merely as a means to an end or deny someone their autonomy. Killing someone (against their will) also interferes with their ability to rationally decide whether they want to continue living. It denies them the possibility of living autonomously. We have a duty, therefore, not to kill other human beings (against their will), and there are no exceptions.

This prohibition doesn't extend to animals, according to Kant. While animals may feel pain and have desires, Kant believed they don't have the capacity to make rational choices. That is, they are incapable of rational self-governance—autonomy. Thus, they don't have the same dignity that humans have. This explains why Kant believed we don't have a duty not to kill animals, like cows, fish, or dogs.

You can probably figure out why Kant believed stealing is wrong. Like lying, stealing denies the one being stolen from the opportunity to rationally decide what to do with their own personal property. It doesn't respect their autonomy. So, like lying and killing, stealing is always wrong.

There are many other behaviors that are wrong because they treat another merely as a means to an end. Hitting someone, entering their property, or burning their building (all without their consent) are wrong because they involve denying another the opportunity to make a rational choice or act autonomously. Breaking a promise is the same. Those who follow Kant believe we can arrive at a complete list of actions that are always wrong by determining what actions deny others the opportunity to make rational choices or live autonomously.

Kant and the Absolute Wrongness of Slavery

To illustrate Kantian ethics further, let's look at one more example. Let's assume slavery doesn't maximize happiness. In that case, a utilitarian would say slavery was wrong. But is that really why we believe slavery is wrong?

Probably not.

Most of us believe slavery is wrong because of the way slaves are treated—as property. Slavery denies people the opportunity to excise their rationality or to pursue their own goals. It strips them of autonomy or uses them as tools that can be bought, sold, and used. It treats the slaves, using Kant's language, merely as a means to an end.

At least for me, Kant's explanation of the wrongness of slavery is superior to the utilitarian explanation.

When we conclude that slavery is wrong, we don't do so because it doesn't maximize happiness; we say it is always wrong in itself because it is treating human beings as objects, merely as a means to an end, and denying them their autonomy and dignity.

Kant and Rodney King

Now it's easy to see why many of us, if we were jurors on the federal case against the police officers, might be disinclined or unwilling to convict the officers if we believed they weren't guilty. Convicting them would be wrong, we believe, because it's wrong to treat a human like a tool, deny them autonomy, or treat them merely as a means to an end to satisfy our own desires or to bring about greater overall happiness.

Social Contract Theory—Another Formulation of Deontology

In this book, I'll primarily focus on Kant's ethics when discussing deontology. That said, I'd like to briefly introduce a formulation of deontology that may be more familiar: social contract theory.

Social contract theory is a moral and political framework that holds an action, law, or public policy is morally right or just if it would be agreed upon by rational, self-interested individuals. Social contract theory is usually appealed to when discussing public policy or laws, but it can apply to personal morality as well.

Thomas Hobbes, a seventeenth century philosopher, is considered by many to be the first and most important modern social contract theorist.

Is Government Morally Justified?

Hobbes explored the fundamental question of whether government was morally justified. After all, governments create laws, and laws restrict our freedom—we are punished if we steal, commit arson, don't pay taxes, stay too long at a parking meter, etc. In contrast, a world without government—Hobbes called this the *state of nature*—wouldn't have any laws. In the state of nature, our freedom would not be restricted. We could do anything we wanted to do.

Imagine living in a *state of nature* or pre-governmental society. You'd have absolute freedom. Sounds good, doesn't it?

The problem, according to Hobbes, is that we're naturally motivated by self-interest. Let's imagine we live

English philosopher Thomas Hobbes (1588–1679) first presented his thoughts on social contract theory in his 1651 book, *Leviathan*.

in a cold climate and winter is approaching. We store food for the winter in our homes, but we know winter may last longer than expected, potentially leading to food shortages. One obvious solution is to steal our neighbor's food. Remember, there are no laws in the state of nature, therefore there is no external deterrent. Our neighbor, thinking along the same lines, might also plan to steal our food. Not only that, but our neighbor knows that we may be thinking of invading and taking his food.

Since our neighbor might be thinking of invading and stealing our food, we might decide to preemptively invade, kill him, and steal his food. The neighbor might be thinking the same. Thus, one of us invades the other. We see, therefore, that a lawless society, a society in which we have complete freedom, might not be what we imagined.

You might suggest that we should make agreements with our neighbors not to invade, but if survival is at stake and there are no laws, it might be rational to break the agreement and invade. Again, since our neighbors understand this, they might invade first. Of course, we are aware of that, so we invade even sooner.

Hobbes famously concludes that life in the state of nature is "solitary, poor, nasty, brutish, and short."

How can we improve our lives if we live in a state of nature? According to Hobbes, if we're rational and self-interested, we should agree to give power to a sovereign or supreme ruler. This sovereign would have the authority to make rules and laws and enforce them. A good sovereign will enact rules, such as don't steal others' food, don't kill others, and don't physically attack others.

If we are rational and self-interested and know the sovereign will punish us if we break the rules, we'll be deterred from doing so. Nor will we fear our neighbor stealing from us, because our neighbor, just like us, is self-interested and doesn't want to be punished.

This move to *civil society* leaves us with less freedom—we aren't free to steal, kill, and so forth—but our lives are significantly better. According to Hobbes, the move to civil society is just because rational, self-interested individuals would agree to it.

Ignorance Is Bliss?

Can we ever make laws that are truly fair or just? If wealthy people make laws, won't they favor wealthy people, even if the lawmakers are trying to be fair and objective? Conversely, if those in poverty create our laws, won't they favor those in poverty? And even more problematic, both sides sincerely believe the laws they made are just or fair. Those in poverty might say fairness means everyone has enough money for food and shelter, regardless of their income. Wealthy individuals might argue that this approach is unfair, discourages hard work, and could lead to societal collapse.

Enter John Rawls, one of the most important twentieth-century philosophers. Rawls tackles this issue by asking us to imagine a veil of ignorance descending over us. Behind this veil, we don't know particular things about ourselves—our financial and social status, age, religion, talents, etc. We do know basic facts about psychology and politics. While imagining we are in behind the veil, we should attempt to rationally determine what principles we would support if we were moderately self-interested. These principles, Rawls claims, are fair and just and should govern our society.

Notice that, since we don't know our actual circumstances, we can't select laws that favor our own specific situation. For example, since we don't know whether we're wealthy or impoverished, we wouldn't support principles that favor the wealthy. Why? We might in fact be impoverished. Rawls argues that behind the veil of ignorance, we would support truly fair principles because they wouldn't reflect the interests of any specific group.

So, what principles would moderately self-interested, rational people choose behind the veil of ignorance? According to Rawls, the first principle we'd embrace would provide the most extensive lib-

(cont. p. 102)

(cont. from p. 101)

erty possible, just as long as everyone could have the same amount of liberty. This would include, he claims, religious liberty, voting rights, freedom of speech, and a variety of other liberties. If we don't know whether we're Christian, Muslim, or Hindu, we wouldn't choose laws favoring any particular religious group, thereby ensuring fairness to everyone. Similarly, if we don't know our political preferences, we wouldn't pass laws that favor one political group or another. Nor would we support laws that restrict voting to one group or another, because we don't know if the law would deny us the right to vote in real life—when we're not behind the veil.

You might think that this approach would back everyone having the same amount of money, but in fact this is incorrect. The second principle Rawls believes rational, self-interested people would support is what's called the difference principle or maxi-min. According to this principle, there could be economic inequalities in society, but they would be limited to those that help the least advantaged. For example, the system might allow doctors and engineers to get paid more than a bakery clerk, because it takes a lot of time and effort to become a doctor or engineer. If we didn't pay them more than bakery clerks, we wouldn't have enough doctors and engineers—everyone would suffer, including the least advantaged. But doctors and engineers wouldn't get paid so much that others in society suffer. Behind the veil, would you conclude that doctors should be paid $400,000 per year and bakery clerks $15,000, or would you want doctors to earn $150,000 and bakery clerks to earn $40,000? Since you don't know which job you hold in real life, Rawls claims that if you're rational you'd favor the latter. Of course, this assumes that, with such a salary structure, we'd have enough doctors.

This is something like a social contract theory, because Rawls claims that if all of us performed this hypothetical thought experiment, all of us would choose these principles if we were rational and moderately self-concerned. Hence, the principles are just.

Social Contract Theory and Moral Principles

Most contemporary social contract theorists suggest that to evaluate the justice of a law in civil society, we must ask whether rational people living in the society would consent to or approve of it. If they would, the law is just. If they wouldn't—again, they must *rationally* disagree with it—the law is unjust.

We can apply the social contract to moral principles as well. We can ask whether rational members of society would consent or agree to a given principle. If they would approve of or consent to it, it is a legitimate moral principle. If they wouldn't, it's not a legitimate moral principle. Using social contract theory, we can arrive at a list of moral principles society ought to follow.

Let's consider how social contract theory might address the issue of lying. We begin by asking whether rational people would embrace a moral principle, such as "Lying is morally wrong."

Lying, we might conclude, undermines trust, and trust is essential for a cooperative society. If we know people are inclined to lie, we will avoid entering into agreements with them. If someone told us, for example, that she'd water our plants tomorrow if we watered her plants today, we wouldn't trust her to follow through. Thus, we wouldn't enter into the agreement, and we'd have to do all the watering ourselves. You can imagine many other instances in which trusting others makes our lives better. We see, therefore, that we benefit more from implementing the principle "Lying is wrong" than from allowing or condoning dishonesty. Thus, the principle "Lying is wrong" is a legitimate moral principle.

Being a liar undermines trust between people, and without that trust in a community it is impossible to form a cooperatively functioning society.

As previously stated, we can use this procedure to generate a list of moral principles that rational people would

support. And once we have this list, social contract theorists would say we have a duty to obey these rules.

So while Kant grounds morality in respect for autonomy and the dignity of persons, social contract theory grounds morality in mutual agreement among rational individuals. But both approaches see morality as something deeper or greater than just maximizing happiness.

Are We Really So Divided?

I'm confident most of us find Kant's theory appealing, even if we don't necessarily believe it's 100% correct. We believe some actions, like enslaving another person or convicting an innocent person, are intrinsically wrong. However, we also believe that at some point consequences do matter. Consider one of the hypothetical cases discussed in Chapter 2 -- you can push a button to prevent the detonation of 20 nuclear weapons, but it would result in the death of one innocent person. Even if you embrace the rule of thumb "It's wrong to kill innocent people," you probably believe this rule of thumb admits of exceptions. You might believe, contrary to Kant, pushing the button was the right thing to do and the rule "It's wrong to kill innocent people" is a rule of thumb as opposed to a rule that never admits of exceptions.

In fact, I've presented this hypothetical to numerous friends and literally thousands of students, and only a small handful of them said we should *never* kill an innocent person. This suggests in high-stakes cases or when the consequences are far reaching, we might reject Kant's theory and lean into utilitarianism.

Many ethicists believe one or another ethical theory is the only right or correct theory and that other theories should, therefore, be rejected. They would claim, for instance, "Utilitarianism is the correct theory and should always be followed," or "Kantian deontology is the correct theory and should always be followed." Not only do I believe these ethicists are wrong, but this commitment to one theory doesn't match how most of us make ethical decisions or experience the moral life.

Most of us shift between these theories. We might appeal to utilitarianism when the stakes are large (say,

A lot of us would probably agree that we should continue to construct bridges, roads, and large buildings for the benefit of our society even though the construction of these structures might cause injuries or even deaths.

killing one to save a million) and deontology when the stakes are smaller (say, killing one to save three, even if saving three would maximize happiness).

Recognizing that almost all of us use different ethical theories at different times or in different situations is important, as it should give you, the reader, insight into your own ethical commitments and how you make moral judgments. I hope that by having a basic understanding of the four ethical theories we'll be exploring in this book (I'll introduce the other two in later chapters), you'll be able to determine what theory motivates your judgments in different situations.

Perhaps of equal or more importance, knowing that we utilize different ethical theories in different situations (even if most people don't know or are unaware they're doing so) helps us better understand others and our disagreements with others.

You might support the death penalty because you believe it deters murder and therefore brings about more overall happiness than not having the death penalty. You're using utilitarianism to justify the death penal-

ty. I seem to be attracted to deontology (when thinking about the death penalty) and believe that even if the death penalty maximizes happiness, it's wrong because we should never risk executing an innocent person and thereby treating them merely as a means to an end or unjustly denying them autonomy.

At first glance, it might seem like our disagreement reveals that we're deeply divided morally, politically, or socially, because one of us uses utilitarianism to support the death penalty and the other appeals to deontology to oppose it. But if we're honest with ourselves, we'd both admit that we sometimes use both theories. You might appeal to deontology when you say it's wrong to cheat on a partner, even if the cheating is never discovered and maximizes overall happiness. And I might appeal to utilitarianism when I say we should build roads and bridges, which in the long run will bring about good consequences, even though doing so will predictably result in the deaths of innocent workers.

So, while we may disagree about the death penalty and use different ethical theories to support our positions, we might come to realize we aren't so different after all. We both embrace and utilize the same foundational ethical theories—utilitarianism and deontology. This recognition, I hope, can help us see that we live in the same moral universe, even if we weigh the theories differently in specific situations.

And realizing we live in the same moral universe has the power to reduce moral hostility, prevent unnecessary division, and preserve relationships. This is the case, even when we disagree with one another over deeply personal or political issues.

Final Thoughts

In this chapter, we explored deontology, particularly Kantian deontology, which holds that actions that treat human beings merely as a means to an end are *always* wrong. Put differently, actions that deny others the opportunity to act autonomously or treat others as a tool to satisfy our own desires are *always* wrong.

Interestingly, when Kant claims we should never treat humanity "whether in your own person or the person of any other" merely as a means, he explicitly

tells us that in addition to not treating others merely as a means to an end, we should also never treat ourselves merely as a means to an end. If we perform actions that deny our own autonomy or our own capacity to make rational choices, according to Kant we are doing something wrong. We aren't respecting our own dignity.

Kant claims, therefore, it's wrong to take one's own life, even if one is suffering. This is the case because we are denying ourselves the opportunity to make rational choices in the future—we are using ourselves as a tool. (In one of Kant's books, he claims both suicide and masturbation are wrong—performing both of these actions involves treating ourselves merely as a means to an end. He adds, with his dry wit: "But at least suicide takes courage.")

Kant also claims it's wrong to lie to ourselves for the same reason it's wrong to lie to others. Obviously, lying to ourselves circumvents our own rationality or interferes with our autonomy (our ability to make rational decisions and act on them).

Finally, Kant believed moderate drinking was permissible, but getting drunk was wrong. You can figure out why: because drunkenness denies us the ability to make rational or autonomous choices.

In the next chapter, we'll explore how motives or intentions affect the morality of our actions.

6: Do Good Intentions Matter?

The Issue: If you do something that benefits others, but you did it for nefarious reasons, are you still behaving in a moral manner?

Imagine you're having lunch with your friend, Kevin, who's married to Sally. With a sheepish grin, Kevin looks at you and says, "You'll never guess what I did last night. I donated all the money Sally and I had in our savings account to a charity called Save the World's Children. The charity's mission is to provide food to malnourished children in the United States and abroad."

Did Kevin do something that's morally good, bad, outstanding, or horrendous? As usual, consider why you believe what you do about Kevin's behavior. In other words, why do you believe donating all his and his wife's savings to Save the World's Children was morally good, bad, outstanding, or horrendous?

Your first impulse might be to say Kevin's action was good or even excellent. That would be my initial thought. It's not every day that someone donates their entire savings to charity, and giving to an organization that helps needy children is something we usually applaud.

However, as you already know, details matter, and you might want to hear more before evaluating the morality of Kevin's behavior. If so, we're in agreement.

Here's some background information. Kevin and Sally are financially comfortable, with good jobs and a history of charitable giving. They regularly attend fundraisers and donate to a variety of organizations but never to organizations that provide food or clothing to

It is surely a worthy cause to give financial donations to a charity that helps children overseas, but some Americans might say we should first make certain all American kids have what they need before sending money to other countries.

children. In fact, at dinner parties, it's not unusual to hear them argue against such charities.

"If parents know charities will step in to save their kids," Kevin once said, "they might not feel pressure to be responsible. It's just unfair to those who do the right thing." At the same party, Sally made her views just as clear: "There's so much suffering in the United States. Poor Americans go to sleep hungry and receive inadequate healthcare. Let's fix our own country first. If there's money left over, we can think about helping others."

Now, what do you think?

In earlier chapters, we explored two different ethical theories or approaches to morality: utilitarianism and deontology. Both can help us make sense of Kevin's donation. And, as I hope you already understand and believe, just about all of us appeal to both theories when trying to figure out what the right thing to do is.

Utilitarianism holds that consequences are the only thing that matters when evaluating the morality of an action. An act is morally right if it maximizes happiness or brings about good enough results. So, if making a hefty donation to Save the World's Children will result in the best or good enough consequences—if it will prevent innocent children from suffering—according to utilitarianism, Kevin's action is morally right or good. This might help explain why many of us are initially inclined to praise Kevin's donation, even if we don't realize we're thinking like utilitarians.

Deontology, by contrast, emphasizes our duty to follow moral principles. Depending on the specific formulation of deontology, Kevin's donation might also be considered morally right. After all, many of us embrace a set of moral principles, which includes the principle "If we have the means, we have a moral obligation to act charitably or help those in need."

One interesting aspect that both utilitarianism and deontology share is that both say little or nothing about a person's intentions, motives, or state of mind when evaluating the morality of actions. In Chapter 2 ("Is It Wrong to Kill One Innocent Person to Save 1,000,000?"), when discussing utilitarianism, we focused solely on outcomes. Whether someone meant well or not didn't matter to the utilitarian. If an act maximizes or brings about enough happiness, the act is right or good—end of discussion.

The same is often true for deontological theories. Consider the Ten Commandments. The Eighth Commandment is: "Thou Shalt Not Steal." Nowhere does this commandment specify that our intention or motive for refraining from stealing must be pure.

What about Kevin's Motive?

Curious and a bit confused at lunch, you decide to ask Kevin, "What made you donate so much money to a charity that helps malnourished children, especially those outside of the U.S.?"

Kevin was sending money overseas to feed hungry children, but his motivation for doing so was not to help the poor but to get revenge on a faithless spouse who he felt only wanted his money.

Kevin tells you to brace yourself. "I've been keeping a secret from you. I don't want to go into too many details, but about a year ago, Sally and I agreed to open our relationship. It was her idea, but I didn't need much convincing. Things weren't great between us at the time. We even considered divorce. But neither of us wanted that, and Sally thought an open marriage might help."

After your initial shock, you ask what this has to do with donating the money to charity.

"Sally and I were seeing a relationship therapist who helped us draft a set of rules. The therapist warned us that opening a marriage is dangerous and can lead to hurt feelings, jealousy, and even divorce. But he said that sticking to a set of clear boundaries helped. One key rule was not seeing the same person more than once. That way, emotional attachments wouldn't form and threaten our marriage."

"Are you and Sally still doing this?" you ask.

"No," Kevin responds. "Last week, Sally told me she was in love with someone—his name is Trent—and wants a divorce. They're planning to get married, and they want to have kids as soon as possible."

"But Sally always said she never wanted to have children," you reply. "That was something that tortured you."

"I know. That makes the betrayal worse. And here's the kicker: Trent was one of my best friends in grade school. And I introduced them. We ran into him at the grocery store a few months ago. Trent and I weren't close friends, but I can't believe either of them did this to me."

Kevin fantasized about the expression on his wife's face when she discovered their savings account had been drained of every last dollar.

"I don't know what to say, except I'm so sorry," you respond, knowing deep down that your response is inadequate.

"After learning about Sally's affair, I wanted revenge. I know that's not something to be proud of, but that's what I wanted. You know how Sally loves money and nice things. We've been saving for a beachfront condo in Florida,

and I realized giving away the money would infuriate her. Then it hit me. I could really hurt and anger her by giving the money to an organization neither she nor I like or respect—Save the World's Children."

"I have to admit," Kevin continues, "it was hard to part with our savings. We worked for years to save the money, and you know I hate the idea of rewarding irresponsible parents. But I knew it would enrage Sally."

Before you have a chance to say anything, Kevin continues, "I know this sounds horrible, but just thinking about Sally's reaction makes me smile."

Now that you know these details, do you see Kevin's action differently? Does learning he was motivated by anger and spite, as opposed to compassion, change your opinion concerning the morality of what he did?

Discussion

As stated above, for the utilitarian, the answer to the previous question is probably "no." Donating the money to Save the World's Children will likely result in far greater overall happiness than would Kevin and Sally buying a beachfront condo. Even if Sally suffers extreme pain upon discovering what Kevin did, the pain is easily outweighed by the many children who will go to sleep with full bellies. Thus, according to utilitarianism the action is morally right, and this is the case regardless of Kevin's motives or intentions.

The same is true for deontology. If donating the money doesn't violate a moral principle—and what could that be—Kevin's behavior was right, even if his motives or intentions were ugly or criticizable.

But for many of us, perhaps most of us, learning about Kevin's motives prompts us to take a new look at or reassess the morality of his donation. We may not say it was morally wrong or bad, but at the very least we might conclude it was less good than if he had been motivated by kindness or concern for others. And if he'd been motivated by care or love, as opposed to spite, hatred, or anger, we'd likely see his donation in an even more positive light. When motives like love or compassion drive an action, it seems more praiseworthy.

Virtue Ethics—
Our Third Ethical Theory

There's a popular ethical theory that captures our belief or intuition that motives, intentions, or character affect or play a role in moral evaluations. This theory is called *virtue ethics*.

Most philosophers identify Plato (429–347 B.C.E.) and Aristotle (384–322 B.C.E.) with virtue ethics. Although it was influential in ancient and medieval philosophy, virtue ethics gradually fell out of favor, and in the past few centuries it has been unpopular among most Western ethicists. This changed recently—about 30 to 40 years ago—when there was renewed interest in Aristotle's ethics and new forms of virtue ethics.

Unlike utilitarianism and deontology, which are primarily concerned with the rightness or wrongness of *actions*, virtue ethics is primarily concerned with good/bad *character* or what it means to be a good person. This is not to say that virtue ethics says nothing about actions; it does. But virtue ethics puts more emphasis on character than it puts on actions.

Virtue ethics can define right and wrong actions by asserting that an act is right if and only if it expresses

Raphael depicted the Greek philosophers Plato and Aristotle (center) at the School of Athens in his fresco at the Vatican Museum, Vatican City.

The Experience Machine

Imagine scientists created an "Experience Machine" that can provide you any experience you desire. Once you're connected to the machine, you can vividly experience winning a sports championship; being in a beautiful and passionate loving relationship, which may or may not include having children; spending great weekends with friends or a lover; living in a peaceful world where people support each other and there is no poverty or hunger; writing a great book and being famous.... You can even have the machine select your experiences in order to ensure you don't miss out on things that might make your life happier. Crucially, if you choose to be connected, you'll stay connected for the rest of your life. Also, once you're connected, you'll forget that you're connected—everything will feel absolutely real "from the inside."

Would you choose to be connected to the Experience Machine?

Robert Nozick, a prominent American philosopher, first introduced the Experience Machine thought experiment in his 1974 book, *Anarchy, State, and Utopia.* The version described above is from his 1989 book, *The Examined Life.*

Nozick believed—and subsequent experimental studies confirmed—that most people wouldn't choose to be connected to the machine. Why not? Because human beings believe a good or fulfilling life consists of more than just happiness. We also value being connected with reality, living an authentic or genuine life, and doing things as opposed to experiencing them. We don't want to feel like we are in a loving relationship or have accomplished something important. We want to accomplish these things and be responsible for accomplishing them.

Perhaps, like those who are attracted to virtue ethics, those of us who wouldn't choose to be connected to the machine believe a good life, like a virtuous or moral life, is about more than just outcomes. That is, a good life is about who we really are. We can feel generous and courageous in the machine, but in reality—even if we don't know it—we did nothing, and that's not enough.

or flows from virtue (good character traits). Notice that such an approach requires us to determine what counts as a virtue (or what it means to be a virtuous person) before we can determine whether an act is right. Hence, evaluations of character precede or take priority over evaluations of acts.

While definitions of virtue vary among theorists, most agree a virtue is a morally good character trait. Some widely accepted virtues include honesty, wisdom, compassion, benevolence, loyalty, courage, generosity, and fairness or justice. Most theorists also agree that a character trait must become habitual to be considered a virtue. For example, let's assume that honesty is a morally good character trait. If we say a person acquired the virtue of honesty, we mean the person will habitually act with honesty.

Back to Kevin

As noted above, from a utilitarian perspective, the answer to the question "Do Kevin's motives matter?" is likely no. Since donating money to Save the World's Children likely produces far more overall happiness than buying a beachfront condo, even if Sally suffers greatly when she finds out, her pain is outweighed by the many children who now go to sleep with full bellies. So, according to utilitarianism, Kevin's action is right, regardless of his motives or inner states.

Although Kevin's act of charity appeared to come from a place of caring and generosity, his motivation behind what he did was truly malicious.

The same is true for many versions of deontology. If Kevin's donation doesn't violate a moral principle, like "Stealing is wrong" or "Don't break promises," then the act is not morally wrong. And this is the case even if his motives were deplorable.

However, many of us, upon learning of Kevin's motives, were unsettled. He didn't act out of the desire to contribute to the well-being

of others or compassion. In fact, his motives were almost the opposite. He was motivated by a desire to hurt someone or make someone suffer, namely, his soon-to-be ex-wife.

If you experienced this reaction, if you were disturbed by Kevin's motives and believe they somehow affect how you morally evaluate his behavior, you're likely attracted to virtue ethics.

Before we learned about Kevin's motives, we naturally or without much thought assumed that his donation, like most charitable donations, flowed from benevolence or compassion. Given that most of us believe benevolence and compassion are virtues or praiseworthy character traits (even if we never explicitly thought about this in the past), we concluded his behavior was morally good or praiseworthy. In addition, his behavior seemed to flow from or express generosity and justice. On the surface, Kevin was extremely generous. He was eager or willing to share his material resources with others. It also seemed as though he was motivated by justice—he was acting out of a desire to help those who were in no way responsible for their own suffering. The children didn't do anything wrong or anything to deserve to suffer from hunger, and Kevin was rectifying this unfair situation.

But once we discovered Kevin's true motives, many of us revised our judgment. If his action flowed from anger, hatred, or the desire to make someone suffer—qualities we see as vices—we likely concluded his behavior was less good than we initially believed, or even morally criticizable.

Polly's Surprise Birthday Party

Revisiting examples from previous chapters can help us appreciate how virtue ethics adds another dimension to our ethical thinking. In Chapter 2, for example, we explored whether it was morally permissible for you to lie to your friend Polly to keep a surprise party a secret. Some of us might have concluded that lying in that situation was permissible, even though we embraced the rule of thumb "Lying is morally wrong." In that chapter, when I introduced utilitarianism, we saw how violating this rule of thumb could be morally justified if doing so maximized happiness.

Now we see that there's more to the story. Some of us might have believed that lying was morally permissible not only because it maximized happiness but also because it was motivated by care or benevolence, and we believe these motives are morally praiseworthy or good—they are virtues. According to virtue ethics, actions that flow from virtue are morally right, giving us another reason to believe lying was the right thing to do.

Ultimately, virtue ethics tells us that motives and character matter. Virtue ethics adds another layer to our understanding of the moral life, offering us a theory we can use alongside, or even in place of, utilitarianism and deontology.

Are We as Good as We Think?

Most of us believe that our moral character is somewhat stable. That is, if we see ourselves as compassionate or courageous, we expect we'll consistently act in that way. We furthermore believe that if we teach our children to be caring and considerate, these traits will guide their future behavior.

But what if our character is less stable than we believe?

In 1971, Stanford psychology professor Philip Zimbardo conducted what is now known as the Stanford Prison Experiment. Newspaper ads recruited participants, offering to pay them $14 per day to take part in a "psychological study of prison life." After assessing the psychological stability of potential participants, 24 were selected, and they were randomly assigned to roles in the prison—either as guards or prisoners.

The prisoners were "arrested" at home, transported in real Palo Alto police cars, and placed in a simulated, realistic prison environment, which included a prison yard and 7-by-10-foot jail cells containing three cots. Prisoners were instructed to stay in their cells or the yard during the course of the study.

The guards were provided uniforms and mirrored sunglasses and told to prevent prisoners from

(cont. p. 119)

(cont. from p. 118)

escaping. Before the prisoners were "arrested," the guards were told they should maintain law and order but shouldn't harm prisoners or withhold food or drink. They were also instructed to call prisoners by their numbers, not their names.

By the second day, guards were humiliating and abusing the prisoners—stripping them naked, verbally abusing them, and denying them food and sleep. One prisoner had what could be described as a nervous breakdown—he was crying uncontrollably and begged to be released. Things just got worse. While some prisoners initially resisted the guards, they eventually began mindlessly obeying them. They became submissive and accepted the abuse as though they deserved it. What was scheduled to be a two-week experiment was terminated on the sixth day, as prisoners had become submissive, depressed, and emotionally distressed. Interestingly, Zimbardo was so caught up in the study that he later admitted he should have stopped it sooner.

The participants were normal college students, probably just like you and me. This study suggests that our moral characters might not be as stable or deep as we believe. Put in the right (or wrong) situation, ordinary people might abandon their values and do things they never thought were possible.

Interestingly, Zimbardo later testified as an expert witness in the defense of a member of the U.S. military who was charged with abusing prisoners. In the early 2000s, it was discovered that U.S. military personnel were abusing prisoners—this included beatings, sexual humiliation, and other forms of dehumanization—at Abu Ghraib prison in Iraq. Zimbardo testified that this military member wasn't a bad person. Rather, like other members in the military who were also charged with abusing prisoners or those in his experiment, he was a good person put in a bad situation. After the prison experiment, Zimbardo probably could have predicted that the Abu Ghraib abuses would occur.

Are We Really So Divided?

As explained earlier, (almost) all of us *naturally* use the ethical theories utilitarianism and deontology—sometimes without realizing it—when we try to justify a past behavior or attempt to figure out what might be the right thing to do at the present moment or in the future. I've now added a third ethical theory to the mix: virtue ethics. And I'm claiming that in addition to utilitarianism and deontology, at times almost all of us turn to virtue ethics when making moral evaluations or decisions.

By recognizing these three approaches, we gain a clearer or more complete understanding of our own moral thinking and the thinking of others. (Spoiler: One final theory or approach will be introduced in Chapter 8.)

Our commitment to three different ethical theories or approaches helps explain why we're often torn, confused, unsure, or pulled in different directions when trying to judge whether an action is morally right or wrong. An action might maximize or bring about enough overall happiness (utilitarianism), but at the same time it may require someone to act disloyally to an employer or friend (virtue ethics). Our commitment to virtue ethics causes us to be repelled by the action, while our commitment to utilitarianism attracts us to it.

Sometimes our disagreements with others are structurally similar to what we experience when we're pulled in two different directions. I might believe that Kevin did the right thing (my utilitarian instincts convince me of this), while my neighbor, Elisa, might disagree and believe what he did was deplorable (her virtue ethics instincts convince her of this).

At first glance, it might look like Elisa and I are divided when it comes to morality and our own moral beliefs. I can imagine an influencer who thrives on stoking division saying: "Here's another example of the division and culture wars afflicting the United States. Gelfand thinks Kevin did the right thing, and his neighbor thinks what Kevin did was deplorable. They, like many Americans, live in different moral worlds. Is there any hope of unity?"

You may already recognize that such an analysis is superficial at best. Yes, Elisa and I evaluate Kevin's be-

havior differently, but that isn't evidence that we're fundamentally divided or living in different moral worlds. Presumably, both Elisa and I embrace the same rules of thumb, including: "It's morally right or praiseworthy to help those in need of assistance." In addition—and this is important when looking at this disagreement—we should remember that Elisa and I almost certainly embrace the same ethical theories. Both of us sometimes appeal to utilitarianism and focus on the consequences of actions, while at other times we appeal to deontology and focus on moral principles or on virtue ethics and focus on motives and character.

In this case, even though Elisa puts more weight on virtue ethics and believes Kevin acted wrongly, she nevertheless recognizes that utilitarianism gives her a reason to believe Kevin did the right thing. I, on the other hand, put more weight on utilitarianism and believe that Kevin did the right thing, even though I recognize that virtue ethics gives me a reason to believe what he did was wrong. In other situations, it might be the opposite. Elisa might put more weight on utilitarianism, while I put more weight on virtue ethics. The fact that we embrace the same foundational ethical theories demonstrates that the imaginary influencer is exaggerating or even incorrect.

The Scale of Morality and Kevin's Behavior

Kevin's Action

1. Utilitarianism: Donating the money brought about the best consequences or more happiness	1. Virtue Ethics: Actions that flow from vicious character traits are wrong or bad
Morally Right or Just?	**Morally Wrong or Unjust?**

If Elisa and I utilize the Scale of Morality to better understand what we think about Kevin's behavior, we'd each place blocks on both sides of the scale. I might assign a slightly heavier weight to the block that's on

the left side, while Elisa would assign more weight to the block on the right side. It might be the case that the weight of the blocks we place on both sides are relatively similar, but we nevertheless disagree over which side wins.

Just to use an arbitrary number, I might assign 54 to the block on the left and 46 to the block on the right. Elisa might do the opposite and assign 46 to the block on the left and 54 to the one the right. So, claiming we are significantly divided or live in different moral worlds would be an oversimplification or exaggeration. We agree that both kinds of considerations matter; we simply differ on which side tips the balance.

In other words, our disagreement isn't deep. It's not the case that we live in different moral worlds.

Sitting with Moral Conflict

You might be wondering how we can resolve for ourselves situations in which we're pulled in different directions. I've wrestled with this question for years.

Human beings have the amazing capacity to look at the same thing from different perspectives to reach different conclusions even when provided with the same information. In many cases, there is no absolute right or wrong answer.

Unlike many ethicists, I don't believe we should strive to find a principle or approach to morality that easily resolves these conflicts. That is, we shouldn't try to determine whether utilitarianism, deontology, or virtue ethics always trumps or wins.

Perhaps instead we ought to learn to sit with moral tension or accept being conflicted. Maybe the fact that we sometimes feel irresolvably conflicted is a sign we're morally aware or mature. After all, as I've said before, morality is complex. That we can experience moral conflict reveals something beautiful about humanity. Isn't it remarkable that we can look at moral questions from different perspectives, even when it's confusing or frustrating? What an extraordinary species we are!

Final Thoughts

In this chapter, we explored a third ethical theory: virtue ethics. Unlike utilitarianism and deontology, which focus on actions, virtue ethics focuses primarily on a person's inner states—motives, intentions, or character traits.

According to utilitarianism, an action driven by bad or deplorable motives can still be morally right as long as it brings about the most happiness. Similarly, such an act could be right according to deontology as long as it follows a valid moral principle. For example, being motivated to help someone because we hate another person (say, we hate someone and help their enemy) can still be right according to both theories. But virtue ethics says otherwise. It claims such an action is wrong because it was motivated by hatred and hatred is not a virtue. Of course, if one performed the same action but was motivated by compassion, virtue ethics would likely view it as morally right.

My hope is that learning about utilitarianism, deontology, and virtue ethics helps us better understand our own moral beliefs or values. In addition—and I want to stress this—I hope learning about these theories gives us insights into the moral perspectives of those with whom we disagree.

Despite what politicians, pundits, and influencers may claim, Americans are not hopelessly divided over moral and political issues. Almost all of us embrace and

utilize utilitarianism, deontology, and virtue ethics—sometimes consciously, other times intuitively. While some of us lean more toward one theory and others might lean more toward a different theory, crucially, almost all of us give some weight to all three theories.

We aren't moral strangers living in different moral worlds. Rather, we're fellow human beings thinking through hard questions with a shared set of tools.

In Chapter 8, we'll explore the fourth and final ethical theory: The ethics of care.

7: Reacting to Hateful Comments

The Issue: What should I do if I hear a racist, sexist, or hateful comment? How should I react? What are my moral responsibilities?

We've all been there. Maybe in a restaurant, an elevator, or a checkout line, and someone says something that's ugly. We look around to see if anyone else heard it. Perhaps the comment repeated a cruel stereotype or a slur. Maybe it was a hurtful or disrespectful comment directed toward someone's partner, or even a child. Is anyone going to speak up? Should you?

During the early days of the COVID-19 pandemic, I had plans to meet a friend in the courtyard of his apartment building. I arrived early with my laptop, and when I tried to sign onto Wi-Fi, I realized I needed the password. Someone sat down at a table next to mine, and after mustering the courage, I asked if he'd share the password. He smiled and gave me the password, and we started chatting.

I learned his name was Burke. He was a server at a local restaurant but dreamed of working in a hospital, maybe as a nurse or physician's assistant. I told him I was an ethicist, specializing in medical ethics.

A few days later I was back in the courtyard, and as Burke walked past me, he waved and then stopped.

"You said you're an ethicist, right?"

"Good memory," I said.

"I have a question."

"I'm listening," I replied, not having the slightest idea that he'd be in tears five minutes later.

"What do you do if you disagree with your parents and oldest friends about ethical issues?"

It's certainly not rare for one generation to have different values than the next generation, but it can be difficult for a son or daughter to stand up for what they believe in when parents do not respect their views.

After I asked him to elaborate, he explained that about a year earlier he had started questioning his political and moral beliefs. A lot of things he'd grown up hearing, especially from his parents, just didn't sit well with him anymore.

"I tried talking to my dad about my new take on the world, but he doesn't take me seriously. He even insulted me, saying that I was still a kid and was too naïve to question his beliefs."

As Burke talked about his relationship with his parents, especially his father, his eyes welled up. "I love my dad, but he doesn't respect me. And it's hard for me to respect him. I just want him to change."

One of the things that troubled Burke deeply was his father's use of the N-word and the way he talked about gay people and immigrants. Burke admitted to having used the same words in the past, but now he thought this was wrong, very wrong.

We chatted for about 15 minutes, and then my friend arrived. I introduced the two of them and offered Burke my phone number.

"Call me anytime. We can talk about the issues we were discussing earlier or anything else—your career aspirations, sports, relationships. I don't care. I just like getting to know people."

Frankly, I didn't expect Burke to call, but about eight hours later my phone rang. After apologizing for calling so late, Burke said he had another question. As he hemmed and hawed, I realized he seemed to be embarrassed about something.

"I get the feeling you want to say something but are afraid I'll judge you," I began. "Trust me, I have no desire to be judgmental. And if I want to judge someone, I can focus on myself and the many things I did in the past that I'm not proud of."

Burke explained that earlier at the restaurant, a customer used a slur to refer to the host.

"I'm embarrassed to admit I pretended not to hear it. I wanted to say something, but I just kept on walking. I don't know if I was scared or just didn't want to cause a scene. What should I have done?"

Of course, I answered: "It depends."

I paused, but before Burke had a chance to say anything else, I told him, "Even though I'm an ethicist, I don't have many answers. But if you tell me more about what happened, we might better understand the situation and your response or lack of response. We might never know for sure what you should have done, but perhaps we can explore how you might want to respond if it happens again."

"My first question," I began, "is: Did the host hear what was said?"

What would you do if you were in a public place—such as a restaurant—and overheard someone loudly using a racist slur to refer the staff?

Why Calling Someone Out Can Backfire

When we call someone out for questionable behavior, what's called Moral Identity Threat might be triggered. Numerous studies demonstrate that when a person's self-esteem or moral credentials are threatened, they tend to become defensive rather than truly evaluate whether what they are being told is true. These studies suggest that we react in this way because we have an innate desire to think of ourselves as being good people, moral people.

If, for example, a liberal is accused of being elitist rather than compassionate, or if a conservative is accused of insincerely promoting family values, both are likely to react defensively instead of reflecting openly on the criticism. Unconsciously, we seek ways to reassure ourselves and others that we have a good moral character.

Sometimes we might think about morally good or praiseworthy things we've done in the past, thereby confirming or reminding ourselves that we are good people. At other times, we might defend what we said and try to explain why it doesn't reveal or suggest what others thought it did. Or maybe we'll convince ourselves that others misinterpreted what we said.

Knowing about Moral Identity Threat might help us recognize our defensiveness and learn from criticism. Recently, I was driving on a narrow street, and the side mirror on the passenger side of my car snapped backward with a bang. The mirror was made to do this, so there was no damage. A passenger said, "You must have gotten too close to a parked car and your mirror hit it." My first response was to deny this—I pride myself on being a good driver. After parking, I thought about what happened and asked myself if maybe my denial was generated by Moral Identity Threat. I didn't want to see myself as someone who wasn't careful enough when driving. I realized that obviously my mirror hit something—most likely a car; it didn't just snap backwards on its

(cont. p. 129)

(cont. from p. 128)

own. This didn't make me a bad person, but I made a mistake, maybe a mistake I could learn from.

Of course, it's easy to recognize that I wasn't being careful enough when driving. What if someone questioned my beliefs or treatment of women? Research suggests that if we tell someone that they aren't living up to their ideals, our words likely won't sink in. If, however, we begin by saying something truthful and positive about their character and then follow this up with our concerns, they're more likely to "hear" what we said. We might say something like, "I know you are committed to equality among the genders, but five minutes ago you said...." Not only will this approach have a greater probability of being heard and understood, but it will likely be less painful or embarrassing for the other person.

Discussion

Let's start with what I hope is common ground: We believe we shouldn't use racial, ethnic, gender-based, and other slurs. We embrace a rule of thumb that looks something like: "It's morally wrong to use racial slurs or hateful, hurtful, or dehumanizing language."

Just to be clear, I'm not suggesting that it's *always* wrong to use this type of language. Like most rules of thumb, it's not difficult to find possible exceptions to this rule. If uttering a slur is the only way we can stop a crazed gun-wielding attacker from killing children on a playground, arguably we should utter the slur. Obviously, this is a pretty far-fetched example.

A more realistic scenario would be an attorney in a courtroom reading aloud from a historical document that contains a slur. Regardless of what you believe about the general impermissibility of using slurs, I think we can all agree that reading an historical document in a courtroom is quite different from using a slur to attack, put down, or hurt someone.

Do you speak up when you hear someone using racist or other hateful language?

The question posed in this chapter isn't just about racial slurs. Rather, the question concerns how we ought to respond if we hear someone say something that's racist, sexist, disrespectful, or just plain hateful or hurtful. This might include someone berating their spouse—maybe telling them they're stupid—or someone telling a cashier at Walmart that they're useless and "I hope you get fired."

So what should we do?

I've said it before, and I'll say it again: Details matter.

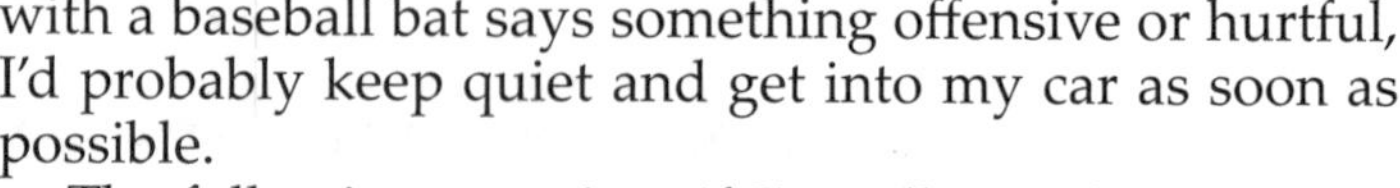
If I'm in a dark parking lot and a tall, muscular, drunk person with a baseball bat says something offensive or hurtful, I'd probably keep quiet and get into my car as soon as possible.

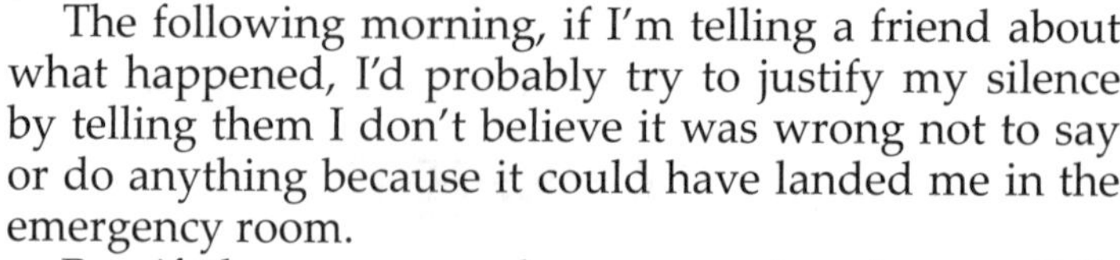
The following morning, if I'm telling a friend about what happened, I'd probably try to justify my silence by telling them I don't believe it was wrong not to say or do anything because it could have landed me in the emergency room.

But if the same words were spoken in a well-lit restaurant with my friends and a security guard nearby, I might feel ashamed if I remained silent.

Although one of the primary aims of this book is to help you better understand your own moral beliefs and commitments, another aim is to help you figure out what sort of person you want to be.

You may know or believe that you wouldn't say anything if you heard friends or a colleague use hateful language to describe members of a particular race or religion, but at the same time you might be thinking you should say something or would like to be the type of person who would say something.

Earlier, we explored three different ethical theories: utilitarianism, deontology, and virtue ethics. Each gives us a different lens or perspective for thinking about what's right. Let's see what they have to say about situations in which we witness hate, cruelty, or deep disrespect.

Utilitarianism and Hateful Language

Utilitarianism, as you already know, dictates that the morally right act is the act that maximizes or brings about enough happiness. So, when we hear something hateful or hurtful, the part of us that's attracted to utilitarianism will try to determine what would be the consequences of speaking up and then compare them to the consequences of pretending we didn't hear what was said and not saying anything.

Let's imagine two different scenarios.

The first is the situation described above. You're alone in a dark parking lot and you hear someone utter a slur—he says something like: "People from that group are dumb." Since you're not a member of that group, you believe the slur wasn't aimed at you. You look around, and it doesn't seem like anyone else is present. When you look back at the speaker, you notice he's holding a baseball bat. Presumably, most of us would be disinclined to confront the person carrying the bat.

In the second scenario you're at a wedding standing next to the bride, who's from X-land (you pick the country), and you hear someone say: "I can't understand why anyone would want to marry someone from X-land. They're all so dumb and lazy." In this situation, many of us, even if we aren't from X-land, would want to say or do something.

Utilitarianism helps us understand why we believe not confronting the speaker or saying anything in the first scenario is the right thing to do, while it might be right to confront the speaker in the second scenario. It's relatively simple.

In the case where the offending person is carrying a baseball bat and looks threatening, it would probably be wise not to engage in a confrontation with them even on moral grounds.

In the first scenario, speaking up could escalate into violence and a trip to the emergency room. Plus, there's little reason to believe the person with the bat will suddenly become more compassionate just because you called him out. So the likely

outcome is more harm than good, and the utilitarian response would be: Stay silent, jump into the car, and try get away safely.

In the second scenario, things are different. If you pull the speaker to the side and calmly explain that her words caused the bride, the groom, their families, and others to experience pain, the speaker might listen. She might realize the power of her words and apologize to those she hurt. Maybe she'll even rethink how she speaks about others in the future. In short, the utilitarian in you might conclude that saying something would likely maximize or bring about maximal or enough happiness and is, therefore, the right thing to do.

Why Smart People Believe Falsehoods

Have you ever wondered how intelligent, sensible people can believe things that you know are false? This might be a belief about something that's trivial and easy to disprove, like swallowed gum stays in your stomach for months or years, or something serious related to politics or society. For example, many liberals believe the richest Americans don't pay taxes, yet IRS data from 2022 shows they paid about 65% of total income taxes. Many conservatives believe immigrants are responsible for more crime than native-born Americans, yet numerous studies conclude the opposite is true. If you don't believe either of these claims, see for yourself.

The Illusory Truth Effect gives us some insight into the question of why people who are usually reliable when it comes to their beliefs might believe false statements. It's pretty simple: The more we hear a statement, whether true or false, the more likely we are to believe it's true. This is the case even if we initially believed the statement was false and didn't receive any information questioning this belief.

In 1997, a research team conducted an experiment and asked participants—college students—to read a list of statements on a computer screen a total of

(cont. p. 133)

Deontology: Should We Be Guided by Principles?

If you tap into the part of yourself that's attracted to deontology or rule-based ethics (and just about all of us do this at times), you might ask yourself whether there's a principle that describes how we ought to act when someone says something hateful or disrespectful. Perhaps you embrace a rule that dictates "We ought to intervene in situations in which we can prevent another person from being hurt or harmed, if doing so doesn't put us at risk of significant pain or harm." This rule would, like utilitarianism, justify not saying anything in the first scenario and saying something in the second.

(cont. from p. 132)

three times at two-week intervals. While most of the statements changed each time, some of them were repeated. By the third time participants read the list, there was a significant increase in the percentage of participants who claimed the repeated statements were true. This and later studies demonstrate that when we hear or read a statement many times, we're more likely to believe it is true—the Illusory Truth Effect. One explanation for this effect is that it's easier for our brains to process statements if we read or hear them numerous times, and as a result, we come to believe these statements are true, even if we initially didn't believe this.

A related phenomenon, the Mere Exposure Effect, might play a role in the Illusory Truth Effect. The Mere Exposure Effect is a phenomenon describing how we are more likely to have a positive feeling about things the more frequently we encounter them. Thus, if we see a picture, hear a statement, or listen to a song a number of times, we feel more comfortable with it. This may cause us to believe the song or picture is good or the statement is true.

As is the case with many phenomena that incline us to make false judgments or believe false statements, if we're vigilant and ready to challenge what we see or hear, we can better protect ourselves from unintentionally accepting false information.

Virtue Ethics: What Would a Good or Virtuous Person Do?

Finally, you might appeal to virtue ethics and ask yourself what a virtuous person would do in each of these scenarios. One of the attractive aspects of virtue ethics is that to some extent the immediate response of a virtuous person is frequently almost automatic, and this response guides their behavior. Virtuous people don't try to calculate what would bring about the best consequences, nor do they think about whether there's a rule they should follow.

In the first scenario, if you were guided by virtue, your compassionate nature might initially be activated. You heard someone use words that were ugly and potentially hurtful, and you wanted to see if anyone was hurt or harmed by what was said. Realizing that no one else heard the words and nothing good will come from confronting the speaker, the compassionate, wise thing to do might be to leave the situation without saying a word.

The second scenario is different. If you were guided by virtue, you might empathize with those who heard the remark and recognize their pain or discomfort. You'd likely be motivated by compassion or justice, again without thinking about it very much, and do what you could to alleviate the pain or embarrassment that others are experiencing. You might want to say something comforting to those who were hurt or insulted, or maybe you'd explain that you believe it's awful that people use these words and that others have to hear them.

At the same time, however, you'd probably be concerned about saying or doing something that would hurt the person who made the remark. Sure, she said something that was hateful or hurtful, and you believe this was wrong. That said, virtuous people are compassionate and don't want others to suffer unnecessarily. For this reason, I suspect that in some (or even many) instances you wouldn't immediately criticize or correct the person who uttered the ugly remark or embarrass them in front of other people. You might instead pull the person to the side and explain how her words hurt those who heard them. You might explain that those people don't deserve this treatment. Perhaps this will result in

the person apologizing and, if luck is on your side, she might realize that she doesn't want to use hateful words in the future.

American History X

I remember watching a movie called *American History X*. In it, a White supremacist named Derek Vinyard is preparing to serve a prison sentence. His younger brother, Danny, idolizes him and shares many of Derek's beliefs.

In one scene, we learn that Danny used a racial slur in a school assignment. Rather than punish him, the school principal, a Black man, asks to meet with him privately. He doesn't raise his voice or scold Danny. Instead, he shares personal stories and tries to get Danny to understand how using racial slurs hurts others. He's trying to engage Danny's empathy.

Essentially, the principal believes that if he can get Danny to empathize or connect emotionally with those targeted by slurs, Danny will naturally recognize that

The Neo-Nazi movement is alive and well in the United States (as well as countries spanning from Europe to South America and Asia). It can be difficult to understand how feelings of hatred for others can generate movements like this even in a free and democratic society. Is lack of empathy the problem or is it something even deeper?

using slurs is wrong. Although the movie doesn't explicitly tell us the principal believes this, it's clear the principal believes that people are naturally empathic and don't want to hurt others needlessly.

Maybe that scene stuck with me because it reminds me to pause and wonder where hateful language comes from. Presumably, those who use hateful language learned to express hate at some time in the past—perhaps from their parents or peers. Like the principal, I can only hope that most people, deep down, are empathic and caring, and if they truly understand the impact of their words, they'll want to change.

Back to Burke

When I spoke with Burke about what happened in the restaurant, he admitted that even though he was uncomfortable and pretended he didn't hear the hateful remark, he wanted to be the sort of person who doesn't pretend he doesn't hear when someone says something hateful.

I told him he wasn't alone. Many of us are uncomfortable and freeze up when we hear people say hateful, hurtful things. Yet we want to say something if it will improve the situation.

As we talked, the conversation circled back to Burke's father. I don't think Burke called intending to talk about him, but this was definitely on his mind.

After giving me some examples of his father's prejudice or racism, I asked why his father might be this way.

Rather than answering my question, Burke responded: "My dad's a good man. He's compassionate and God-loving, and he'd never intentionally hurt anyone."

"Does that include someone of a different race or religion or someone who isn't heterosexual?" I asked.

"Absolutely. He seems to look down on these people, or maybe he's angry at them. But he doesn't want to harm them."

At some point, I asked Burke if his father picked his parents or had any control over who were his role models while he was growing up. My goal was to help him realize that his father, like all of us, was shaped by his upbringing.

"Of course not," he replied.

Before I could say anything, Burke was back to de-

Nobody in this world is either all good or all evil. Everyone has some of both, although they might lean one way or the other. We should recognize this before judging others as hopelessly different from us.

fending his father. He wanted me to know his dad wasn't all bad, that in many ways his father was a good person and a good parent. He told me his father loved him and tried to be a good parent. He told me about ways in which his father assisted those in need, including one time when he stopped on the highway and picked up a hitchhiker. Burke was proud his father regularly volunteered to work at church events.

I gently pointed out that Burke was confused and being confused was a good thing. "Whenever you start to tell me things that bother you about your dad, you switch directions and tell me the good things about him. I wonder if you do this because you have a tendency, a tendency that many of us have, to think of your father as being either a good or bad person. It seems like you want me to know that your father does some good things so I don't label him as a bad person. Or maybe you're saying these things to convince yourself that he's not a bad person."

We talked about the danger of using general moral labels and whether it's a mistake to characterize people as being either good or bad.

"Aren't most or all of us a mixture of both?" I asked.

Perhaps, I suggested, the same is true with respect to calling someone a racist. Rather than label his dad a racist or not a racist, it might be helpful and more accurate to say his dad does or says some racist things but also does or says things that aren't racist.

"Might I suggest that when thinking about your father, it might make more sense and be more honest to take a nuanced approach and recognize that he, like all of us, does some good things and some bad things? No one, including your father, is completely good or bad, moral or immoral."

We also explored Burke's apparent need to change his father. Was it about control? Was it about improving

their relationship? Or was Burke motivated by a desire to protect others from his father's ugly, hateful language? As might be expected, we never came up with a clear answer to these questions.

I told Burke that I believe that not arriving at easy answers is part of the beauty of learning about ethics. We can think and talk about ethical issues for days, months, and years, yet we still won't know all the answers or can't be sure we are getting it right. But that's not a flaw. That's what makes morality so powerful. It reflects the complexity of humanity and living a morally good life.

We can think and talk about ethical issues for days, months, and years, yet we still won't know all the answers or can't be sure we are getting it right.

We also talked about how almost all of us want to be good people. When we do something that might be seen as wrong, we often rush to defend ourselves and explain why it wasn't really wrong. Sometimes this involves convincing ourselves we did the right thing or rationalizing what we did.

As I'm prone to do, I asked Burke to consider these aspects of human behavior and morality. I think he came to share my belief that our seemingly innate desire to be good people and do the right thing is beautiful. Not only that, but the moral world in all its complexity is also beautiful, and maybe the fact that we often can't easily determine what's the right thing to do contributes to this beauty.

Burke and I still talk.

Not long ago, I reminded him of how we met. He told me he still felt a little ashamed for using slurs and stereotypes in the past, but he is well on the way to self-forgiveness.

Things with his dad have improved, and his dad no longer uses slurs—at least not when Burke's around him. He wants to ask his mom whether his dad uses them when he's not there, but he's afraid of the answer.

Whether Burke will speak up the next time he hears someone say something hateful is still an open question. He knows what sort of person he wants to be, but he recognizes he isn't there yet. I try to remind him he may never get there and that he's not alone, but that's another beautiful thing. We can always improve.

Are We Really So Divided?

Are Americans truly divided on whether it's morally right or wrong to use racial, ethnic, religious, or other slurs? Or whether it's okay to use hateful language in an effort to hurt or demean others?

According to a 2019 Pew Research public opinion poll, the answer is: No, or not very divided. Only 3% of Americans answered that it was always acceptable for White people to use the N-word, 6% said it was sometimes acceptable, and 13% said it was rarely acceptable. 70% said it was never acceptable. (Of course, some of those who answered "rarely" or "sometimes" may have been thinking of cases like reading aloud from a novel or legal document. Reasonable, caring people might believe that quoting a slur in a courtroom isn't the same as using it to hurt or put down others.)

I suggest that while most Americans believe it's almost always wrong to use racial slurs or hateful/hurtful language, there is disagreement as to how we should respond when someone crosses the line. As I discuss in Chapter 12, in which we explore political correctness and wokeness, many Americans believe they're being observed by thought and language police who love pouncing on, chastising, or demeaning those who say the wrong thing. That fear can lead to silence or even resentment and makes it harder to have open, honest conversations about race, gender, and other difficult issues.

The vast majority of Americans support minorities and treating them with respect. A Pew Research survey showed that 70% of Americans felt it was never acceptable to use racial slurs, and another 13% said it was only very rarely okay to do so.

It should be obvious by now that I'm not going to tell you what's right or who I believe is right. Rather, I want to reiterate that even though Americans, especially those on the left or right, disagree over the issue of how to best combat or address racism, they agree that it's wrong.

That's not something to dismiss lightly. It marks progress and is a big change from the past.

Final Thoughts

In this chapter, I address the question of how we might respond to those who utter racial slurs or other hateful, hurtful, disrespectful words. Whether we're looking through the lens of utilitarianism, deontology, or virtue ethics, we find general agreement that using slurs and other hateful language to demean or harm others is morally wrong. They furthermore tell us that how we should respond to hateful language depends on the circumstances related to the situation in which the language is used.

Before we close this chapter, I again encourage you to reflect on what sort of person you want to be. Would you prefer to remain silent when confronted with hateful language, or do you want to respond, and if so, how? Do you want to immediately challenge or chastise the person directly? Do you want to empathize with and speak with those who were the object of the language?

What is it that motivates you to want to be a specific sort of person? Do you want to be a person who strives to maximize overall happiness or someone who obeys a set of moral principles? Or do you want to be a virtuous person who is loyal and honest? Do you want to empathize with others and strive to contribute to a just society in which well-being is possible for everyone? I wouldn't be surprised if all these approaches resonate with you to some degree.

8: Favoring Family and Friends

The Issue: We are naturally more likely to help a family member or a friend over a stranger, but, objectively speaking, is this kind of favoritism moral?

About 15 years ago, my daughter was getting ready to start elementary school. My wife and I faced an important decision: Where should she go?

We'd heard our neighborhood school was mediocre, but a nearby public magnet school had an outstanding reputation. Several of our friends sent their children there, and the school's small class sizes were exactly what my daughter's teachers believed would help her thrive.

The only catch? Admission was determined by lottery, and to even enter the lottery, parents had to attend a mandatory presentation outlining the school's mission, expectations, and goals.

We settled on trying to get our daughter into the magnet school, trying our luck with the lottery. But then we ran into a problem.

That year, I was on sabbatical from my university job, and we were spending a few months overseas. When the dates for the presentations were released, we learned that they'd all take place during our time away. Flying back was out of the question—it was simply too expensive.

One afternoon, I was on the phone with a friend whose child also wanted to attend the magnet school. He'd gone to the presentation the night before and he was raving about the school.

"You guys are entering the lottery, right?" he asked.

"We can't," I said. "I called the school and asked if it was possible to enter the lottery without attending the

Imagine that you wanted to get your child into a small magnet school, but the only way to do so would be to tell a white lie. Would you be justified in doing so if the end result were positive, or is lying always wrong even if it greatly benefits your kids?

presentation, and they said the only exceptions were for emergencies, like if a child or family member was in the hospital. We're stuck, out of luck."

My friend paused and then asked, "Have you thought about telling them your mother's ill and you have to stay in Florida taking care of her?"

"Truth be told," I replied, "I fantasized about doing something like that, but you know I can't. Would you?"

"I don't know," he admitted. "But it's not your daughter's fault you're out of the country, and she shouldn't have to suffer because you're on sabbatical, doing what's best for you."

That night I told my wife about the conversation. We both agreed the school's policy was fair. At the same time, we believed this small school would be best for our daughter and wanted her to at least have the opportunity to enter the lottery.

Would a small lie to help someone we loved really be so wrong?

Part of me felt guilty for even considering it. Like most people, I embraced the rule of thumb "Lying is

morally wrong." But the thought of giving my daughter a better chance at success made the idea tempting.

So, what do you think? How would you morally evaluate the behavior of parents who lie to get their child into the school that best fits their child's personality and would provide the best education? Why?

For me, this is another "It depends" question.

On the one hand, most of us embrace the rule of thumb "It's morally wrong to lie," which suggests we shouldn't lie to get our children into what we believe is the best elementary school for them. At the same time, as we've already discussed, rules of thumb aren't chiseled into stone. We use the term "rule of thumb" to describe a rule that usually holds, but there are exceptions. We often start evaluating actions, perhaps instinctively, by appealing to rules of thumb. We then might consider whether the situation allows for an exception to the rule.

In this case, the exception wasn't obvious. Is there an exception that says we can violate rules of thumb if doing so will improve the life of a loved one? Such an exception seems odd. Isn't the whole point of morality to help us make decisions fairly and impartially, without favoring those close to us?

American psychologist and feminist Carol Gilligan (1936–) is well known for her work on ethical relationships and community and for her 1982 book, *In a Different Voice: Psychological Theory and Women's Development.*

Until recently, most philosophers and ethicists would have answered the last question in the affirmative. There's a long tradition in Western ethics that basically says we should treat everyone equally, without bias towards friends and loved ones.

But this tradition was challenged in the early 1980s by psychologist Carol Gilligan, who published *In a Different Voice: Psychological Theory and Women's Development*. Gilligan questioned whether it really is praiseworthy or right to treat strangers the same as our loved ones when making moral decisions. She suggested it might be morally permissible or

even praiseworthy to prioritize the well-being of family and friends.

Gilligan's book sparked a major shift in ethical thought, leading to the development of a completely new ethical theory: the ethics of care.

Could this new theory justify lying to get my daughter into a better school?

As we explore the ethics of care, we'll consider whether morality should sometimes make room for the deep obligations we feel toward family and friends.

Discussion

Prisoners and Breaking the Rules for Love

The movie *Prisoners* gives us insight into the question of when it might be permissible to break rules of thumb for the sake of loved ones.

In the film, two young girls vanish after a Thanksgiving meal. They were last seen playing near an RV, and the police soon locate a vehicle matching its description. The RV's occupant, Alex, is arrested but later released after authorities concluded he lacks the mental capacity to have kidnapped the girls.

Outside the police station, the father of one of the girls confronts Alex and assaults him. During the attack, Alex utters a chilling phrase: "*They didn't cry 'til I left them.*"

Convinced Alex knows more than he admitted to the police, the father abducts him. Along with the second girl's father, he brutally tortures Alex, desperate to uncover the truth about their daughters' whereabouts.

Watching this unfold, many of us are deeply conflicted or of two minds. We're reluctant to side with the fathers because we embrace at least two rules of thumb that tell us what they're doing is wrong: "Kidnapping is morally wrong" and "Torturing another human being is morally wrong." Yet at the same time, we sympathize with the desperate parents of the kidnapped girls. On some level, we might believe there could be an exception to these rules of thumb, if breaking them is the only way the fathers can save their daughters' lives.

We might be thinking: What the fathers did was wrong, but wasn't it also, in some way, right? Or perhaps: I know it's usually wrong to kidnap and torture someone, but if my own child or someone I loved deeply were kidnapped, I hope I'd have the strength or courage to do whatever it takes, even kidnapping and torturing the kidnapper, to save them.

Driven to desperation, a father whose daughter has been kidnapped finds and tortures the kidnappers in order to get them to reveal the child's location. While we know torture is wrong, who wouldn't be sympathetic to the father in this case—at least a little bit?

Why do so many of us feel this tension?

I think it's because we recognize the fathers' actions are motivated by care or love as opposed to greed or cruelty. If they had kidnapped and tortured someone to steal a winning lottery ticket, I'm confident we'd feel and think differently. We might also feel and think differently if the fathers were torturing Alex after he revealed where the girls were being held. In the latter case, the fathers would most likely shift from desperation and love to, among other things, hatred or revenge, and we don't believe these motives are praiseworthy or morally good.

In short, their motives matter.

The Ethics of Care—Motives Matter

If we believe the fathers' actions are permissible (or less bad than the typical case of kidnapping and torture) because they were motivated by care or love, we might embrace or be drawn to a moral principle that says something like: Actions that flow from care, concern for others, or love are morally right. We might furthermore believe that actions that flow from motives far away from or in opposition to care or love are morally wrong, bad, or deplorable. Even if we've never heard of this ethical theory, if we find ourselves evaluating mo-

rality in this way, we are attracted to the ethics of care, our fourth and final ethical theory.

Just as we might automatically appeal to utilitarianism to justify sacrificing one life to save many (see Chapter 2), or deontology to condemn convicting an innocent person even though convicting them would maximize happiness (see Chapter 5), almost all of us, at some point, appeal to the ethics of care when evaluating or justifying moral choices.

Let's consider another scenario that shows how motives can shape our moral judgments.

Charles, Clarise, and Their Dogs

Suppose two people, Charles and Clarise, each have an elderly dog named Cookie. One day both visit the same veterinarian, Dr. Porter, and receive the same di-

Would You Save Your Pet or a Stranger?

Imagine you're hiking next to a fast-flowing river when suddenly your beloved pet slips and falls into the water. Just as you're about to leap to its rescue, a nearby stranger falls into the river. You must instantly decide: Will you save your pet or the stranger? What do you think most people would do in this situation?

Studies suggest that many individuals claim they'd choose to save their pet over a stranger. In a 2013 study, participants were asked to imagine that a bus is traveling down a busy street and their pet (or an imagined pet if they didn't have one) ran in front of the bus. At the same time, a foreign tourist stepped in the path of the bus. Participants were asked: If you could only save the life of your pet or the person, "who would you save?"

The researchers asked this question multiple times, changing the nature of the relationship of the person in the road and the participant. These included choosing between one's own pet and a hometown stranger, distant cousin, close friend, grandparent,

(cont. p. 147)

agnosis: Cookie has suffered a stroke and will likely live for a week or two, but with poor quality of life.

After thinking about it all afternoon, both Charles and Clarise decided to put their dog to sleep.

Did Charles do the right thing? How about Clarise?

At first glance, it seems as though the moral quality of both their actions are the same because they did the same thing. If Charles's action was morally right, shouldn't the same be said of Clarise's action? If we were to appeal to utilitarianism, for example, we'd likely conclude that both actions should receive the same moral evaluation because they would both bring about the same or similar amounts of happiness or sadness.

But now, imagine you discovered that while Charles was weighing his decision, he decided to sneak a small camera into Dr. Porter's office and record the death of Cookie. Why? Because he hoped a video of Cookie's

(cont. from p. 146)

and sibling. They changed the relationship of the pet to the participant, asking them what they'd do if it was their own pet or someone else's pet.

Approximately 40% of participants claimed they'd save their own pet instead of a foreign tourist, and 37 % chose their own pet over a hometown stranger. As the closeness of the relationship between participant and person increased, the percentage of people who chose their pet decreased: distant cousin—23%; close friend—5%, grandparent and sibling—2% to 4%. Similarly, if one was choosing between someone else's pet and another person, a smaller percentage claimed they'd choose to save the pet of another.

An interesting aspect of this study is that most of us claim we value human life over animal life. The researchers concluded that this study demonstrates that many times when we make moral choices, they are based on emotions rather than rationality. That is, if we love a pet, even if we value human life more greatly than animal life, our emotional connection with it will affect the choice of whom we choose to save, a human or a pet.

What if a dog owner agreed to let a vet put their pet to sleep but only in the hope of putting the procedure on social media in order to get followers?

death might go viral on YouTube and that would jump-start a lucrative career as a content maker. You also learn that he told a close friend: "Truth be told, I couldn't care less about preventing Cookie's suffering, but if I can make money off his death, I'll definitely put him to sleep."

Now imagine you also learn about Clarise's thought process. When she went home to think about Cookie's future, she also spoke to a friend and said, "I'm not ready to put Cookie to sleep. But because I love him, I want to minimize his suffering. I guess I'll put Cookie to sleep this afternoon, but I think I'll sneak a small camera into the treatment room. I'm confident I'll feel better knowing I have a video of his last moments, even if I never watch it."

I suspect that almost all of you, like me, believe that Clarise's behavior is morally better than Charles's. You might even consider Charles's behavior to be morally repugnant or wrong, while finding Clarise's morally praiseworthy.

Yet, I repeat, they did the same thing. If outcomes were all that mattered and we were utilitarians, we'd judge them equally. But many of us don't.

And that's where the ethics of care helps us make sense of our moral thinking. By appealing to the ethics of care, we can explain (to ourselves and others) why we believe that Charles's behavior is morally worse than Clarise's. We believe that motives matter, and actions motivated by care (or empathy or love) are morally superior to actions that flow from motives far away from care, like greed or callousness.

This example again highlights the complexity of the moral life. On the one hand, we frequently use utilitarianism to determine whether an action is morally right or wrong, and utilitarianism tells us that Charles's and Clarise's actions should receive the same evaluation.

Yet, because we also embrace the ethics of care, part of us believes that Clarise's action was morally better than Charles's.

In practice, we don't appeal to just one ethical theory. We move between them, sometimes looking at consequences, sometimes at principles or duties, sometimes at virtues like honesty, courage, and justice, and sometimes at motives and relationships. At times this makes things complicated, but it also aligns with our moral experience, and doing this well may be a sign of wisdom.

Back to My Daughter's School

So, would it have been morally permissible for me to lie and say I was taking care of my sick mother to qualify my daughter for the lottery?

First, it's obvious that lying violates the rule of thumb "Lying is morally wrong." But we know that rules of thumb admit of exceptions, and this is when we appeal to ethical theories for guidance.

Let's begin with utilitarianism. A utilitarian might argue that if only one person lies in this situation, the overall impact on happiness would likely be negligible. Let's say 200 families attended the presentation and chose to take part in the lottery, and 100 children would be admitted to the school. Presumably, the well-being of these 100 children will be increased by admittance to the school. Even if I lie to get my daughter's name in the lottery, 100 children will still be admitted—99 of the original 100 and my daughter. Thus the well-being of 100 children will still be increased, and we have reason to believe the consequences of lying are no better or worse than the consequences of not lying. If this is correct and there are no further consequences of lying, lying would be morally permissible.

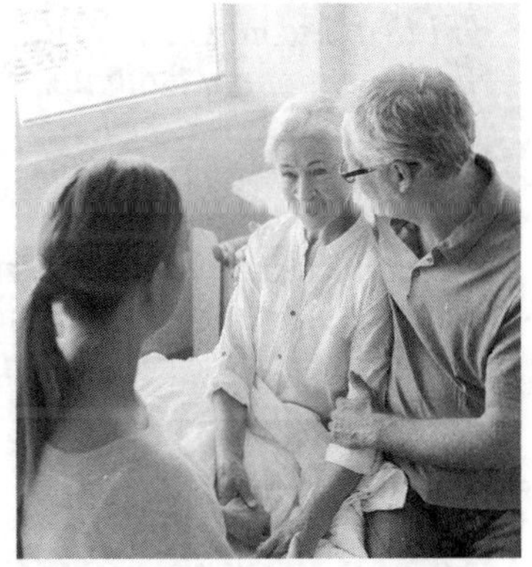

Lying about seeing one's sick mother as an excuse to get around the rules of a school admission process is disingenuous at best, blatant cheating at worse. Could you live with yourself in such a case?

However, the calculus changes if others learn or suspect people are lying to get their children into the school. If families start to believe the system is unfair and that others break the rules, they might feel pressure or permission to do the same. This would likely have negative or bad overall consequences because widespread dishonesty could erode trust in the government or school system or even trust in each other. If this were the case, utilitarianism would deem lying wrong due to the negative ripple effects. That said, utilitarianism might justify lying just as long as others don't discover the lie. But most of us need to talk, and this talking involves sharing with friends things we did to help our children. In this case, the friend might tell someone else, who tells someone else, and eventually the lie is known by many. This results in the same consequences discussed above and again suggests lying would be wrong according to utilitarianism.

While many of us appeal to utilitarianism to evaluate situations like this, we might also intuitively appeal to virtue ethics. What would a virtuous person do in this situation?

Of course, we believe honesty and justice are virtues. Honesty dictates that lying is wrong. Justice might do the same. Justice is often believed to be synonymous with fairness. Would it be unfair to lie and thereby get my daughter's name in the lottery? I think so. After all, everyone whose name is included in the lottery had a parent or guardian attend the school's presentation. For some this was likely a small sacrifice, but for others it might have been a huge sacrifice. If I lied, I would have gotten the benefit of my daughter being included in the lottery, but I wouldn't have had to make any sacrifice. That would be unfair. We can see that virtue ethics likely tells us lying would have been wrong.

If I lied, I would have gotten the benefit of my daughter being included in the lottery, but I wouldn't have had to make any sacrifice. That would be unfair. We can see that virtue ethics likely tells us lying would have been wrong.

Another virtue, however, is care or compassion. Would a caring or compassionate person lie to get their

The ethics of care suggests that the qualities of caring for another person (compassion, love, empathy, and so on) are the most important factors in making moral decisions. But a caring person might go either way when it comes to making a choice, depending on who is the object of compassion.

child's name in the lottery? Before exploring this question, I think it's important to distinguish virtue ethics and the ethics of care.

Interestingly, the ethics of care is frequently conceived of as a special kind or formulation of virtue ethics. Whereas virtue ethics is usually thought of as a theory that's concerned with a list of virtues—honesty, loyalty, courage, justice, wisdom, compassion, and others—the ethics of care claims that there is only one virtue: care (or compassion, empathy, or love).

With the above in mind, let's see what the ethics of care would say about lying in this situation. As I already explained, when trying to evaluate the morality of an action or justify a choice, many of us appeal to the ethics of care, which, like virtue ethics, shifts our focus to the motives behind an action. The central question is: Why would I lie to get my daughter in the lottery? Would I be motivated by care or a motive close to care, like compassion or love, or would my motive be far from care, like selfishness or callousness?

I think it's safe to say that if I had lied in this situation, I would have been motivated by love, care, and the desire to improve the well-being of my daughter. Like any caring person, I want those I love to flourish and suffer as little as possible.

That said, the ethics of care doesn't give us a blanket check to prioritize our loved ones at all costs. It's more nuanced. Even if I love my daughter and want her to flourish and not suffer, if I am truly a caring person, I want others to flourish and don't want them to suffer. I might realize that it's possible that my daughter would be admitted to the school, and as a result some other person would not be admitted. This person lives in my city and may be in a worse school district than my daughter's. That is, they might suffer if they aren't admitted to the magnet school, while my daughter wouldn't suffer

if she had to attend our neighborhood school. She might not do as well as she'd do at the magnet school, but I repeat, she wouldn't suffer. Surely, this realization causes me to question whether it's right to lie in this situation.

The Complexity and Beauty of the Moral Life

At this point, you might be thinking: "Come on, Gelfand. Tell us what a caring person would do. Is it okay to lie in this situation?"

Truth be told, I'm really not sure what a caring person would do in this situation. Perhaps I should say that some caring people might lie, while others might not lie.

This answer, or lack of an answer, is a frustration that we've experienced throughout this book. We've seen that it's not always obvious what is the right thing to do. In this case, as caring people, we deeply love our family members and want to act in their best interests. Yet we also care for and have a natural desire to contribute to the well-being of friends, neighbors, work colleagues, and even strangers. This makes using the ethics of care to answer moral questions challenging or frustrating.

Although at times we may wish there was a way to easily answer moral questions, when we think more deeply we may come to value this difficulty. Isn't it extraordinary that we, humans, can think, talk, and feel so passionately about what is right? Our ability to balance love for those closest to us with care or compassion for others, even strangers, complicates moral decision making, but it also showcases the profound beauty of the human condition.

Are We Really So Divided?

Throughout this book, we've seen how moral reasoning involves both rules of thumb and the different ethical theories. Our initial response to moral questions usually begins with the rules of thumb. These rules are useful, and they often feel so obvious we don't even stop to question them.

In the lifesaver scenario, you have one lifesaver but there are two people in the ocean drowning: one is a loved one and the other is a complete stranger. Again, most people would rescue the loved one, but what if the stranger is a brilliant scientist who is close to curing a deadly disease?

For instance, if asked whether stealing a bicycle is morally permissible, we might immediately respond, "No. Stealing is wrong," and consider the matter settled.

Sometimes, however, we recognize, intuit, or sense that these rules of thumb don't fully apply or don't tell the whole story. We might learn that someone stole a bicycle to save three lives. Without realizing it, we shift into the utilitarianism mode and immediately assert that while stealing is usually wrong, in this situation it was morally right because it prevented a lot of pain and sadness or brought about the best consequences.

In other situations, we instinctively appeal to the ethics of care. Imagine you're on a boat in the middle of the ocean, and a loved one and a stranger fall overboard at the same time. You have one lifesaving ring.

Without hesitation, some of us, perhaps most of us, would throw the ring to our loved one. If asked to justify our behavior, we'd say something like: "I saved someone I loved. Surely, morality can't demand I save a stranger over someone I love." This justification is grounded in the ethics of care, which dictates that an act is right if it was motivated by care or love.

Some of us in this situation, however, might try to quickly decide whether saving the life of a loved one or a stranger would be best for the world or maximize happiness and then throw the ring to that person. Although you may believe that the ethics of care is best in this situation, it's essential to remember that almost all of us appeal to utilitarianism sometimes. Thus, it's not necessarily appropriate to criticize the person who used utilitarianism in this situation. We might disagree with them, but at the same time we can relate to them and remember our shared commitment to the same ethical theories.

My Neighbor, the Bread Thief

Let's look at a different scenario.

Consider a scenario where you learn that your neighbor was recently arrested and charged with stealing bread from a grocery store. A quick online search reveals that this isn't the first time he's stolen bread; there are videos showing him stealing bread two to three times per week.

What is your initial reaction?

I imagine I'd initially react with disapproval, appealing to the rule of thumb "Stealing is wrong." But after this initial reaction, I might want more details. I might want to know why he stole the bread.

Maybe I should talk to my neighbor. Suppose my neighbor tells me, "I give the stolen bread to hungry, unhoused families." He furthermore explains that, like me, he embraces the rule of thumb "Stealing is wrong." But he also believes his behavior is an exception to the rule.

"I am confident," he might explain, "that stealing a few loaves of bread and bringing them to a shelter for unhoused families causes minimal harm to the grocery store, but it prevents families, especially those with children, from going to sleep hungry." Your neighbor may not realize it, but he's making a utilitarian argument to justify a behavior that we usually think is wrong.

Or maybe your neighbor offers a different explanation. He might explain that when he thinks about children going to sleep hungry, he can't just sit back and do nothing. "Stealing the bread will alleviate so much suffering. I don't think I could sleep at night if I knew I could help these children and chose not to. Surely, we shouldn't follow rules if doing so would require us being callous or uncaring."

That's the ethics of care speaking. He's not just calculating outcomes. He's responding from empathy or care.

Even if you disagree with your neighbor's justification, recognizing that you sometimes use utilitarianism or the ethics of care to justify your own behavior can foster understanding. Perhaps you'll realize that your neighbor isn't simply a petty thief. Instead, like you, he sometimes appeals to utilitarianism and the ethics of care in an effort to do the right thing.

The Scale of Morality to the Rescue

The Scale of Morality might be useful when trying to understand this disagreement.

Stealing Bread

1. Utilitarianism: Stealing maximizes or brings about enough happiness
2. The Ethics of Care: A caring agent would steal the bread if it was the only way to stop suffering

1. Deontology: It's wrong to steal

Morally Right or Just?

Morally Wrong or Unjust?

Many of our moral disagreements stem from the different weight we attach to the blocks representing the various ethical theories.

In one situation, I might prioritize or put more weight on deontology, focusing on moral principles like "It's never permissible to steal," whereas my neighbor prioritizes or puts more weight on utilitarianism and the ethics of care. But in a different situation, I might prioritize utilitarianism and the ethics of care while my neighbor prioritizes deontology. The scale helps us recognize that there is common ground, and this recognition can help prevent moral disagreements from harming or destroying relationships. It helps us disagree without dehumanizing each other.

How Ethical Theories Shape Social Policy Debates

Not only do we appeal to different ethical theories at different times when attempting to determine whether an act is right, but we also appeal to different ethical theories when thinking about social policy. For divisive topics like the death penalty, abortion, or affirmative action, sometimes we might appeal to utilitarianism, while at other times we appeal to virtue ethics, deontology, or the ethics of care.

Consider the debate over removing statues of historical figures who were slaveholders or supported slavery. From an ethics of care perspective, which dictates caring/loving acts are morally good, we might ask ourselves whether a caring person would support or oppose the removal of the statues. If keeping the statues will likely cause significant pain while removing them causes only minor disturbances, we'll likely opt for removal.

But suppose your neighbor disagrees. At first you might think, "How could she not care about those who suffer every time they see these statues? How can I be friends with her?"

But what if you talk with your neighbor and learn that she is a caring person. Perhaps she wants the statues to remain because she believes keeping them reminds us of the complex history surrounding slavery and race and their presence may prompt important conversations. These conversations, she might believe, will in the long run improve relationships and the lives of those who currently suffer when they see the statues.

Statues honoring Confederate soldiers like this one in North Carolina were removed around the country after Americans protested that they praised a rebellion against the United States and also disrespected African Americans. A caring person could still argue that the statues should go untouched as an important reminder of the past and the tragedy of slavery.

I'm not trying to argue for or against the removal of statues. I'm trying to demonstrate that even if we disagree with one another concerning what's the right social policy, this disagreement doesn't necessarily reveal that we're very divided. Although at the policy level we disagree with our neighbor, at a deeper or more foundational level we're in agreement. We disagree over what policy is right or best, but we appeal to the same ethical theories when attempting to justify why we support one policy or another.

We're often told society is hopelessly divided or polarized, whether it's liberals and conservatives, urban and ru-

ral, or the young and old. As I've suggested, maybe we aren't so different. Regardless of where we fall on the political spectrum, we use the same ethical frameworks or theories when making moral judgments. We all value fairness, consequences, compassion, and loyalty. The difference between us is how much weight we attach to each of these.

We're often told society is hopelessly divided or polarized, whether it's liberals and conservatives, urban and rural, or the young and old.... Regardless of where we fall on the political spectrum, we use the same ethical frameworks or theories when making moral judgments.

Maybe, just maybe, recognizing our shared commitment to an overwhelmingly similar set of moral commitments can move us beyond "Us vs. Them" thinking. Perhaps in its place we can move towards meaningful, empathic, productive discussions. These discussions, I think, are way less threatening than the discussions many of us currently experience. They allow us to share important things about ourselves—our values and positions on issues that affect all of us—without the threat that these discussions will destroy our relationships with others. They may, in fact, deepen them.

Final Thoughts

In this chapter, we explored a fundamental ethical question: Is it morally permissible to prioritize the well-being of our loved ones over that of strangers? One example was whether it's permissible to throw a lifesaving ring to a loved one, knowing that doing so would result in a stranger drowning. Historically, most ethicists advocated for *impartialist* ethical theories. Impartialist theories claim we should be unbiased when trying to decide what is right. We shouldn't put priority on our loved ones. According to these theories, saving a loved one isn't right just because the person we're saving is a loved one.

But in the 1980s, a new voice emerged. Carol Gilligan, and subsequently others, challenged the idea of impartialism in moral decision-making and introduced

the ethics of care. The ethics of care is an ethical theory, and it claims that *partialism*, putting more weight on the well-being of certain people or groups of people, is sometimes permissible or even praiseworthy. More specifically, some versions of the ethics of care claim that when making moral decisions, it's morally praiseworthy to favor friends, family, and those close to you. According to the ethics of care, motives play a central role in morality, and love, empathy, and care are the highest or best motives. Motives far away from love, empathy, and care—say, indifference, callousness, or hatefulness—are among the worst. For example, the ethics of care would likely justify choosing to visit a sick family member in the hospital as opposed to visiting a stranger, assuming one has the right motives. If one visits a loved one out of genuine concern, their action is praiseworthy or right. If, however, one visits a loved one just to look good on Instagram, their action is morally worse or even deplorable.

Crucially, the permission to favor those close to us doesn't negate our obligations to strangers; rather, it suggests a spectrum of care, allowing deeper concern for those close to us and a less intense, but present, meaningful care for those who are less close.

Finally, we explored how different ethical theories shape not just personal decisions, but social or political ones as well. Whether it's a debate over drug allocation, school admissions, or public memorials, many of our disagreements aren't about *whether* to be moral, but about which ethical theory we're applying in a given moment. If you step back, you may realize that you appeal to utilitarianism in some situations. So do I. And I appeal to the ethics of care sometimes, and so do you.

In other words, we're not always divided by competing values. Often, we're united by the same values, but we prioritize them differently depending on the case.

As we continue to explore the complexity of moral and political decision-making, we'll ultimately address a fundamental question: What sort of person do you want to be? This reflection on personal character and ethical identity will tie together the various moral frameworks we've discussed, helping us navigate the complex landscape of moral decision-making in our lives.

9: Giving to Charity

The Issue: Do we have an obligation to give to charities? Putting all the ethical theories we have learned so far, let's see how they apply to the concept of being charitable.

I met José several years ago, while I was drinking a café con leche at a small café in Barcelona. José, a retired businessperson, spoke Spanish and English, and it didn't take long for him to realize my Spanish wasn't great. After a short conversation, he offered to give me free Spanish lessons. I jumped at the offer.

The first phrase José taught me was *por si acoso,* which means "just in case." To illustrate how to use the phrase, José said: *"Por si acaso, todas las mañanas compro un billete de lottería."* Translation: "Just in case, every morning I buy a lottery ticket."

I never saw José after that first lesson. When I texted to schedule a meeting, he was "too busy."

Fast-forward to last summer: I returned to Barcelona, and, as fate would have it, the apartment I rented online was located above a tiny store that sold lottery tickets. Remembering José's lesson, I decided to buy two tickets every week—just in case.

The first week I won 50 euros (about $55).

The second week, I handed my ticket to the lottery agent. She scanned it and then went to the back of the store and consulted a colleague. I had a hunch I won something more than 50 euros.

When she returned, she confirmed my hunch. I won a little more than 5,000 euros (about $5,500)!

As I was hiding my winnings in various spots around my apartment, I was thinking about what to do with the

money. My first thought was to tip the agent who sold me the ticket. I figured she wasn't earning much, and she was the one who took the time to explain the many different lotteries in Europe. In fact, she suggested I buy two tickets for *La Primativa*, the very lottery I won.

Then I remembered José. We hadn't spoken in years, but I decided to give him a call. Although he didn't remember teaching me *por si acaso, todas las mañanas compro un billete de lottería*, he laughed when I told him the story. He still buys a ticket every day.

Before we hung up, José asked me what I was going to do with the money, and he suggested, "Why not give a little to charity? After all, you weren't expecting the money."

When I hung up the phone, I thought about Jose's suggestion and whether we have a duty or obligation to act charitably—to donate money to charities or volunteer to spend time teaching kids to read, working in a soup kitchen, or doing something else.

What do you think?

The Morality of Found Money

Imagine you're strolling through a parking lot and stumble upon a roll of money secured by a rubber band. You glance around, trying to see if anyone else was around, while also trying not to attract any attention to yourself.

"Theft by Finding" laws say that if you discover money just lying around somewhere, you are obligated to take it to the police to see whether they can identify the owner.

You pick up the money roll and discover it contains 20 crisp $100 bills, a total of $2,000. You look around again. You might be trying to find the owner, or maybe you're looking to see if anyone saw you find the money, hoping that you can keep it.

What do you do next?

For some reason—maybe you're in a good mood or just want to do the right thing—you post a flyer in the parking lot. You don't want to give the money to the wrong

person, so you keep some information to yourself. The flyer, which includes your phone number, says: "If you recently lost something valuable in this parking lot, please contact me." Two weeks pass. No calls. No texts.

What now? Do you keep all the money? Do you have a moral obligation to donate some of it to a charity that helps those in need? What about the law? Do you have a legal obligation to turn the money in or do something else?

You go online and learn that some states have finders keepers laws and you get to keep found money if no one claims it. In other states—I'd look it up—you don't get to keep it, even if no one claims it.

Charity: Genuine Altruism or Self-Interest?

Philosophers, psychologists, and others have long debated whether charitable acts stem from true altruism or self-interest. Those who believe the latter claim that at the deepest level, charitable acts are rooted in self-interest. This position is grounded in or based on a position known as psychological egoism.

According to psychological egoism, humans are constructed in such a way that they cannot perform actions that aren't in their own self-interest. Thus, if I act charitably, I do so because I'll feel good afterwards or want to avoid feeling bad if I don't do so. Or maybe I act charitably because I know others will look at me with admiration. This will positively affect my social status and reputation. Some claim that even if we aren't aware that our charitable acts are motivated by egoism, they nevertheless are.

Those who believe in the possibility of altruism claim that common sense and reflection refute psychological egoism. For example, some of us make anonymous gifts—some of these have been huge. If we were motivated by self-concern, wouldn't we want to bask in the glory of making these gifts?

Of course, a psychological egoist could claim that we feel good or morally superior when we make anonymous gifts. Thus, even though we don't get some of the benefits from acting charitably—e.g.,

(cont. p. 162)

(cont. from p. 161)

a good reputation or praise from others—we are nonetheless motivated by self-concern, as we want to feel good or morally superior.

But what about anonymously donating a kidney to a dying stranger or running into a burning building to save a child? Surely, these seem like altruistic acts. Can the benefit of feeling good about ourselves outweigh the risk of death?

Others say focusing on how we benefit from our charitable behavior is missing the point. Even if we do feel good, it doesn't necessarily follow that we're motivated by an initial desire to feel good. Consider the act of going to a dentist to get a cavity filled. You know it's going to hurt, but this doesn't mean that your initial motivation was a desire to experience pain. Rather, you were motivated by a desire to keep your teeth, and whether getting a tooth filled brings pleasure or pain, it doesn't follow that you were seeking those feelings. Similarly, even if we know we'll feel good after making a charitable contribution, it doesn't follow that our initial motivation was to feel good.

A final defense of altruism is to consider the meanings of words. Would we say that a generous person who truly cares about others feels bad after helping through charity or feels good? Presumably, the latter. Thus, it makes sense to say that charitable people may feel good after contributing to charity, and this is evidence they are generous or altruistic, not selfish or motivated by self-interest.

Discussion

Is Charity a Moral Obligation or a Personal Choice?

When it comes to charity, we don't seem to have a widely accepted rule of thumb. Surely, no one would says it's wrong to donate found money or lottery winnings. But that's different from saying we have a moral obligation to act charitably or make charitable contributions.

We're taught from a young age that giving money and time to charitable causes is a moral obligation that all good people do.

In fact, I suspect most people believe we have no moral *obligation* to make charitable contributions. We don't embrace a rule of thumb that dictates "It's morally wrong not to donate money to charity." Instead, we tend to view charitable giving as discretionary. We believe it's morally good or praiseworthy to contribute to charity, but not required. If we decide not to give, we aren't doing something that's morally wrong or deplorable.

Is this belief defensible?

Should we treat charity as discretionary or optional but never morally required? Or should we believe the opposite, that charity is obligatory, and failing to give (assuming we have enough time and money to take care of our own basic needs) is morally wrong?

Singer's Drowning Child

Consider this scenario: Imagine you're walking past a shallow pond and see a small child flailing in the water, clearly drowning. You look around to see if the child's

parent or caretaker is present, but you don't see anyone. You realize if you don't act quickly, the child will drown.

The problem is your new cellphone is in a case attached to your belt. There's no time to remove it. If you rush into the pond to save the child's life, your cellphone will be destroyed.

Would you hesitate? Would you let the child drown?

You see a child drowning in a pool. With no time to spare, you must jump in immediately to rescue him, but your new expensive cellphone is in your pocket. Philosopher Peter Singer would say to forget about the phone and save the child.

This hypothetical case is based on an essay written by Peter Singer, an Australian philosopher. Singer believes almost all of us will agree we have an obligation to save the child, even if doing so would destroy our cellphone (or, as in his essay, an expensive pair of shoes).

Do you agree with Singer?

Suppose that while reading this book, you learned I was in the situation described above and allowed a child to drown because I didn't want to destroy my new phone. What would you think of me? Am I selfish? Am I moral monster?

I imagine most of you would say yes to both of these questions. In fact, I'm confident most of you would question whether you should continue reading this book. What can a selfish, moral monster tell you about morality?

Here's where Singer's thoughts get interesting, challenging, and disconcerting.

If you believe it would be wrong to let the child drown in order to save my phone, Singer says you should also believe we have a moral obligation to donate money to effective charities (again, assuming you have enough money to take care of your daily needs). That is, contributing money to charity is not, like many of us believe, discretionary. Essentially, Singer believes not donating to charity is morally equivalent to not saving the drowning child.

Let's imagine my cellphone cost $500. If you believe it's wrong for me to let the child drown to save my

Australian philosopher Peter Singer (1946–), the Emeritus Ira W. DeCamp Professor of Ethics at Princeton University, has written that charitable giving is a moral imperative.

phone, you believe I should be willing to sacrifice an item that's worth $500 if that's the only way I can save a child from drowning. This is straightforward.

Luckily, most of us will never be in a position in which we have to sacrifice a new cellphone to save a drowning child. But maybe we're in the position more often than we think.

Singer claims that when you, I, and most others contemplate buying a new cellphone, we're in the same position, morally speaking, I was in when I saw the drowning child. We have an option or choice. We can buy the cellphone or not buy it and send the $500 to a charity that will use the money to feed and thereby save the life of a starving or malnourished child.

According to the World Food Program, it costs $0.43 to provide food and nutrition to a child facing famine. Even if we more than double that number and round it up to $1 per day, if we send the $500 to a reputable, efficient charity, we could feed a child experiencing famine for over a year. That is, we could save a child's life.

If *you* believe it would be morally wrong for me not to save the drowning child, even if doing so would cost me a $500 cellphone, then, according to Singer, it's equally wrong for you to buy a $500 cellphone when you could instead send the $500 to a reputable charity. Put differently, according to Singer, donating money to charity isn't discretionary. We have a moral obligation to donate, and this obligation is just as strong as the obligation I had to save the drowning child. If I would have been a moral monster if I didn't save the child because I didn't want to destroy my phone, you're a moral monster if instead of donating money to a charity, you buy a new cellphone (or television, car, or other unnecessary item).

What do you think? Are you convinced? Can you tell what ethical theory Singer is implicitly utilizing?

Singer's a utilitarian, and he's essentially saying that it would maximize happiness to wade into the pond and save a child from drowning, even if doing so would destroy one's cellphone. Thus, we have an obligation to save the drowning child.

Similarly, he's claiming that it would maximize happiness—by saving a child's life—if we donated the money we'd otherwise spend on a new cellphone to a charity helping children suffering from hunger or malnutrition. Therefore, choosing to buy the phone, instead of donating the money to charity, would be morally wrong. Put differently, charity is not discretionary—we have an obligation to give to charity (assuming our basic needs are being met).

How the Different Ethical Theories Understand Charity

What do the other ethical theories say about charity?

Let's begin with virtue ethics. As you know, this approach focuses on the virtues that underpin moral behavior. If our behavior flows from, is motivated by, or reflects virtue, it is right. If it flows from or reflects vicious motives, it is wrong. What virtues might be activated when contemplating the morality of charity?

The first and most obvious is compassion. When we witness someone acting out of compassion or the willingness to go out of one's way to help another, we react with approbation or a sense of approval. Conversely, we react with disapproval when someone exhibits callousness or cold indifference when confronted with a situation in which someone is suffering or in need of assistance. If, according to virtue ethics, an act is right if it flows from virtue—in this case compassion—then acting charitably is morally right or praiseworthy. And if never acting charitably reveals a lack of compassion, then never acting charitably is morally wrong.

A second virtue closely connected to charity is generosity. Many of us admire generosity—the willingness to give of oneself, whether time, resources, or emotional support. We react with approbation or a sense of approval when we contemplate actions that flow from generosity. From this perspective, charitable actions that flow from the virtue of generosity are virtuous, good, or

Donating one's time as a volunteer is also a form of charity, of course. And giving of yourself is considered just as generous—maybe more so in some ways—as giving money to a cause.

praiseworthy. By contrast, actions that flow from selfishness or greed are morally criticizable.

A third virtue that might be linked or connected to charity is justice. In this context, justice involves a commitment or desire to act fairly or treat people equitably. Some claim that a just person, upon realizing others lack the resources to meet their basic needs (e.g., food and shelter), will feel compelled to address these inequities.

Importantly, the motive of justice differs from compassion or generosity. A just individual might explain their charitable actions by saying something like: "It's unfair that some people go hungry while I have more than enough. The system works for me. I work hard, and as a result I earn enough money to buy food and rent a decent apartment. I know there are others who work as hard as I do (or would work as hard as I do if they were able to find a job), but for a variety of reasons they can't pay for their basic needs. This is unfair, so I regularly donate to charity in an effort to address this unfairness."

Depending on your own beliefs concerning compassion, generosity, and justice (or even just one of these), you might agree that acting charitably is consistent with these virtues, making acting charitably the right thing to do. (I'll get to some arguments claiming we don't have an obligation to give to charity shortly.)

The Ethics of Care

The ethics of care, you might already have realized, also supports an obligation to make charitable contributions. Recall that the ethics of care is usually conceived of as a form of virtue ethics. However, unlike most virtue ethics theories that claim there is more than one virtue, the ethics of care claims there is only one virtue: care, compassion, or love. In the same way a caring person has a natural desire to save a drowning child—they don't even think about it; it's their nature—that person will feel an impulse to help those who go to sleep hungry or don't have a safe place to sleep.

While our desire to assist neighbors, others in our community, or even strangers is less intense than our desire to help friends and family, it nevertheless is significant.

You might also recall that the ethics of care highlights the importance of relationships. A proponent of the ethics of care might claim that caring (or virtuous) individuals have a strong, natural desire to contribute to the well-being of their friends and family. While the desire to assist neighbors, others in our community, or even strangers is less intense than the desire to help friends and family, it nevertheless is significant. Accordingly, if the needs of my family and friends are being met, I'll have a natural desire to act charitably, as doing so will help others in my community, those residing in my state or country, or strangers living halfway around the world.

What Does Deontology Say?

Now let's consider deontology, focusing on the version associated with Immanuel Kant (discussed in Chapter 5). Kant argued that morality is founded on our capacity for rational thought and autonomy, which gives humans a unique dignity and worth.

A Kantian might argue that rational individuals would recognize that all of us depend on one another and that any of us may need assistance in the future. Rationality thus requires us to foster communities where mutual aid is a norm. Since acting charitably sustains these communities, charitable giving isn't just commendable, it's morally obligatory.

We see that the four ethical theories suggest charity is not discretionary or optional. Put differently, they suggest that we have an obligation to act charitably and help those in need of assistance. Just to be clear, these theories don't claim that we must always act charitably or always help people if we recognize they're in need of assistance. Rather, they suggest that acting charitably should be part of one's life plan.

Laughing at Misfortune

Many of us get easily upset by life's minor inconveniences. A delayed flight, spilled coffee, or a minor setback often prompts complaints and frustration. And if we experience a major tragedy, like the death of a close friend or a family pet, many of us break down and cry and are saddened or distressed for days.

If we had lived in Athens or Rome in ancient times, we might have reacted to life's ups and downs—whether minor inconveniences or major tragedies—very differently. If we lost a scroll or a sandal, we'd have told ourselves: "I lost an object. It's just a thing." And we'd have continued living without feeling angry or frustrated. Similarly, if a loved one died, we'd have recognized that death is just a part of nature, not something that should distress us for days.

This philosophy or approach to life is known as Stoicism, and the Stoics strived to focus solely on what they could control: thoughts, judgments, and actions. Everything else—like wealth, other people's opinions, the prospect of our own death, and the deaths of others—shouldn't disturb our peace of mind or command our attention. Rather, these things should simply be accepted as a part of life.

When Zeno of Citium, the founder of Stoicism, learned he had lost his ship and all its cargo and was

(cont. p. 170)

(cont. from p. 169)

bankrupt as a result, he is claimed to have calmly said: "Fortune bids me to be a less encumbered philosopher." Rather than dwelling on his loss, Zeno traveled to Athens, learned about Socrates, and became one of history's most important philosophical figures.

The Stoics thought that life is like a theater, and we are actors playing roles we didn't choose. Our job is to do the best we can with our role, since we can't escape it or rewrite our scripts. If our house burns down—it's just a thing. If our romantic partner runs off with someone else—that's their choice, not ours.

Complaining or feeling sorry for ourselves, according to Stoicism, is pointless or even ugly. After all, we can't go back in time and change roles. What we can do, however, is use our power to play the role as well as we can. This may involve focusing on things we can control. As Marcus Aurelius, a Roman emperor and Stoic, believed, we should play our part or role with virtue, grace, and dignity.

There's been a resurgence of interest in Stoicism in the last couple of decades. Some believe it's a result of economic insecurity—e.g., the 2008 financial crisis or post-COVID inflation—or awareness of global challenges or crises—e.g., pandemics, climate change, and political division.

Are There Arguments Claiming Charity Is Discretionary or Optional?

There are some arguments supporting the claim that while charity is praiseworthy, it isn't obligatory.

One of the most compelling arguments claims that addressing basic needs is the responsibility of the state or our government, not individuals. Those who make this argument claim that governments exist, in part, to ensure everyone has enough essential goods, like food and shelter.

This doesn't mean that giving to charity is wrong. It just shifts the burden from individuals to institutions.

In the same way the government should develop a national defense to protect us from invasion, it should ensure no one is left without their basic needs being fulfilled.

One school of political thought is that governments should be responsible for ensuring that their citizens' basic needs are met, which is the philosophy behind social programs such as Medicaid, food stamps, and public schooling.

Deontology provides a second argument supporting the claim that charity is discretionary. Some deontologists claim people have a fundamental, natural right to control their own time and resources. It follows from this that people are morally entitled to spend their own time and money however they choose, even if this includes buying things like concert tickets or expensive meals or gambling in a casino.

One who makes this argument could consistently claim that donating money or time to organizations that help those in need of assistance is praiseworthy or a good thing, but we shouldn't make the mistake of believing doing so is morally required. We might say donating time or money to charity goes above and beyond one's minimal moral obligations. Philosophers call actions that go above and beyond the minimum *supererogatory* acts.

(Notice that the conclusion of this deontological argument—acting charitably is praiseworthy or good but not obligatory—is different from the Kantian deontological argument discussed above. It isn't unusual for two individuals to appeal to the same ethical theory or approach and arrive at different or even opposing conclusions. Recall that in Chapter 2, I explained that one utilitarian might support the death penalty because she believes it will deter crime and therefore bring about more overall societal happiness than not having the death penalty. A second utilitarian might oppose the death penalty because he believes it won't deter crime and will result in less overall happiness. Again, we see that ethics and morality are complicated. But that com-

plexity, I submit, is part of what makes our moral lives and moral thinking so beautiful and human.)

Charity in These Divided Times

Let me begin by reminding you of something important: The goal of this book is *not* to dictate what you should believe or how you should live. I'm not trying to convince you, for example, that you have an obligation to give to charity. Rather, my aim is to help you better understand your own moral commitments and the processes you use to make moral decisions and judgments. I hope you recognize that even before you read this book, you were already using the four ethical theories we've been exploring, most likely without even realizing it. Not only have you been using them to make moral decisions, but you've also likely appealed to one or more of them to justify your political beliefs.

A second goal is to offer insight into the moral and political beliefs of others. You already know I believe, contrary to the divisive rhetoric we often hear, that Americans share a remarkably similar set of moral commitments. Most of us not only embrace the same rules of thumb but, even more importantly, also embrace the same foundational ethical theories. As I've said before, this is important because these theories provide support for our rules of thumb and deviations from these rules.

An ethical argument can be made both *for* stealing medication from a pharmacy to help a poor ill person and *against* doing so because it denies the pharmacist autonomy over her own decisions and ends up raising drug costs for others to cover losses.

When examining the issue of whether acting charitably is discretionary or obligatory, I might justify my belief that it's obligatory by appealing to utilitarianism and claim that acting charitably is obligatory because a world where people help one another without expecting anything in return is a happier world than one in which people don't do so. That is, in such a world there is far more happiness and less pain and suffering.

You, on the other hand, might disagree and justify your position by appealing to deontology. You might argue that we have an obligation to respect others' autonomy, and this obligation extends to recognizing that individuals have the right to decide how to use their own time, money, and other resources.

At first glance, this might look like yet another example of Americans being divided over morality. But step back, and you'll notice something deeper: Both of us are appealing to the same ethical theories nearly everyone accepts. Our disagreement isn't about what the core moral values are; it's about how to weigh the competing core values that we all embrace.

We've seen this before. One person believes that it's wrong to steal medicine from a pharmacy, even if doing so is the only way to save a person's life. Another believes that stealing the medicine is the right thing to do.

The first person might appeal to deontology and claim stealing the medicine is wrong because it doesn't respect the right of the pharmacist (an autonomous person) to decide what she wants to do with her own property. The second person might appeal to the ethics of care and claim that any caring agent would steal the medicine because a caring person would value life over property rights.

Both people want to do what's right. Both appeal to widely accepted ethical theories to support their beliefs concerning the rightness or wrongness of stealing the medicine. And, crucially, if they reflect on their own moral reasoning, both will likely realize they sometimes use the ethical theory that the other person is using now.

This kind of moral disagreement doesn't suggest we're deeply divided. On the contrary, it suggests we share a common moral foundation but differ in how we prioritize its parts. That's a subtle but important point. When we understand it, we open the door to greater empathy and better conversations, even in these divided times.

Final Thoughts

In this chapter we explored the issue of whether charity is discretionary or whether we have an obligation to act charitably. We examined an interesting argument proposed by philosopher Peter Singer, who claims that charity is obligatory or nondiscretionary. We then explored what the four ethical theories tell us about this issue.

While all four theories provide strong cases for charitable action, they differ in their reasoning and emphasis. Utilitarianism appeals to consequences, while virtue ethics focuses on character. The ethics of care highlights relationships, compassion, and empathy, while deontology focuses on rights, principles, and obligations.

Together, these four theories make up a rich moral landscape and give us insight into our own beliefs and those of others. And importantly, remembering that we all embrace or use the different theories in different situations reminds us that even though it may appear or seem we're divided, the fact that we use the same theories reveals that our division isn't as deep as many might want us to believe.

In the next chapter we'll explore how we might manage friendships with those whose moral and political views are different from our own.

10: Can We Still Be Friends?

The Issue: Is it possible to maintain friendships or relationships with family members when their political or moral views differ dramatically from our own?

Several years ago, after the final exam for my Introduction to Ethics class, a student—let's call her Wendy—approached me and asked if we could talk. She looked troubled.

Wendy confided that she was married to a White supremacist and her parents and husband frequently used racial slurs, including the N-word, and openly expressed hateful views. She admitted she had once believed the same things. But now, something had changed. She had come to see how wrong these beliefs were. Even more surprising, she now believed all people—regardless of race, religion, or ethnicity—were fundamentally the same and deserved equal respect. She literally used the word *respect*.

"I don't know what to do," Wendy said, visibly distressed. "I haven't told my husband or parents about my change of heart because I don't want a divorce, and I love my parents. I'm scared. Last week I couldn't bring myself to sit in the same room or sleep in the same bed with my husband. He knew something was wrong, but I was afraid to tell him how I felt. Every time I looked at him, all I could think about was how different we were. When my mom called, I let the calls go to voicemail. I just couldn't talk to her. What should I do?"

If a colleague or neighbor confided something similar and asked for advice, what would you say? What guidance would you offer?

My initial impulse was to give my usual answer: "It depends." But that response wasn't adequate, and she

might have seen it as dismissive. Wendy was suffering and needed something more than what might seem like a philosopher's shrug.

After a moment's thought, I told her, "You probably know by now I don't claim to have definitive answers to most moral questions. But that doesn't mean that I don't have thoughts about your situation. If you're open to it and have time, let's talk this through. Let's try to figure out what's motivating you and your family members. Maybe we can gain some insights into why this is so upsetting for *you*. I can't promise we'll find a solution to your problem, but maybe we can understand things more clearly."

Wendy's story isn't unique. In recent years, I've watched as more and more relationships —between family members, close friends, and even spouses—fracture over moral and political disagreements. And every time I hear a story like this, it breaks my heart.

During the Trump and Biden presidencies, too many students have come to my office seeking advice or wanting to talk about strained or broken relationships. The COVID-19 pandemic, and particularly debates over the vaccines, exacerbated these tensions.

Some of my students believed the vaccines were dangerous and dreaded sitting down at the dinner table with their pro-vaccine parents. "How can I stay at my parents' house when they're forcing my siblings to get vaccinated and spreading the word the vaccines are safe? They weren't tested properly! What if they change our DNA or cause cancer? I can't respect my parents anymore."

It is readily apparent that the Trump presidencies have driven apart the people of the United States by emphasizing differences over the things that Americans all have in common.

Other students took the opposite stance, confident in the safety and efficacy of vaccines. They were furious with family members who spread what they viewed as dangerous misinformation on social media. "How can I face my parents and pretend everything's fine when their posts

The COVID-19 pandemic elicited a surprising debate between those in favor of the mRNA vaccine as a treatment and the "antivaxxers" who feared that the vaccine was unsafe because it was developed too quickly in the lab.

encouraging vaccine refusal are putting lives at risk. I feel embarrassed and ashamed, and I don't think I can be around them."

It wasn't just students grappling with these issues. Two friends of mine ended our relationships because of differing political views or disagreements about the pandemic. And I know I'm not alone. I suspect many of you reading this have had similar falling-outs with people you care about because of disagreements about moral or political issues.

So, what *should* you do if someone close to you holds moral or political beliefs you find repugnant? How should you respond if a friend supports a political candidate—either Democrat or Republican—you see as a threat to democracy or the well-being of our country? What if a family member uses slurs or expresses hatred toward a group of people? Can you, or should you, maintain these relationships? Should you welcome such people into your home, or does doing so compromise your own values or integrity?

These are difficult questions, but in a divided world, they're worth asking.

Can we still be friends with those on "the other side"?

Discussion

Wendy trusted me, or at least I think she did. She wanted to talk. As we walked back to my office, I scrambled to fill the silence with small talk, asking her about the weather, where she lived, and her plans for the semester break. I wasn't really listening to her answers as I tried to figure out how to approach our conversation.

"I know that relationships with parents and spouses are among the most important relationships we have,"

I began cautiously. "Far be it from me to tell anyone whether to end one of these relationships, or in your case, both."

Wendy nodded, so I continued.

"I don't know you very well, and obviously I've never met your parents or your husband. Even if I knew all of you, I couldn't and wouldn't tell you what I thought you should do. If I were in your shoes, it might take me weeks, months, or even years to decide what was best. And even then, I'd probably second-guess myself, wondering if I did the right or best thing."

"I understand," she said softly.

"But," I continued, "as I mentioned before we walked over here, I do think we can gain valuable insights if we talk. We might get a better sense of who you are, who you want to be, and what's driving your distress. Maybe we can also better understand the roots of your parents' and husband's beliefs. This might help you decide what to do."

"Okay," Wendy whispered.

"I think you know I value a range of perspectives on moral and political issues," I said. "Remember our discussion on the morality of abortion in class? I tried to show the class there are good arguments supporting both sides. I hope you also discovered that I don't share my personal beliefs with students. But since the semester is over, I'll take the risk. I need to say up front that I think White supremacy is different from abortion or the other issues we discussed in class."

Again, Wendy nodded her head.

"I can't tell you there are two reasonable sides to this issue. Unlike abortion or cloning, unlike capital punishment, I believe White supremacy is indefensible and unjustifiable. That doesn't mean your parents and husband are terrible people. Again, I don't know them. It does mean, however, that they hold some horrible beliefs, and those beliefs can lead to horrible actions."

"I think they're horrible, especially my husband."

"We can discuss that, but maybe not just yet," I suggested. "For now, I think it might be helpful to discuss why your parents and husband believe what they believe. Let me ask you this: Why did you believe what you believed? Why were you a White supremacist?"

"I was born that way."

"Let me get this straight," I said, smiling. "You be-

lieve you came out of the birth canal as a White supremacist?"

Wendy gave a forced laugh. "No. I was raised that way. I never learned anything else. My parents and their friends were White supremacists. I was home schooled, and I just always believed what they taught me."

"I see. Here's another question: Do you think you're responsible for being a White supremacist? Think before answering this."

"I guess so. I don't know," she replied.

At that point, I wasn't entirely sure where the conversation was heading, but I decided to introduce an idea from moral philosophy: *moral luck*. Moral luck is a philosophical term that refers to situations in which someone receives moral praise or condemnation, even though their behavior is influenced by factors beyond their control or by luck.

Moral luck is a philosophical term that refers to situations in which someone receives moral praise or condemnation, even though their behavior is influenced by factors beyond their control or by luck.

"Imagine two people born in Germany in 1920, about two decades before World War II and the Holocaust began. One, Hans, is brought to the United States as an infant. The other, Horst, grows up in Germany and becomes a Nazi prison guard. If Hans had stayed in Germany, he might have become a prison guard too, contributing to the deaths of many innocent people. Hans was lucky he didn't have to stand up to the familial and other social pressures that might have led him to do the things Horst did."

I paused to let the idea sink in and think about what to say next.

"Most philosophers believe if moral luck plays a significant role in a person's behavior, that person isn't fully morally responsible for their actions. Hans doesn't deserve moral praise for not becoming a prison guard. That was luck—good luck. And bad luck helps explain why Horst became a prison guard. Sure, Horst did horrible things, but it doesn't follow that he is fully blameworthy for doing these things or was a horrible human being. Maybe we'd have done the same had we been raised like he was, if we had the same bad moral luck."

If a person was born and raised in Germany before World War II and eventually became a guard at a Nazi concentration camp, how much could what they did as a guard be attributed to how, when, and where they grew up and how much to their own moral character?

I then quoted St. Ambrose to underscore the point: "'If we have not committed the sins that others have, perhaps this is because we did not have the opportunity—the situation and circumstances were different. In each person there is something good and something bad....'"

I asked Wendy what she thought Ambrose was saying. Before she could answer, and hoping to take the pressure off, I continued, "He was trying to point out that all of us have the potential to believe the wrong thing or act immorally. So much depends on how we were raised and what we were exposed to. If your parents or your husband were raised in families with different beliefs, they probably wouldn't believe what they believe now. In a way, it was bad luck that led them to where they are today, or at least bad luck played a part. Does this make sense?"

Wendy nodded, but I wasn't confident she agreed with me.

"The same goes for you," I added. "Luck may help explain why you believed what you believed. As you said, your parents raised you to become a White supremacist. And you didn't choose your parents. I'm hoping this recognition will help you be less hard on yourself. It might even help you empathize with or understand the people who play such a large role in your life."

"I don't know if I'll ever forgive them," Wendy replied. "Or myself."

"That's okay. I'm not suggesting you should. Seriously, I have no idea about that. What I do know is that true forgiveness, if it ever comes, takes time and effort. I believe it's something you shouldn't force, and I don't believe it's something you owe others. What is important, and this may take months or even years, is

figuring out what sort of person you want to be. Once you've done that, maybe you'll know whether you want to forgive your parents, husband, or even yourself. If that happens, it would be a beautiful thing."

By the end of our conversation, Wendy still didn't want to be around her parents and husband. We had a lot more to think about and discuss, and I invited Wendy to continue our talks during the semester break. She called once, saying she was more confused than ever, and I tried to explain that confusion is frequently the beginning of growth.

To this day, I occasionally wonder what happened with Wendy. Did she continue rejecting White supremacy? Did she discuss her beliefs with her parents and/or her husband? Did she decide to rebuild or redefine her relationships with them? Was she at peace with whatever she decided? I'll probably never know, but I'm confident that if she did find her way, the path was messy and uncertain.

I continue to ponder whether we can or should be friends with those who perform seriously immoral or repugnant acts or hold repugnant beliefs. I keep going back and forth on this one.

We're Neither All Good nor All Bad

As I hint at above, one common mistake many of us make, myself included, is trying to sort people into simple categories: good or bad. A close friend and I were recently discussing someone we knew from high school, and she bluntly told me: "Based on what he's done, he's a piece of garbage."

When I objected and tried to remind her of some of the good things he did in the past, she replied: "You have to draw a line somewhere. Some people are just bad. Take a stand."

I'm guessing my friend, without being aware of it, was trying to keep things simple. Labeling someone as a bad person makes it easier to end a friendship. But if they're just a person who's done a mix of good and bad things, maybe even some really bad things, it becomes complicated. Ending the friendship doesn't seem to be the obvious course of action.

This reminds me of Paolo Di Canio, a famous Italian soccer star. In his autobiography, Di Canio praises former fascist dictator Benito Mussolini, stating that he was "basically a very principled, ethical individual" and claiming that he was misunderstood. In fact, Di Canio describes himself as a fascist. This alone might be enough for some to conclude Di Canio isn't a good person.

But there's more to the story, as you probably already imagined. In 2000, Di Canio was playing for West Ham United in a match against Everton. The score was 1–1, and Di Canio's teammate passed him the ball in front of the goal. Di Canio saw Everton's goalkeeper on the ground, injured. Instead of trying to shoot the ball into an open net, he caught the ball, using his hands, and play stopped immediately. The crowd gave him a standing ovation, and the following year Di Canio was awarded the FIFA Fair Play award.

So, how do we label someone like DiCanio? Maybe we shouldn't try. It might be more honest or accurate to acknowledge that all of us have good moments and bad moments, sometimes great and sometimes horrible. Instead of saying "Di Canio is a horrible person," we might say "Di Canio, like everyone else, did some good things and some bad things. Some of the things he's done are very bad, but let's not forget what he did during that game. He probably also did other good things."

Paolo Di Canio (1968–), a popular Italian soccer player from 1985 to 2008 and a team manager from 2011 to 2013, is also a fascist who admires Benito Mussolini.

Resisting the urge to label someone as either good or bad provides us with a better, truer, and more nuanced understanding of them. After all, we've all done some regrettable things. I don't deny that some people do more bad things than most others or do worse things than most others, but maybe some of these same people do more good things than others as well.

Here's the rest of the St. Ambrose quote from above:

Saint Ambrose of Milan (c. 339–397) was a bishop and ethical commentator who was also known for developing the Ambrosian chant. He asserted that while everyone has good and bad in them, people always tend to focus on just the vices in others.

"In each person there is something good and something bad; we usually see only the vices in people and we see nothing that is good."

You might be thinking that resisting the urge to label people makes it tougher to decide whether to continue a friendship or relationship with someone whose moral, political, and religious beliefs are different from your own. I think you're correct. If you're okay with this or value the complexity of many of the issues we've explored in this book, welcome to my club. As I've said before and will say again, when I began studying ethics, I was frustrated because I didn't find the answers I was looking for. Eventually, I discovered that ethical and moral issues are complex, and this complexity is beautiful. Isn't it remarkable that we're capable of thinking so deeply about whether we should continue or end a friendship?

An Old Friend Who's Changed

Let's look at the issue from a different perspective. Imagine running into an old friend, Phillip, in the grocery store. After catching up for a few minutes, you discover that Phillip has changed. He says some crude, denigrating things about women and uses a slur when someone asks if you can move so they can get something off one of the shelves.

Your initial excitement at seeing Phillip vanishes. Now, you're just uncomfortable. You question whether you want to spend time with him or see him again, as he suggested. You might be thinking: "What if he asks for my phone number. Should I give it to him or maybe 'mistakenly' give him the wrong number? I need to get out of here before he asks for it."

But let's say you do exchange contact information. You were smart enough (or lucky enough) to realize that if you gave him the wrong number, he could easily find your work number and call you there. You've agreed to stay in touch, but now you're questioning what you should say if he calls.

Your first instinct might be to ghost him. This might be the easiest thing to do, but is it the best?

Do you want to be the sort of person who ghosts someone because it's easier than having a hard conversation? Might there be a better way to let him know you're not interested...?

Do you want to be the sort of person who ghosts someone because it's easier than having a hard conversation? Might there be a better way to let him know you're not interested in restoring your friendship?

Now imagine you spoke with me about the issue, and I smiled and asked, "Have you thought about whether spending time with Phillip might have a positive influence on him? He didn't hold these ugly beliefs in the past, and maybe after talking with you he'll come to see that he's somehow gotten off track. This discovery might be good for him and the world."

I might remind you that this is an example of utilitarian reasoning and then say, "You know I don't know what you should do, but I think it's worthwhile thinking about this."

You might agree that continuing to talk with Phillip will potentially be good for Phillip and the world. But then again, the personal costs of associating with him, even if you might have a positive influence on him, might be too great. Perhaps after spending time with him, you'll be depressed or outraged. Or maybe you're concerned that others, including your current friends, boss, and colleagues, might discover that you have this hateful friend, and this might cost you your job or negatively affect some important relationships. And then there's your moral integrity. Perhaps you believe continuing to pass time with Phillip will somehow negatively affect it or compromise who you are.

What do you think you would do in this situation? What should you do or what would you do if you were the person you want to be?

Camila: Parents with Problematic Beliefs

Let's change the situation. Suppose a different friend, Camila, confides in you that she recently discovered that in the past her parents were part of Weather Underground, a radical left-wing organization that advocated violent revolution to overthrow the U.S. government. The organization carried out bombings and other direct actions in the past, and her parents were currently trying to revive the organization. Camila despises their beliefs and feels lost and confused. Years earlier, she shared that she was adopted when she was five years old. Later, as a teenager, her parents admitted that they didn't really want a child when they adopted her, but they believed the foster care system was horrible and wanted to save a child in the system. They also told her they came to believe it was the best thing they ever did.

I pose this hypothetical case to reiterate that for most of us there isn't a clear-cut answer as to whether we should maintain relationships with people whose moral or political views we find immoral or even repugnant.

Like most children, Camila had disagreements with her parents while she was growing up, but she loved them, and they loved her. Now, she turns to you for advice: "What would you do if your parents turned out to be bad people?"

What should your friend, Camila, do? What advice might you give her?

Might it be helpful for Camila to resist labeling her parents as bad people? Might you say something like: "Obviously your parents hold some ugly, hateful, and dangerous beliefs, but from what you've told me, they've done some beautiful things in the past. How many people adopt a child they initially didn't want just to save him or her from foster care? I know it's heartbreaking and it makes you angry to think about their current beliefs, but at the same time you and I know that your parents have done some amazing things, things that most people would never even consider. I think it's important to remember both the good and the bad and recognize the complexity of who they are."

I pose this hypothetical case to reiterate that for most of us, there isn't a clear-cut answer as to whether we should maintain relationships with people whose moral or political views we find immoral or even repugnant. I imagine that if Camila was my friend and asked for advice, I'd be pulled in different directions.

One part of me would believe that Camila should cut ties with her parents, as this might be better for her own mental health. Additionally, perhaps ending or minimizing her relationship with her parents will send them a message. They might realize they're alienating their daughter, and this might at least motivate them to question their beliefs.

Why Do Trolls Troll?

When we hear the word "troll," most of us immediately think of internet trolls, but trolling isn't new—it's been around for centuries. Before the internet, pamphleteers played a similar role. In the fifteenth century, the printing press was invented; by the seventeenth and eighteenth centuries, printing presses were accessible throughout most of Europe. Armed with this relatively new technology, would-be trolls were ready to ply their craft. They could inexpensively print pamphlets that were easy to distribute by slipping them under doors, posting them in town squares, taverns, or churches, and throwing them into a large group of people. Perhaps most importantly, they could maintain their anonymity while provoking and mocking others.

While many pamphleteers made legitimate claims about society, others didn't care about the truth. For example, during the late 1700s, pamphleteers accused French queen Marie Antoinette of sexual deviance, incest, treason, and extravagant cruelty without any proof.

Recent research has shed light on the minds of internet trolls, and they discovered (perhaps not surprisingly) that trolls tend to have four dark personality traits known as the Dark Tetrad: Machiavellianism, Narcissism, Psychopathy, and Sadism.

(cont. p. 187)

But another part of me would hesitate. Continuing the relationship would give Camila opportunities to talk with her parents about their beliefs (and her own). There's a chance—and this might be a longshot—that these conversations will motivate her parents to question their beliefs. And who knows, maybe Camila might learn something.

And then there's the unique and special quality of the parent-child relationship. I'm not suggesting it should be preserved at all costs, but for most of us the situation must be pretty bad if we believe terminating a parent-child relationship is the right thing to do. Ulti-

(cont. from p. 186)

While the Dark Tetrad is not listed in the *Diagnostiic and Statistical Manual of Mental Disorders* (DSM) as a mental disorder, those with high scores are frequently self-centered, popular—but their relationships tend to be superficial—prone to lying and bullying, and jealous. Perhaps more concerning is that they lack compassion, and rather than help people in need of assistance, they're prone to laughing at others or even try to make bad situations worse.

So, how should we respond to trolling? For many of us, our initial desire is to retaliate or set the record straight. We might be motivated by a need for justice or by the natural motivation to respond and defend ourselves against threats, whether physical or psychological. But this plays right into the hands of trolls.

Fairy tales like "The Three Billy Goats Gruff" or "Rumpelstiltskin" suggest a smarter approach: ignoring or outsmarting trolls. Responding or paying attention to them is exactly what they crave. If we're feeling particularly generous, we might want to try to empathize with them or try to understand what's motivating their behavior. On a good day, when I think about trolls, I feel a sense of pity for them. I recognize that their harmful behaviors likely stem from deep personal wounds, often from childhood, and that something has gone terribly wrong to produce these destructive behaviors.

mately, only Camila (and her parents) can assess whether the costs associated with maintaining the relationship are worth it.

While this may seem to be wishy-washy, perhaps wishy-washiness is called for.

Are We Really So Divided?

A few years ago, during the heated Trump vs. Biden presidential campaign, I was talking with a former student, Nathan, about the divided nature of the United States.

Nathan was all-in for Trump and told me he proudly displayed a Trump sign in his front yard. His next-door neighbor had a Biden sign. Up until this campaign, the two had a friendly relationship. They'd frequently chat for a few minutes when they saw each other outside, and his neighbor would occasionally invite him over for a barbecue with friends and family members.

Sad how the same neighbors who used to invite each other to barbeque parties now barely talk to each other, thanks to the horrible political situation currently ongoing in the United States.

"Things changed this year," Nathan said. "We barely say 'hello' to each other. It's obvious he doesn't want to talk with me, and frankly, I'm not sure want to talk with him. If he's voting for Biden, we don't have much in common."

Although I never spoke with Nathan's neighbor, I figured he was thinking the same about Nathan.

"Are you okay with this?" I asked Nathan.

"It is what it is," he said with a shrug.

"That's not saying much," I replied. "I get the sense that you're resigned to the situation but not necessarily happy about it."

"I guess so. But there's nothing I can do about it."

"I wonder," I began, "if there's much difference between not having a relationship with a neighbor because of his race or religion and avoiding him because of his political views or affiliation." As I frequently do, I asked Nathan about his neighbor's basic moral commitments, and his replies were unsurprising.

Nathan told me his neighbor always seemed to be a good person. He believed his neighbor would help him and others in an emergency and drive his child to school if his own car didn't start.

"Do you think he'd lend you a cup of sugar?"

"He used to invite me to barbecues, so obviously he'd lend me a cup of sugar. In fact, before this election, if I was out of town and couldn't cut my lawn, I'm confident he would have happily done so."

"It sounds to me like he's a good neighbor, and at the very least a decent person," I said.

"It does, doesn't it?" Nathan laughed, but it seemed forced.

"So, how's your reaction to him different from someone who learns the religion of their neighbor and then terminates or minimizes their relationship? I'm not asking you this to make you feel bad. I know that lots of people are in the same situation that you're in. It just seems like when you attached the label 'Biden supporter' to your neighbor, you saw him differently."

"But it is different," Nathan insisted. "Biden lies all the time. I value truth. I don't want friends who value lying."

"I'm not going to get into a debate over who lies more, Biden or Trump," I replied. "Let me ask you this: Why do you think your neighbor doesn't value the truth?"

On the Trump side of the camp, a large segment of the American population felt that Joe Biden was a fraud from the start and hated many of his policies.

"Like I said, Biden lies all the time, and he supports Biden."

"Is it possible he knows Biden lies and doesn't like lying, but he cares more about other issues? Again, I'm not going to try to figure out who lies more, Biden or Trump. It's somewhat irrelevant. Maybe your neighbor believes that Biden's economic policies are way better for those in poverty than are Trump's. Or he believes that Russia is a threat to the U.S. and the world order, and Biden would address this better than Trump. I ask you again, is it possible he hates lying but believes the most important issues right now are helping those in need and slowing Russia's international influence?"

"I guess that's possible."

"My point is," I continued, "you thought he was basically a good person before the signs went up. You used to go to his house for barbecues. Maybe he hasn't changed much at all. Sure, he's voting for someone you dislike or even despise—but you told me he was a decent person and the two of you had a good relationship until the signs went up."

I paused and saw him thinking. "I suppose my question is a question you've heard me ask in the past," I said. "What type of person do you want to be? Do you

want to end relationships with neighbors and maybe friends because they support one candidate or another? Or do you want to be a person who maintains these relationships until you learn that they do bad or immoral things?"

Nathan and I discussed whether he should talk to his neighbor and explain his concerns. I admitted I might not have the courage to do this and that it might make things worse. That depends on how the two interact with each other.

As he was leaving, I realized I might have nudged him to talk with his neighbor. "Nathan, before you leave, I want to make it clear that I wasn't trying to convince you to do anything. I truly don't know what you should do. And remember not to be too hard on yourself. You might decide that something is the right thing to do, but at the same time you might not be able to do it."

"I'm not sure what you mean."

"Sometimes we don't have a choice. We can't continue living next to someone without having the difficult conversations. Other times, their views and the way they communicate might be so off-putting that we can't force ourselves to interact with them even though we might think it's the best or right thing to do. Don't make any rash decisions, and hopefully you'll be comfortable with whatever choice you make."

Final Thoughts

In this chapter we explored the issue of whether we should maintain friendships with people whose moral and political views differ greatly from our own. This issue is especially salient in the United States, where our moral and political divisions seem to grow greater every year.

We looked at extreme cases, like White supremacy and neo-Nazism, and everyday ones, like political division between neighbors. And we explored the concept of moral luck. I suggested that many of us might have become White supremacists if we had been raised in environments that promoted White supremacy and were never exposed to differing viewpoints. We might want to say that we were just lucky that we didn't become

White supremacists. Recognizing this can make it easier to empathize with, rather than hate, those whose views we find repugnant.

We also looked at our tendency to label people as "good" or "bad." It's much easier to end a relationship with someone we've labeled as bad. But these labels are distorting or overly simplistic. Everyone does good and bad things. Recognizing this and refraining from using the labels "good" and "bad" forces us to see people in a more nuanced light, making the decision to end or maintain a relationship more challenging—but maybe it should be.

In the past, Americans went to the voting polls with varying social and political opinions, but after the election they came together and supported the democratically elected officials. Nowadays, it seems different. If we view those with opposing views as immoral and untrustworthy, as bad people, how can we put aside our differences after elections?

If we believe those with opposing views are immoral and untrustworthy and are bad people, how can we put aside our differences after elections?

I don't have a definitive or neat answer, but I do think it's important to remember that most of us embrace the same basic moral principles and rules of thumb. We believe it's usually wrong to lie, to break promises, and to steal. We believe we should help people in need of assistance if it doesn't cost too much (in time, money, and/or energy), and we value loyalty, generosity, and fairness. We also draw from the same ethical theories or moral frameworks—utilitarianism, virtue ethics, the ethics of care, and deontology—even if we weigh them differently.

So, should we stay friends with those on "the other side"? Maybe. Maybe not.

But remembering our shared values helps us see that those with different political views and affiliations don't have to be enemies. Maybe we can, maybe we should, continue some of our challenging friendships and relationships and not others. Perhaps continuing challenging friendships is inherently good. Or doing so might improve the life of our challenging friend or the lives

of others who interact with this friend in the future. That said, some relationships might be best terminated if they cause too much pain because we find the other person's beliefs and actions to be repugnant.

Ultimately, we might want to remain open to changing our minds. We might want to remember that whatever decision we make might not be the best or correct one. Perhaps, that is the best or most moral approach.

11: Fair Hiring Practices

The Issue: Experience shows us that sometimes people are hired into positions even though there are more qualified candidates out there. Are there circumstances in which this might be justified?

We've all heard stories about someone with weaker credentials being hired for a job or admitted to a college or university. Maybe it's because of affirmative action. Or maybe it's due to personal connections or a university's legacy admissions policy—someone is admitted because a family member previously attended the university.

When I was in law school, a classmate who worked in the admissions office claimed to have stolen internal, confidential data. While we were studying together, they told our group that the stolen records revealed that Black applicants were often admitted with significantly lower grades and test scores than White applicants. At the time, I dismissed the story, thinking they were just trying to impress us by boasting about stealing confidential information.

Several years later, over dinner with a friend, the topic resurfaced.

"Did you hear about the article in our law school's student newspaper?" my friend asked.

"What article?"

She told me about an article, entitled "Admissions Apartheid," written by a student who had worked in the school's admissions office. This student claimed to have accessed confidential files and alleged that Black students, on average, were admitted with far lower grades and test scores than White students.

Confidence vs. Competence: The Dunning-Kruger Effect

As a mentor of many students, I often talk with thoughtful, intelligent individuals who claim that they do poorly in job interviews and as a result don't get hired. They tell me how classmates or others applying for the same job are confident and strong in these interviews, while it's unnatural for them to brag or even believe they're the best.

Sometimes I wonder if these students should somehow mention the Dunning-Kruger effect during their interviews. About 25 years ago, David Dunning and Justin Kruger identified a cognitive bias known as the Dunning-Kruger effect. Their research revealed that individuals with low competence in a specific area tend to overestimate their abilities. In contrast, highly competent individuals frequently underestimate themselves. Thus, in a job interview, for example, less-competent applicants may believe they are better qualified than competent applicants, and this belief will bolster their self-confidence. Meanwhile, those with high competence will underestimate their own abilities, and this will decrease their confidence. The upshot: The less qualified person is hired.

(cont. p. 197)

"What do you think of this?" my friend asked.

"What do I think of what?" I responded. "Do I believe the claims? Or are you asking about the morality of stealing and publishing of confidential information? Or maybe you want to know whether I think the school's admission process is fair, assuming the allegations are true."

"I guess the last one," she answered.

This conversation raises some important questions. What would you think if you heard a local law school or university admitted Black, Hispanic, or any other group of students with lower grades and test scores than White students? Would your opinion change if the reverse were true, if White students were admitted with grades and test scores lower than Black applicants? Whatever your stance, what values and beliefs motivate your position?

(cont. from p. 196)

The Dunning-Kruger effect isn't limited to self-assessments of how one will perform a job. It seems to play a role in the different tasks we confront. As a professor, I realized early on that students who volunteer to answer challenging or subtle questions frequently don't understand what we're discussing. Not only that, but those who hesitate to say something or begin their answers with "I'm not sure this is correct, but…" are often more likely to provide thoughtful answers to challenging questions than those whose hands immediately go up. Sometimes I tell my students, "If you think that you understand this well and that the material isn't complicated, there's a good chance you're confused." I then explain Dunning-Kruger.

Although many of us are frustrated by those who suffer from the Dunning-Kruger effect, Dunning and Kruger pointed out that those so afflicted suffer a dual burden. First, they make many mistakes. Second, they don't have the cognitive skills to recognize they make these mistakes. Should we respond with pity as well as resentment?

Discussion

Like many of the issues explored in this book, my views on hiring or admitting the "less qualified" candidate are a work in progress. Part of me believes at least some of these policies can be justified and should be supported, while another part of me believes they're unfair and should be discontinued. As with other issues or questions discussed in this book, like the morality of abortion or breaking promises, I trust that by the end of this chapter many of you will find your own views on the issue to be more nuanced than you may have initially thought. I furthermore suspect that many of you, like me, will come to realize you both support and oppose policies that result in the "less qualified" candidate being hired or admitted.

Colleges and universities present a variety of arguments to justify admitting students whose formal qualifications seem to be weaker than those of applicants

who were denied admission. Employers frequently appeal to the same or similar reasons when explaining why they might hire individuals whose formal qualifications seem to be weaker than those of applicants who weren't hired.

Affirmative Action

One of the most controversial approaches associated with these practices is affirmative action. Yet, as with many of the issues discussed in this book, there is disagreement concerning what actually counts as affirmative action.

Some claim policies aimed at ending discrimination qualify as affirmative action policies. A notable example is President John F. Kennedy's 1961 executive order, which is often cited as the first affirmative action policy in the United States. It instructed government contractors to "take affirmative action to ensure that applicants are employed, and that employees are treated during employment, without regard to their race, creed, color, or national origin." Today, most people support Kennedy's order and believe prohibiting discrimination in the hiring process shouldn't even count as an affirmative action policy. Basic fairness dictates that hiring practices that allow for discrimination based on race, religion, and ethnicity are wrong. The same goes for the treatment of employees.

Following Kennedy's executive order, affirmative action policies proliferated. In 1969, President Richard Nixon, a Republican, issued the Philadelphia Order, requiring those in the craft and construction industries to set goals and timetables reflecting a commitment to overcome hiring biases against Black individuals. Around the same time, some colleges and universities began implementing affirmative action policies of their own. Some of these policies explicitly stated that points would be added to the admissions scores of mem-

"Affirmative Action" is a collective term for policies and laws designed to end systemic discrimination in business, education, and society in general.

bers of specific groups of people or that a minimum number of places would be reserved for them. Similar measures were adopted by some police and fire departments as well as private corporations. One of the stated goals of these policies was to create workforces or student bodies that better reflected the racial, religious, or ethnic makeup of their communities.

Opponents of affirmative action often sought recourse through the courts. In 1978, the U.S. Supreme Court addressed the issue in *University of California v. Bakke*. The Court ruled that race could be a factor taken into account by admissions committees deciding who should be accepted into medical schools. However, the Court explicitly rejected the use of *numerical quotas* (policies requiring a fixed number or percentage of positions for underrepresented or targeted groups).

More recently, the Supreme Court and other courts have been increasingly reluctant to condone affirmative action and have limited its use. In 2003, the Court revisited the issue in *Grutter v. Bollinger* and *Gratz v. Bollinger*. While the Court upheld the principle that colleges and universities could favor "underrepresented minority groups" in order to provide students the educational benefits associated with a diverse student body, it prohibited awarding extra points to the admissions scores of all members of a group. The Court held that candidates for admission must be looked at on an individual basis, assessing each individual's qualifications and circumstances. Presumably, the Court tried to balance the need or desire to diversify student bodies and the value of fairness.

Reverse Discrimination and the Wrongness of Affirmative Action

One of the most common arguments against affirmative action begins with a moral claim most of us embrace: Discrimination based on race, religion, ethnicity, and gender (and perhaps other factors) is inherently wrong or unjust. Certainly, if we learned a university refused to admit Black or women students, we'd immediately identify that as wrong or unjust, because discrimination based on race or gender is wrong or unjust.

Critics of affirmative action then claim that affirmative action policies discriminate against White men.

If a college only admitted white students into its academic halls, we would easily conclude they practiced discrimination. But isn't deliberately *not* admitting a qualified white student a type of discrimination, too?

And if it's wrong to discriminate based on race or gender, then it follows that affirmative action policies that discriminate against White men must be wrong. Discriminating against White men, they say, is no better than discriminating against Black people, women, or other minorities in the past. This argument is frequently called the reverse discrimination argument against affirmative action.

If we think about the ethical theories we've already explored—utilitarianism, deontology, virtue ethics, and the ethics of care—the reverse discrimination argument probably falls into the category of a deontological (or rule-based) argument. In this case, the relevant rule is something like: "It's wrong (or unjust) to discriminate on the basis of race, sex, ethnicity or religion." Since affirmative action policies discriminate on the basis of these factors, the argument concludes that these policies are wrong.

It's likely that most of you embrace the principle "It's morally wrong or unjust to discriminate on the basis of race, sex, ethnicity or religion." For this reason, the reverse discrimination argument against affirmative action may resonate with you or align with your beliefs.

If affirmative action truly discriminates on the basis of these factors, it seems logical to conclude it is wrong or that we have a reason to believe it's wrong—but there may be other reasons that lead us to believe it's right or permissible.

Merit Is What's Most Important

In addition to the reverse discrimination argument, many of those opposed to affirmative action advance a second argument, which is also deontological. They begin by claiming we should embrace an ethical principle, which states hiring and admissions decisions should be based on merit and only merit. Philosophers and ethicists call this the *principle of meritocracy*.

They then claim affirmative action, which to some extent bases hiring decisions on race, gender, and religion, violates the principle of meritocracy. Thus, affirmative action is wrong. This is the case, they claim, regardless

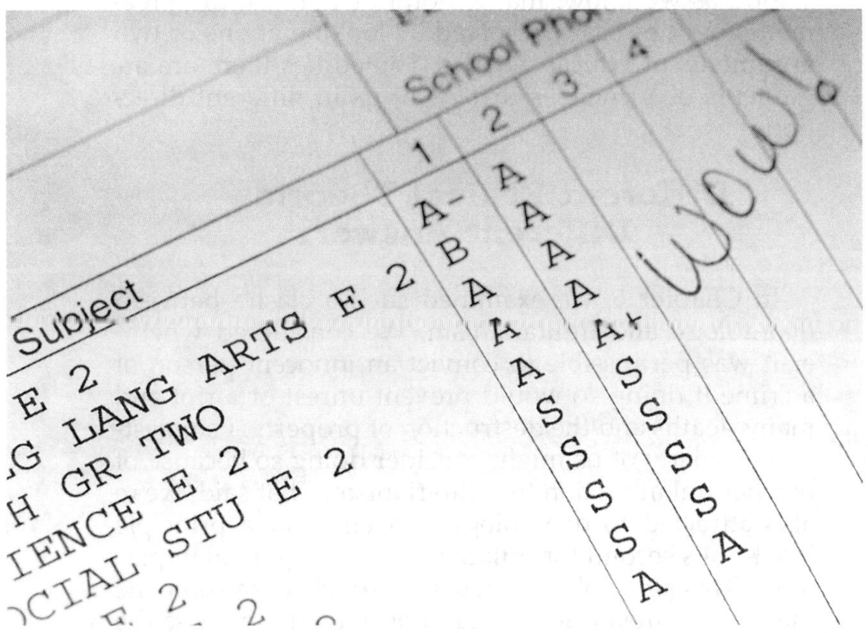

A meritocracy asserts that people should be rewarded based on their talents and skills. A school teacher should therefore give a student an A only if they deserve the grade, and those who earned mediocre grades should not be admitted to a university ahead of better students regardless of race, creed, sex, or other factors.

of whether in the past (or in the present) marginalized groups suffered from unjust discrimination. Two wrongs don't make a right.

Regardless of whether we support or oppose affirmative action, the meritocracy argument resonates with most of us. Think back to high school. Imagine that one of our teachers told us that final grades would be determined by pulling names out of a hat (say, the first five names get an A, the next five a B, and so forth). Most of us would have objected and argued that grades should be based on merit, on the scores of that semester's tests and assignments. Similarly, if our boss announced half the workers will get raises and they'll pull names out of a hat to determine who gets a raise, we'd likely believe this was unfair or wrong. This is the case because these practices violate the principle of meritocracy.

Given that we embrace the principle of meritocracy and believe affirmative action violates this principle, we now have a second deontological argument in opposition to affirmative action.

But, as we know, many moral or political disagreements can't be easily resolved by looking at one or two arguments or ethical theories. Sometimes there are arguments or principles that point us in different directions.

Different Ethical Theories—Different Answers

In Chapter 5, we examined such a clash—between deontology and utilitarianism. We considered whether it was permissible to convict an innocent person of a crime if doing so would prevent unrest or a riot and many deaths and the destruction of property. I suggested that many of us might consider doing so because of our natural attraction to utilitarianism. That said, we're also attracted to deontology and embrace a principle like Kant's second formulation of the categorical imperative. This principle dictates it's wrong to use someone merely as a means to an end or as a tool to increase the well-being of ourselves and others (without regard to how this behavior would affect the one we are using). I suggested that some of you might conclude convicting the innocent person was wrong, or put differently, you believed deontology in that situation trumped utilitar-

ianism. Others might conclude utilitarianism trumped deontology and, therefore, convicting the innocent person was the best thing to do.

I then returned to a hypothetical case introduced in Chapter 2. This case involved the choice of pushing one of two buttons. If you pushed the first, your friend would kill an innocent person, but it would prevent 20 nuclear weapons from exploding in 20 large cities. If you pushed the second, your friend wouldn't push the button and the nuclear weapons would detonate, killing 1 million people. I speculated that even though most of us might be torn—deontology would tell us to push the second and utilitarianism would tell us to push the first—at the end of the day almost all of us would push the first. That is, almost all of us believe utilitarianism trumps deontology in this situation.

These hypothetical scenarios demonstrate how we navigate situations in which two different ethical theories suggest or justify two different actions. With this in mind, let's look at arguments that support affirmative action.

Why Is My Boss So Incompetent?

We've all heard someone claim that their boss or manager is unqualified, and sometimes those making these claims assert that they should be the boss or manager. Are these grievances rooted in jealousy, misjudgment, or genuine insight?

In their 1969 book, *The Peter Principle*, Lawrence J. Peter and Raymond Hull explore management and the seeming truth that managers are frequently less qualified than those they manage. According to Peter and Hull, supervisors recognize which of their employees do the best job, and these employees are selected for promotion. So far, so good. Shouldn't it work this way?

The problem is that as these employees continue to be promoted, eventually they're promoted to positions for which they are unqualified. Their lack of qualifications usually isn't a lack of intelligence; rather, it's that the new job requires a skill set that's different from the skill set that allows them to excel in their current job, and they don't have this new

(cont. p. 204)

(cont. from p. 203)

skillset. The Peter Principle explains this phenomenon: "In a hierarchy, every employee tends to rise to his level of incompetence."

Imagine an organization that has six levels of management, 1 being the highest (CEO) and 6 the lowest (Shift Supervisor). Susan is hired for a level 6 Shift Supervisor position and excels. When there's an opening at a level 5 Team Manager position, her supervisor promotes her. Again, she excels. She is next promoted to a level 4, Division Director. Her supervisor notices that she's not doing well at this level—that she's incompetent to do the job—and she never receives another promotion.

According to Peter and Hull, this was bound to happen. Susan possessed the skillset necessary to do well at levels 5 and 6. But level 4 required a different skill set that she didn't possess. As a result, she'll never be promoted again but likely won't be fired either. She'll continue in a job that she may not like and cannot do well. Those who work under her are the ones we meet at a party who tell us: "I could do a better job than my boss!"

Interestingly, Peter and Hull's book was originally written as a satirical critique of management, but their thesis—that employees are frequently promoted to a level of incompetence—resonated with many and began to be taken seriously. For example, the 2019 study "Promotions and the Peter Principle" by Alan Benson, Danielle Li, and Kelly Shue concluded that in many organizations the top salespeople are promoted to management positions. Even though these employees are excellent at sales, they don't have the best skill set for management and frequently perform poorly.

The solution? Organizations shouldn't base promotion solely on how well employees are doing in their current jobs. Instead (or in addition), they should focus on the skills that predict success in the new position and attempt to determine whether the candidate possesses these skills. Of course, this isn't as easy as it sounds. If you're the best person at your level and someone else is promoted, you'll likely cry foul.

Affirmative Action as Repayment for Past Injustice

The most prominent argument supporting affirmative action policies claims beneficiaries of these policies are owed a debt, and affirmative action is a good way to repay it. This argument, known as the *compensatory argument* in support of affirmative action, claims members of various groups suffered discrimination in the past and as a result were unjustly denied benefits they deserved or had a right to—most notably opportunities for jobs and education. While the specific groups affected may vary, most agree Blacks, Latinos, and women have historically been the object of discrimination and denied both educational and career opportunities. The compensatory argument maintains this past injustice must be addressed and rectified, and the best way to do this is to implement affirmative action policies that compensate those affected.

Notice that the compensatory argument, like the meritocracy and reverse-discrimination arguments, is a deontological or rule-based argument. It's motivated or rooted in a principle like: If a person was unjustly harmed or wronged or unfairly denied a benefit or an opportunity in the past, fairness dictates they should be compensated. Failing to do so, proponents of this argument claim, perpetuates unfairness.

If you're attracted to Kant's deontology, you might say that not compensating a person who deserves compensation would be treating her unfairly or merely as a means to an end. It's similar to not paying someone after wrongfully destroying his car. He is owed a debt and deserves to be paid. I think most of us, regardless of whether we sup-

It can easily be argued that a large portion of minority students in America—especially if they live in inner cities—receive inadequate educations at underfunded schools and that much of this is the collective effect of racism in this country. Therefore, this should be a factor for consideration when reviewing college applications.

port affirmative action, embrace this rule. If someone steals and destroys your car, you'd believe you deserve to be compensated. Presumably, the most fitting compensation would be a car of equivalent value.

Similarly, consider a case in which Bob applies for a job and Carie steals and alters Bob's resume to make him look less qualified than he is. Carie then submits her own résumé. Let's assume Bob would have been hired for the job if Carie hadn't altered his résumé. But Carie did alter it, and Carie was hired because her résumé revealed that she was a better candidate than was Bob, based on his altered résumé. I assume most of us would agree Bob deserves compensation, such as being offered the position Carie unjustly secured.

These examples reflect our shared belief that compensating for past injustices is essential to fairness. If we believe certain members of certain groups were unfairly denied opportunities in the past, the compensatory argument suggests that affirmative action might be justified.

Now that we've looked at what deontology has to say about affirmative action, let's see what the other ethical theories tell us. Does utilitarianism support or oppose it? What about the ethics of care?

Utilitarianism and Affirmative Action

The utilitarian analysis of affirmative action is intricate, as it depends on whether such policies maximize societal happiness. Advocates argue affirmative action fosters diversity in the workplace and educational institutions, which, they claim, increases overall happiness.

You might be wondering why anyone would believe diversity leads to greater happiness. Proponents of affirmative action offer many arguments, including: (1) Members of all ethnic, religious, and racial groups have the same basic capabilities. This also extends to gender, age, and disability cohorts. If these groups are underrepresented in the workforce or student body, we miss out on valuable talent; (2) Diverse teams bring together ideas and viewpoints from different perspectives, which can lead to more creative ideas or better solutions to challenges. When certain groups are kept

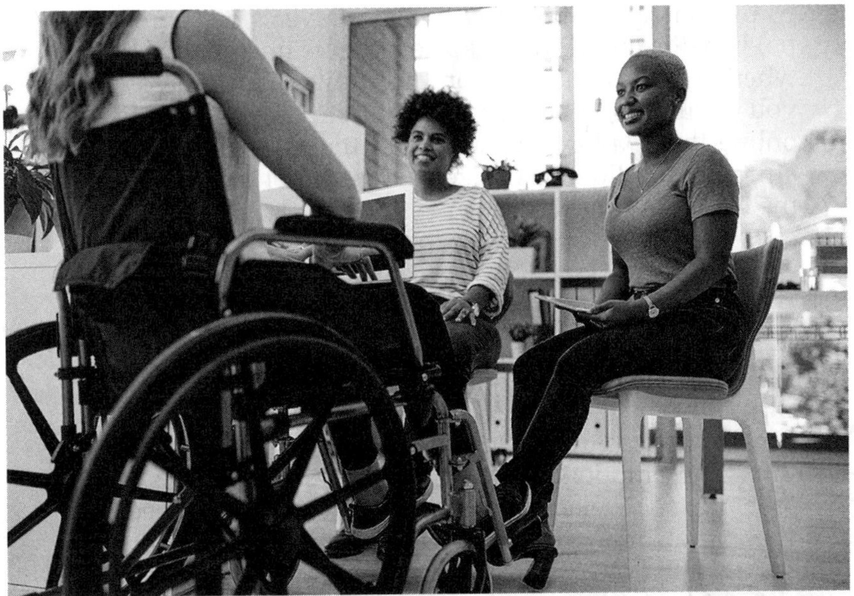

Several factors go into analyzing how affirmative action policies can increase happiness in a workplace based on utilitarian principles. Work teams can produce better results when exposed to diverse opinions, abilities, and backgrounds among their members.

out or underrepresented, we risk losing key insights or innovative proposals; and (3) Members of diverse teams are more likely to remain objective—they're more willing to challenge each other's ideas, which helps avoid groupthink and encourages more rigorous, creative decision-making. Together, these arguments suggest that diversity results in greater productivity and innovation, which brings about increased societal well-being. Those who accept these claims often conclude that affirmative action is justified because it is the best means of achieving diversity.

Even if affirmative action improves workplaces or educational institutions, some claim it may still fail to maximize overall happiness or bring about the best (or good enough) consequences. For example, it might generate resentment or anger among members of majority groups who feel or believe they are unjustly disadvantaged by these policies. This resentment can, in turn, fuel prejudice or bigotry, which may undermine societal harmony and reduce happiness.

Ultimately, a utilitarian analysis reveals both potential benefits and drawbacks, leaving us uncertain about whether affirmative action maximizes happiness. If you're curious, there are plenty of articles and studies online that explore diversity and the issue of whether affirmative action maximizes happiness or brings about the best consequences.

The Ethics of Care and Affirmative Action

Things get even more complicated when we look at affirmative action through the lens of the ethics of care. Recall that the ethics of care is concerned with relationships and emotional connection. Advocates of this approach (and I believe we all are attracted to this theory at one time or another) ask whether a caring individual would support affirmative action policies. They might attempt to determine whether it fosters or harms relationships between individuals and communities. Does affirmative action improve relationships by addressing historical wrongs, or does it create or enhance divisions by engendering feelings of unfairness?

Proponents of the ethics of care might also pay special attention to motives. As discussed above, critics of affirmative action sometimes argue that it is wrong because, like past discrimination, it makes decisions based on race, gender, or religion. But from an ethics of care perspective, the motives behind those decisions matter.

Historically, discrimination was fueled by hatred, fear, or at best indifference or callousness. The goal was exclusion, keeping Black Americans and members of other groups out of schools, jobs, and positions of power.

Historically, discrimination was fueled by hatred, fear, or at best indifference or callousness. The goal was exclusion, keeping Black Americans and members of other groups out of schools, jobs, and positions of power. Those motives are far away from or the opposite of care.

In contrast, supporters of affirmative action often act out of care or concern. They might claim that even if an affirmative action policy disadvantages White men, it stems from praiseworthy motives, namely, care, com-

passion, and/or concern for others as opposed to hatred or fear. This gives us a reason, they claim, to support affirmative action or to believe that affirmative action is appropriate or just.

Are We Really So Divided?

Almost all of us believe discrimination based on race, religion, and similar factors is wrong. So if affirmative action discriminates against members of these groups, we have a reason to believe it's wrong. Additionally, we believe decisions concerning school admissions and whom to hire should be based on merit, and affirmative action is criticizable because it bases these decisions (at least to some extent) on something other than merit.

At the same time, we also believe people should be compensated if they were treated unfairly or wrongly denied something in the past—a reason to support affirmative action. And we believe policies that bring about significantly increased (or maximal) happiness are right or just. Given that affirmative action may increase happiness by enlarging the pool of good candidates or diversifying a workforce or student body, we have a reason to support it. But then again, perhaps it won't, in fact, increase overall happiness, as some may feel resentful towards beneficiaries of affirmative action policies and that could diminish social harmony.

Motives also play a role in the evaluation of policies and laws. Even if affirmative action results in unequal treatment, it's driven by care or compassion, not hatred, hostility, or fear. This may weigh against the reverse discrimination argument. I suggest we can imagine reasonable, caring agents either supporting or opposing affirmative action.

If this is correct, it's not a stretch to say that we both support and oppose deontological, utilitarian, and ethics of care arguments pertaining to affirmative action. We might want to further state that even though this is the case, at the end of the day we're more attracted to or feel a stronger pull toward one position or the other. Or perhaps we're stuck in the middle and can't make a decision concerning affirmative action.

It might make sense to say that with respect to many of the issues that divide Americans, regardless of which position we hold, we're attracted to the other side. Or at the very least, we understand the other side and can see how someone might support it. This is where the Scale of Morality comes in. It helps us visualize why we feel conflicted about complex issues like affirmative action.

Affirmative Action

1. Compensatory Argument
2. Utilitarianism—Affirmative action results in a larger pool of talented candidates; decisions made by a diverse group are usually more creative; there's more objectivity with diverse teams
3. Ethics of care — Addressing historical wrongs improves relationships; the motives of those who support affirmative action (e.g. care and compassion) are praiseworthy, but the motives of those who discriminated in the past (e.g. hatred and fear) are not praiseworthy

1. Reverse Discrimination Argument
2. Meritocracy Argument
3. Utilitarian Argument — Affirmative action results in feelings of resentment towards beneficiaries of these policies
4. Ethics of Care — Addressing historical wrongs might engender resentfulness

Morally Right or Just? **Morally Wrong or Unjust?**

Regardless of whether we support or oppose affirmative action, if we're honest with ourselves, we recognize that we put weight on most or all of the blocks on the scale. That is, we believe or embrace all these principles. However, if we believe affirmative action is just or moral, we put more combined weight on the left, and if we believe it's unjust or immoral, we must be putting more combined weight on the right. Regardless of which side

It could be argued that the federal government policy of, in some cases, preferentially hiring veterans for jobs violates the principles of employment based on merit.

we believe has more weight, we can reflect and ask ourselves if we believe we're putting the correct amount of weight on each. We may come to discover that we can't answer that question.

Still Confused?

At this point, many of you, like me, may be uncertain or confused about affirmative action. Deontology supplies arguments both for and against it, and it's not obvious that affirmative action maximizes happiness.

Some of you, I imagine, believe that even if affirmative action increases happiness, it nevertheless can't be justified because it violates the principle or meritocracy and the principle of nondiscrimination (if you believe it truly is reverse discrimination). Others believe that both the compensatory and utilitarian arguments outweigh these deontological arguments.

My hope is that at least some of you recognize the complexity of this issue and haven't yet made up your minds. I know that I can't determine with clarity my own beliefs concerning how much weight to attach to these different considerations. Because I attach significant weight to each of them, I'm not sure whether affirmative action is moral or just. I wonder whether some of you agree.

I also recognize that if most of us embrace these different considerations, we may not be as divided as we think. Most of us rely on the same moral principles—compensation for past injustice, the importance of merit, respect for fairness—as well as the same four ethical theories when trying to determine whether to support affirmative action (and other social policies). I take this as strong evidence we live in the same moral world.

Finally, I'd like to suggest that the confusion concerning affirmative action that many of us experience may help explain why the affirmative action issue is so divisive. When we're torn between two positions—supporting a policy on one level and objecting to it on anoth-

er—we may reflexively dig in and defend our position rather than admit to our uncertainty. This reaction often stems from fear of being wrong, as well as the discomfort resulting from being uncertain about our policy preference and knowing that our perspective might be flawed.

Before moving on to the next section, I'd like to briefly explore other policies that, like affirmative action, violate the principle of meritocracy. For example, many states and the federal government often advertise jobs that give preference to military veterans. This practice clearly violates the principle of meritocracy or the claim that jobs should go to the most qualified candidate based on formal credentials. Yet, this policy is often justified on the grounds that veterans risked (or were willing to risk) their lives for the good of the country and, therefore, deserve some form of preferential treatment.

I'm not denying that many veterans risked their lives for the good of the country. Clearly, they did, and I deeply appreciate this. That said, if we embrace the principle of meritocracy, which claims that merit is the only thing that should matter when making hiring decisions, the fact that they risked their lives shouldn't play a role in hiring practices. If, like me, you do think one's military service matters or should play a role in hiring decisions, notice that you are rejecting or allowing an exception to the principle of meritocracy.

If we accept this exception to the principle of meritocracy, it raises a question: Shouldn't beneficiaries of affirmative action programs, who suffered from unfair discrimination in the past, also be granted an exception?

I'll leave it to you to figure out what you think about this question.

Another exception to the principle of meritocracy can be found in college and university admissions policies. Many colleges and universities give preference to legacy applicants (i.e., those whose parents or other relatives attended the same school). While these institu-

Many colleges and universities give preference to legacy applicants (i.e., those whose parents or other relatives attended the same school). While these institutions may justify this practice by claiming it supports alumni fund-raising or strengthens ties with alumni, it undeniably violates the principle of meritocracy.

tions may justify this practice by claiming it supports alumni fund-raising or strengthens ties with alumni, it undeniably violates the principle of meritocracy. If such a violation is deemed acceptable, does it further open the door to accepting affirmative action as a permissible exception?

A third widespread violation of the principle of meritocracy occurs in hiring practices that prioritize personal connections. We've all heard of cases where someone was hired because his family or friends made phone calls to influential decision-makers. Sometimes the person hired is the most qualified or competent applicant, but in many cases the chosen candidate—the boss's nephew or the child of the boss's best friend—is not the best-qualified person for the job. This too represents a clear departure from the principle of meritocracy.

Recognizing these exceptions to the principle of meritocracy just complicates what is already a complicated, divisive issue. If we accept these and other deviations from this principle, we might want to ask ourselves if affirmative action is also a justified or acceptable deviation.

These examples complicate the conversation, but they also enrich it. By grappling with these nuances, we can better understand the depth of the debate and why it might be difficult to determine whether we should support or oppose affirmative action. We might also better understand why reasonable people might disagree with us.

Final Thoughts

In this chapter I explored the issue of affirmative action or, more broadly, whether it's just or permissible to admit or hire someone who doesn't have the strongest formal qualifications.

Personally, I find this issue to be complex in the same way that other divisive issues, like the issue of abortion, are complex. Not because the arguments are hard to grasp, but because I find myself genuinely pulled in both directions. That's not to say I don't have an opinion; I do. But to say I am *convinced* that the arguments on one side are better than those on the other side might be too strong. Not only that, but I can't say with any

certainty that I won't weigh these arguments differently in the future.

Am I willing to argue for the position I currently embrace? Yes, but at the same time I understand why someone might disagree with me, and this person's values are probably not so different from my own. Knowing this last point affects my attitude when I discuss affirmative action with people who disagree with me. I realize that we aren't so far apart and that if my life experiences were different, I might weigh the arguments differently.

This recognition—that we aren't so different from others—engenders productive, interesting, and respectful dialogue.

In the next chapter, we'll explore another social/political issue: Has Wokeness/Political Correctness Gone Too Far?

12: Wokeness and Political Correctness

The Issue: Have "wokeness" and political correctness gone too far? Does the preoccupation with not offending anyone result in poor decision-making? Might being too PC actually harm people?

Not long ago, I was chatting with a friend, Phil. He told me a story about Jackie, a woman who works in a coffee shop and loves her job. Recently, though, the shop hired a new employee, and Jackie's work-life changed.

"After about a week on the job," Phil explained, "Jackie's new colleague approached her with a question: What are your pronouns?"

Jackie, who is a biological woman and uses the pronouns "she" and "her," didn't think the question was necessarily unreasonable. In fact, Phil emphasized that Jackie values inclusiveness. But something about the interaction felt off to her. She had the feeling her colleague was fishing for more than just her pronoun preferences. It seemed like a political litmus test and her colleague was trying to find out whether she held the "right" beliefs.

"Jackie's known for her warmth and friendliness," Phil explained. "She's one of those people that make you feel comfortable when you're chatting with her. But after this exchange, she felt pressured, like she couldn't be herself at work anymore. And she didn't want to get caught up in other people's political agendas."

Phil continued, "Jackie wanted to tell her colleague to mind her own business. Instead, she told her: 'You can call me anything or use whatever pronouns you want.'"

Later that afternoon, Jackie was summoned to meet with her manager. Much to her surprise, she learned a

complaint had been lodged against her. According to the manager, Jackie wasn't respecting others. "If someone wants to be called he, she, or they," the manager told her, "you should respect their choice."

Jackie tried to clarify the situation and explain that she respected people's right to share or not share their pronouns. But she also felt caught in the middle of something bigger, something political. Before she was able to defend herself, the manager ended the meeting.

Phil wanted my opinion. Did I think Jackie handled the situation poorly? What about her new colleague or the manager? Has wokeness or political correctness gone too far?

What do you think? Did Jackie do anything wrong? Why or why not? Was it wrong not to share her pronouns? What about the manager?

As usual, my answer was: It depends.

I needed to hear more context. For instance, did Jackie refuse to share her pronouns because she thought doing so would make her new colleague feel uncomfortable? Was she perhaps avoiding her own discomfort? What was the manager's agenda?

Details matter in these conversations.

Discussion

Few topics seem to ignite more heated debate than "political correctness" and "wokeness." These terms are complicated, emotionally charged, and often poorly defined. As a result, they tend to provoke strong reactions and a remarkably wide range of opinions.

I want to say from the outset that this chapter will not be an exhaustive analysis of the arguments both for and against political correctness and wokeness. Instead, I aim to explore, with the help of some examples, why some embrace political correctness and wokeness while others believe they have gone too far. As usual, we'll focus on the values that underlie both sides of the issue.

Defining the Terms

First, let's distinguish the terms "politically correct" and "woke." In the late 1980s or early 1990s, the term "political correctness" came to be associated with efforts

aimed at minimizing or eliminating language and behaviors that might offend or harm members of disadvantaged or marginalized groups. Examples of political correctness from this time include using gender-neutral language, such as "firefighter" instead of "fireman" and replacing the term "cripple" with "person with a disability." Similarly, the adoption of terms such as "African American" instead of "Black" and the term "Native American" instead of "Indian" reflected a broad societal push toward inclusivity and respect.

The movement was particularly influential in educational institutions. School curricula were scrutinized and sometimes revised in an effort to avoid language that might hurt members of disadvantaged or marginalized groups. In the spirit of inclusivity, textbooks aimed to include a wider range of perspectives. History textbooks, for example, were changed to include the roles and experiences of more women, non-White people, and people from non-Western countries/civilizations.

The term "woke," by contrast, has a different origin and focus. In the early to middle twentieth century,

The movement toward "political correctness" encouraged white people to refer to minority groups in more sensitive terms such as "African American" instead of "black," "Asian American" instead of "Oriental," and "Latinx" instead of Latino. Derogatory words met with fierce disapproval.

"woke" was used primarily by Black Americans to signify awareness of various forms of social injustice, like racism and discrimination. By the early twenty-first century, the term gained broader usage and came to signify awareness of a much larger class of social injustices, including those affecting LGBTQ+ individuals, indigenous people, immigrants, and others. While political correctness focuses primarily on language and behavior, wokeness emphasizes being awake or aware of societal or structural inequalities and social injustices that negatively affect members of marginalized groups. To be woke is to acknowledge how historical and systemic factors contribute to injustices faced by members of these groups.

Over the last decade or so, "woke" has become politicized and, for many, has taken on negative connotations. Critics often use it to describe excessive reactions in the pursuit of social justice.

Although the terms "politically correct" and "woke" are often conflated, their differences lie in their emphasis or implications. If one is politically correct, they might assert we ought to avoid the use of racial and ethnic slurs (and others) because these words hurt and demean members of the group to which the slurs refer.

THE INAUGURATION

Pardons for 1,500 1/6ers

A WHACK ON WOKE

Exec orders kill DEI & recognize 2 sexes only

Energizer Donny

'Equal treatment'

Feds vs. trans

Wasting no time

President Trump wasted no time signing a slew of executive orders on Day 1, including these that:

Among MAGAs and other right-wingers in America, "woke" has become a pejorative term associated with insulting images of weak, avocado-toast-eating leftists who want to suppress free speech and enforce politically correct language. President Trump has used this misinformed hatred to promote his anti-diversity and anti-immigrant policies.

If one is woke, they might claim that the use of slurs is wrong because it perpetuates prejudice and discrimination, which might make it easier to see certain groups as being inferior. This could result in people believing that members of these groups don't deserve equal treatment or opportunities, which might then result in unjust laws, institutions, and social policies. Of course, these are issues of social justice.

Public Opinion

When I started writing this chapter, I assumed about half of all Americans, mostly conservatives and/or Republicans, opposed wokeness and political correctness or believed they had gone too far, and the other half, mostly liberals and/or Democrats, supported wokeness and political correctness or believed that they hadn't gone too far. I also expected generational differences, with younger people being more supportive of wokeness and political correctness than older people, in the same way that younger people tend to be more supportive of same-sex marriage.

But the data told a more nuanced story. In 2018, the organization More in Common released a public opinion survey showing that 80% of Americans reported that they believed excessive political correctness was a problem in the United States. That means significantly more than half of *both* Democrats and Republicans held this view.

Other public opinion polls show a similar, yet somewhat different, picture. A 2021 survey conducted in Illinois by Eighteen92 (on behalf of the conservative-leaning American Council of Trustees and Alumni) offered slightly different results. It found that 42% of respondents believed that Americans were too politically correct, 32% said Americans were not politically correct enough, and 10% said the amount of political correctness was just right. When the data was broken down by political affiliation, 70% of Republicans and 21% of Democrats said that Americans were too politically correct.

Clearly, discomfort with political correctness isn't limited to one side of the political spectrum.

Political Correctness Protects People from Hurt/Harm

Supporters of political correctness claim that it protects people from being hurt or harmed, promotes fairness, and challenges unfair discrimination. They point out that slurs and stereotypes aren't just words and that using slurs or appealing to stereotypes can have deeply hurtful impacts. They furthermore claim that not using politically correct language perpetuates prejudices.

In a 1991 commencement speech at the University of Michigan, Republican president George H. W. Bush acknowledged this. Bush said that the political correctness

Ancient Cancel Culture: Ostracism

It's often said that history repeats itself, and today's cancel culture seems to be a good example of this phenomenon. About 2,500 years ago, Athens had its own form of canceling: ostracism. Once a year, Athenian male citizens—those who had full political rights—voted on whether to hold an ostracism. If the vote was in the affirmative, citizens wrote the name of the person they wanted ostracized on a pottery shard. The "winner" was exiled, but after 10 years they were allowed to return to Athens, regaining their property and political rights.

Ostracism was usually used as a political tool, and it's claimed that one of the purposes was to protect Athens from dangerous but popular politicians. Themistocles, for example, was a popular naval hero, but some Athenians believed his political aspirations were overly ambitious and might lead to tyranny. Enough people voted to ostracize him, and he was exiled for 10 years.

Sometimes ostracism was used—perhaps misused—to rid Athens of an irritating individual. Aristides "the Just" was an Athenian statesperson who, as his name implies, was known for his integrity and moral rectitude. Many Athenians resented him or his reputation; it is said some were just tired of hearing people refer to him as "the Just." Enough Athenians voted to ostracize him, and he was exiled for 10 years.

(cont. p. 221)

movement "arises from the laudable desire to sweep away the debris of racism and sexism...."

But he also warned that political correctness can replace "old prejudice with new ones."

We see that this Republican president embraced the values or ideals that motivate political correctness: fairness, justice, ending unfair discrimination, and not hurting or harming others. Surely, these are values that almost all of us embrace. That said, Bush's quote also reveals that over 30 years ago, he and others believed it had gone too far.

(cont. from p. 220)

Contemporary cancel culture, which usually plays out on digital platforms, can be seen as a contemporary variant of ostracism. Hashtags, instead of pottery shards, are used to mobilize public opinion against individuals seen as harmful, out-of-touch with prevailing values, or offensive.

Although contemporary cancel culture bears striking similarities to ostracism, some important differences exist. Ostracism was a structured, civic procedure that included a democratic process requiring widespread participation. In contrast, modern cancellations occur informally without clear rules or consistent standards. In addition, ostracism included the expectation that those exiled would return—that is, there was a clear path for returning to society with one's political rights and property holdings intact. This isn't necessarily the case with cancel culture.

The informal nature of cancel culture has the potential to destroy people's lives – sometimes innocent people's lives. In 2017, anonymous online accusers claimed that Benny Fredrikson, actor and managing director of the Stockholm City Theatre, tolerated sexual harassment in the workplace. Fredrikson, who denied the allegations, resigned from his position at the theatre. A formal investigation was launched, but three days before a final report was published, Fredrikson died by suicide. The report stated that no evidence of sexual harassment was found. Most cases of cancellation don't result in death or suicide, but they can have devastating effects on people's careers and personal lives.

President George H. W. Bush felt that being too politically correct could turn into another form of prejudice.

Slurs and Hate Speech

Let's take a closer look at two types of speech that fall under the umbrella of political correctness: slurs and hate speech.

Slurs can target someone's race, religion, ethnicity, disability, sexuality, or other aspects of their identity. As stated in Chapter 7, I'm confident that most Americans, regardless of their political commitments and identities, agree it's morally wrong to use slurs in most circumstances.

If asked why we believe this, most of us would state that the answer is simple: Slurs have the potential to deeply hurt or harm the people they target. And because most of us embrace the rule of thumb "It's wrong to unnecessarily hurt or harm others," we believe it's morally wrong to use slurs in most situations.

A second category of politically incorrect language is hate speech. While definitions of hate speech vary, most agree it includes: (1) communication, whether spoken, written, or behavioral (2) that is directed at or referring to individuals or groups based on characteristics like race, religion, ethnicity, and/or nationality, and sometimes including other factors pertaining to one's identity, such as sexual orientation, gender, or age; and (3) this communication has the potential to incite hatred or violence against its targets.

Based on my experience and the survey data discussed above, I think it's fair to assume almost all of you oppose or think it's wrong to use hate speech. Why? Because, like me, you recognize our words matter. We know we can usually choose to express our ideas without using language that has the potential to lead to violence or hated—and it takes little or no effort to use these words as opposed to words that are hateful and dangerous. Given that we embrace the rule of thumb

"It's wrong to unnecessarily harm others" and our caring and compassionate natures, we're more than willing to avoid the use of hate speech.

So, why do a majority of Americans believe political correctness has gone too far?

Political Correctness Suppresses Free Speech

Some critics of political correctness claim it suppresses free speech and honest dialogue. According to this view, political correctness creates an atmosphere in which people refrain from communicating or talking about controversial issues, like race, gender, or religion, because they fear saying the wrong thing or offending others.

I'm confident almost all of us embrace free speech and honest dialogue, the values and ideals that motivate this argument. If a policy undermines these values, we are naturally inclined to question its merit.

One common concern is that political correctness fosters an atmosphere of fear, specifically fear of talking about controversial issues. This, some claim, effectively creates an informal kind of censorship. People with minority viewpoints may fear being labeled as bigoted or offensive if they share their beliefs. As a result, they remain silent.

In more extreme cases, critics argue that political correctness is sometimes weaponized to attack the character of those who (unintentionally) run afoul of its rules. This leads to the perception of "language police" who are ready to pounce on us if we say the wrong thing, even when no malice was intended.

Book Bans

Another concern is the impact of political correctness on education, especially when it comes to banning books. Take, for instance, *To Kill a Mockingbird* or *The Adventures of Huckleberry Finn*. These classics are frequently challenged or banned from school curricula because they contain racial slurs, especially the N-word. Supporters of these bans argue that such language can deeply hurt Black students by making them feel uncomfortable in classrooms or by undermining their dig-

Books containing racial slurs—even critically acclaimed books like *To Kill a Mockingbird*—have been banned in American schools. Most educators would agree that this censorship prevents young people from reading important works of literature.

nity. They also worry that reading such material might normalize the use of slurs or send the message that it's not wrong to use them.

Opponents of book bans, however, emphasize the educational value of these books. Some argue these books are classics that provide students valuable insight into our history and culture. They capture the attitudes of another era, provide teachers and students an opportunity to discuss the issue of race, and may provide students an opportunity to develop empathy and the courage necessary to fight injustice. Denying students the opportunity to read these books, therefore, deprives them of important learning experiences and, potentially, the opportunity to develop strong characters.

We Don't Want to Be Wimps

Critics of political correctness may also claim it shields people from hearing criticism about themselves or ideas they oppose. They worry that shielding people from criticism, like banning books, may foster weakness. For example, even if a book contains hateful and hurtful language, encouraging students to read and critically discuss it can teach our children to think deeply, build resilience, and develop the skills to navigate uncomfortable situations.

What about Bigger Problems?

Finally, some argue that political correctness places too much focus on symbols and not enough on substance. For example, replacing offensive terms is good,

but what about addressing the policies or power structures that perpetuate inequality? Critics worry that we may be content to clean up our language, while leaving deeper injustices unaddressed. Put differently, it creates the appearance of progress without requiring meaningful change.

Good Arguments on Both Sides

As with most issues or topics explored in this book, most of us embrace the values associated with arguments in support of political correctness and those that underlie opposition to it. We care about others and don't want them to suffer unnecessary pain. We believe everyone deserves respect and wants to live in a fair society that doesn't discriminate against people based on traits like race, gender, and religion (and maybe others, like sexuality or age).

At the same time, however, we value open dialogue and want to live in a society in which people feel free to express themselves. We also want our children to have a true understanding of our history, and we want to help them develop the strength of character necessary to deal appropriately with criticism, to hear things they don't want to hear, and to respond to viewpoints that are different from their own.

Whether we support political correctness or believe it's gone too far is a function of how we weigh different values. The scale might be helpful.

Political Correctness

Not Too Far	Too Far
1. Prevents hurt or harm	1. Inhibits open dialogue
2. Promotes fairness	2. Erases our history
3. Challenges discrimination	3. Undermines strength of character

Not Too Far **Too Far**

Remember, the scale helps us visualize and thereby better understand why we might be pulled in different directions when thinking about moral or social issues. As stated above, most or all of us believe it's morally bad or wrong to unnecessarily hurt or harm others. We

also value fairness and want to prevent or decrease discrimination. Thus, we have reasons to believe political correctness is a good thing.

At the same time, we value free speech and open dialogue, a true and correct understanding of our history, and strength of character. These values push us away from political correctness or motivate us to question whether it has gone too far.

Depending on how much weight you attach to these different values or concerns, you'll believe political correctness has gone too far or it hasn't. I wonder whether many of us, if we're honest with ourselves, are confused. We embrace the values on both sides and can't say with confidence which side is correct or most convincing.

That too, is part of the beautiful moral landscape. Morality is frequently complex, and that's one reason it's so fascinating.

Wokeness

Now let's turn to the issue of wokeness. Much like political correctness, I suspect most of us will discover we embrace the values that underlie both support for wokeness and concerns that it has gone too far.

We All Want to Live in a Just Society

At its core, being woke involves believing that prejudice and discrimination have resulted in unjust social practices, laws, and institutions. Thus, many who identify as woke believe that political correctness—e.g., trying to eliminate the use of slurs and hate speech—while important, is insufficient to address deeper systemic issues impacting marginalized groups.

> *Studies consistently show that schools with the highest concentration of Black, Latino, and Native American students receive significantly less funding than schools with the lowest concentrations of these students.*

Take school funding, for example. Studies consistently show that schools with

the highest concentration of Black, Latino and Native American students receive significantly less funding than schools with predominantly White populations. This disparity often translates into fewer teachers, outdated resources (such as textbooks and computers), and worse buildings. As a result, students who attend these schools face greater challenges in obtaining a quality education, which can lead to fewer career opportunities and lower earnings later in life.

I imagine almost all of us can agree that everyone, regardless of race or ethnicity, deserves equal access to good schools and good jobs. But notice that political correctness—not using slurs or stereotypes—doesn't fix or address this problem. It's a structural issue that requires something different. That's why many who identify as woke believe in doing more than changing words or individual behavior if we want to live in a just society.

Structural Racism: A Provocative Term

This belief often leads to the concept of *structural racism*. Some Democrats, liberals, or progressives use this term to describe laws, policies, and institutions that provide unfair disadvantages for certain groups, even if unintentionally. They might argue, for example, that school funding disparities, which disadvantage certain minority groups, perpetuate injustice rooted in historical (and maybe ongoing) prejudice and discrimination. They may furthermore believe the only or best way to address this injustice is by changing our institutions—reforming the way cities and states fund schools.

However, "structural racism" is a provocative term, often driving the division between the woke and anti-woke. Many Americans see themselves as fair and nondiscriminatory, believing they treat everybody equally. For these individuals, the suggestion they might be complicit in racism, simply because they don't view systemic inequities as rooted in racism, can be offensive or off-putting.

Some might claim, for example, that individuals and families living in under-resourced neighborhoods can work hard, make smart financial decisions, and eventually move to areas with better schools or work to

Poorer neighborhoods in America tend to have higher percentages of minorities, which leads to poorer schools and education, putting minorities at a disadvantage through no fault of their own but rather because of systemic racism.

improve their own schools. While they may recognize the challenges associated with these choices, they believe personal effort can overcome them. They may also claim that those wanting change should become more politically involved, and they should vote for better representatives at local and state levels. (The feasibility of these solutions is something I'm not going to discuss. My focus is on explaining the concepts of political correctness and wokeness and exploring the reasons behind the divisions they create, not to settle policy debates.)

Implicit Bias

Wokeness also encompasses concerns about diversity, equity, and inclusion (DEI) issues as well as the concept of implicit bias. Let's briefly explore the latter.

Implicit bias refers to unconscious attitudes or beliefs that influence how we think and act. For instance, when thinking or talking about engineers, many of us automatically think of men, but while thinking or talking about elementary school teachers, we picture women. How many of us have asked, "What's his name?" or "Where's his office?" when a friend tells us they just hired an engineer to survey the safety of a house they want to buy? Or "What's her name?" when talking about a young child's teacher.

According to many supporters of wokeness (and maybe some who oppose it as well), these biases can have wide-ranging effects on individuals and society at large. It may unconsciously motivate some women to become teachers, even when they have the aptitude and personality to excel as engineers. Similarly, some men may be unconsciously guided toward becoming engineers, even if teaching may be a better career fit.

This implicit bias may also affect educators and school counselors, who might inadvertently steer students toward careers that fit traditional gender expectations.

Beyond career choices, some argue implicit bias contributes to broader disparities. For instance, it may result in people respecting and trusting male engineers more than female engineers, perpetuating gender-based disparities in the field of engineering.

Finally, some argue this bias affects more than just one's career choice. Since engineers' salaries are usually much higher than teachers' salaries, those who become engineers will likely live in better neighborhoods, their children will attend better schools, and they will be able to access better health care.

Focusing on implicit bias falls into the category of wokeness because, rather than focusing on eliminating the use of words or actions that hurt members of marginalized groups (political correctness), the emphasis is on repairing what some believe is an unjust or unfair system. In a just, fair world, they claim, gender wouldn't negatively (or positively) affect so many aspects of people's lives.

The Pronoun Problem—Respect or Overreach?

Another flashpoint in the wokeness debate is pronoun usage. I imagine all of us know someone (usually thought of as being woke) who believes everyone should have the right to choose which pronouns they will use to refer to themselves. Some go further and claim we should respect and use a person's chosen pronouns when we refer to or communicate with them. Focusing on pronouns can be considered woke because the goal is to create a more just society that's inclusive of everyone, including LGBTQ+ individuals.

Critics may reject this view because they believe gender is fixed at birth. They may believe that referring to someone by pronouns that differ from their biological sex is confusing, unnecessary, or even dishonest. (Again, I'm not going to weigh in on this issue as my goal isn't to settle this debate but to explore the values behind each position.)

Microaggressions

Microaggressions are words or actions that (usually) unintentionally communicate prejudice towards others based on race, gender, religion, age, disability, sexual orientation, etc.

About a decade ago, I accompanied a guest speaker who was blind to her hotel, talking with her as she navigated with a white cane. When we reached the front desk, the receptionist directed all his words towards me. I must admit, at the time I didn't realize that this was happening. He then asked a question clearly pertaining to her. I can't remember what it was, but he directed it at me. She calmly but firmly stated: "Please talk to me. I can answer all your questions."

This is an example of a microaggression. I'm confident the receptionist didn't intend to be disrespectful. Nor did he consciously think, "The guest who is blind can't think for herself." If, however, we unconsciously disregard the presence of those who are blind or otherwise disabled, we may act in ways that are hurtful and disrespectful. We might be subtly saying that they are less competent or even less present.

A similar thing happened several months ago, when I took my mother on a tour of a retirement community. The community's representative looked at me and my mother as she described the community and the numerous activities. However, when the conversation shifted to financial details and costs, she directed her words and questions exclusively to me.

I felt uncomfortable, and while I wanted to tell her my mother was fully capable of answering these questions, I hesitated. I worried such a comment might be perceived as confrontational and potentially lead to my mother being treated poorly if she chose to move there.

As we walked toward the car, my mother told me she felt disrespected. "Did she think that I couldn't understand what she was saying?"

My mother, who takes pride in her physical and mental well-being, was hurt and offended. I'm confident, however, the representative didn't intend to hurt or disrespect my mother, nor did she have any idea that she had done so.

These examples may seem like matters of political correctness, but they also fall under the umbrella of woke-

A couple takes their aging mother to a retirement home for a tour, and when it comes to money the manager giving the tour only talks to the the younger people. This is a type of microaggression caused by the manager making wrong assumptions about the older woman.

ness. Unconsciously viewing the elderly as incapable of taking care of their own affairs or understanding issues related to their own finances can affect hiring decisions, healthcare treatment, and educational opportunities. At some point, these aren't just about language—they become matters of social justice.

Has Wokeness Gone Too Far?

I repeat, I believe most Americans support the core values underlying or motivating the examples of wokeness discussed above: quality education for all, fair treatment for the elderly, and basic respect for people's identities. Even if we don't support people choosing their own pronouns, we do embrace the rule of thumb "It's wrong to unnecessarily hurt or harm others."

So, why do so many believe that wokeness has gone too far?

To answer this question, I spoke with people across the political spectrum. Interestingly, most of them, including people I would label as super-progressive,

The Paradox of Tolerance

In 1945, while the ashes of World War II were still smoldering, Karl Popper, an Austrian-British philosopher, published a book titled *The Open Society and Its Enemies*. Popper, who fled Vienna in 1937 to escape the rise of Nazism, was concerned (and that's an understatement) with the ways in which Nazis exploited Germany's free speech protections to usher in a fascist regime that didn't allow free speech.

Popper explained that complete freedom or tolerance of political speech could ultimately destroy the freedom it aims to protect. He wrote: "Unlimited tolerance must lead to the disappearance of tolerance." Thus, to maintain a politically tolerant society, political tolerance itself must sometimes be limited. This is the Paradox of Tolerance.

As Popper explains, if we value freedom of speech, we should be willing to tolerate speech that we disagree with. But what if someone uses that freedom to advocate for a society in which people no longer have the right to free speech? If we tolerate all speech, including speech that calls for censorship, it would seem inconsistent to censor those who advocate limiting free speech. Yet if we allow such advocacy to spread unchecked and it succeeds in gaining enough support, we may find ourselves in a society in which we no longer have free speech. Put differently, if we don't limit our tolerance of political speech, we may end up losing political tolerance altogether.

(cont. p. 233)

didn't identify themselves as woke. A common theme emerged: many believed wokeness was a problem because of the ways in which its ideals are communicated.

The word "elite" came up frequently, and Republicans (and some Democrats) explained that woke individuals and the woke movement views those who disagree with them as being ignorant, stupid, uneducated, or even racist. They furthermore described woke individuals as unwilling to hear or consider ideas and per-

(cont. from p. 232)

If, on the other hand, we argue that certain political ideas, like those that include widespread censorship, should be censored or not tolerated, then it seems as though we are contradicting ourselves and advocating for something that we claim we don't support—censorship or limited toleration of freedom of speech.

Is there a solution? Many theorists have struggled with this paradox. Popper claims that being tolerant of free speech includes the right to suppress speech that advocates for intolerance. He goes so far as to say: "But we should claim the right to suppress" the utterance of intolerant philosophies "if necessary, even by force...." Popper realized, of course, that some might claim he was being hypocritical.

Rainer Forst, a German political philosopher currently at Goethe University Frankfurt, provides a different solution to the paradox of tolerance. Forst proposes a framework he calls "reason-based toleration." Essentially, Forst argues that tolerance should extend to any political speech that is grounded in universally acceptable reasons. These are reasons that all individuals would support or recognize as legitimate. Central to his view is the principle of reciprocal respect. If I want the freedom to express and advocate for my own political views, I should embrace a framework that allows others to advocate for what they believe. This principle, he claims, would exclude intolerant speech, because such speech explicitly rejects reciprocity by denying others the right to freely advocate opposing views.

spectives that are different from their own and are quick to censor dissenting views.

Whether a significant percentage of woke individuals genuinely believe anti-woke individuals are ignorant, uneducated, or racist is something I don't wish to explore. What matters is the perception: If a sizable group of people believes woke culture disrespects or devalues them, this perception must be taken seriously. A healthy society can't function or flourish if large segments of the

population believe they are disrespected, looked down on, or believed to be unworthy of respect.

In 2020, during the run-up to the presidential campaign, I listened to a podcast addressing this issue. The hosts interviewed a man living in Pennsylvania, a hotly contested state, and he said that for the first time in his life he planned to vote Republican (for then President Donald Trump). He explained he treated everyone equally and didn't consider race when interacting with others. He resented or even felt insulted by being labeled a racist by woke Democrats. Towards the end of the interview, he explained that President Trump didn't make him feel bad about himself, while Democrats did.

This story is not unique. Like many of those who believe wokeness has gone too far, he opposed racism and valued social justice. His concern was the way the woke message was communicated and how woke individuals perceived him.

A 2023 *USA Today*/Ipsos public opinion poll reveals that 56% of Republican respondents and 18% of Democrats believed being woke meant one was overly politically correct and policed others' language. The results also revealed that 60% of Republicans, 42% of Independents, and 25% of Democrats believed that being described as woke was an insult.

White Privilege

One of the most contentious topics under the wokeness umbrella is "White privilege." Woke advocates claim being White in the U.S. confers many unearned advantages that make it easier to succeed and live a good life. These advantages include not having to worry about police racial profiling; feeling confident that one's race or ethnicity won't negatively affect job prospects; having access to better schools; and receiving better healthcare. Studies, for instance, reveal that Black people are more likely to be undertreated for pain medication than are White people with the same symptoms. A recent study, the results of which were presented at the 2024 Anesthesiology Annual meeting, reveals that Black patients are 29% less likely than White patients to receive the safest and best pain management options and 74% more likely than White patients to receive only highly addictive opioids.

Generally an accepted principle among those on the left end of the political spectrum is the idea that whites enjoy privileges (economic, educational, social) that others do not.

Critics of White privilege, however, offer different perspectives. Some claim these advantages stem more from socioeconomic class than race, claiming many White individuals face hardships that wokeness fails to address. They point out many White people live in poverty and attend poor schools, and the woke aren't concerned with addressing issues that may negatively affect their life prospects. Others claim focusing on White privilege amounts to reverse discrimination, and reverse discrimination is just as bad as other forms of discrimination. Finally, some claim that while racism and sexism were major problems in the past, we have largely overcome them.

Are We Really So Divided?

It would be naïve or even dishonest to claim Americans aren't divided over political correctness and wokeness. And this isn't just an American phenomenon. Studies from other countries show similar divides. But as I've tried to demonstrate in this chapter, the division may not run as deep as it sometimes appears.

I suggest that the politicization we see has been magnified, or even manufactured, by politics and the media. A 2023 King's College of London and Ipsos public opinion poll reveals that 62% of those in the United Kingdom believe that politicians invent or exaggerate culture wars for political reasons. Perhaps our own politicians, media personalities, and social media influencers chasing clicks exaggerate our political divisions, including our disagreements over political correctness and wokeness, for their own good. They know that if I fear those on the other side, I'm more likely to vote, donate, and stay loyal to those who claim to protect me.

Sometimes I wonder if we should stop using the label "politically correct" when referring to the rejection of slurs and hate speech. What if, instead of framing it as a matter of political correctness, we simply said that this kind of language is wrong because it's needlessly hurtful? Calling someone a slur is legal, just as it's legal to tell a loved one (or stranger) they're "dumb as a rock." But legality doesn't automatically make something morally right. Words can inflict deep emotional pain. In that light, rejecting slurs isn't about being politically correct; it's about basic human decency. Reframing the issue in this way might even have the long-term effect of reducing the appeal of identity politics—something many on both sides of the political continuum would welcome. Rather than seeing people as members of (opposing) interest groups, we might start seeing them more as individuals.

Perhaps it would be helpful to go further and drop both the labels "politically correct" and "woke" altogether. Doing so would allow us to focus on real disagreements rather than demonize those on the other side. In the same way that labels ratchet up the emotions associated with political correctness, some of the strong emotional responses associated with woke behavior might be mediated by more careful use of language.

For example, instead of branding someone as woke for believing prejudice and discrimination result in some groups not having access to good education, we could simply acknowledge their position. If we disagree with their claim, we could explain why. Maybe we believe it's the responsibility of the family, not the government, to secure such opportunities. Rather than angrily labeling the government-focused advocate as woke, we could calmly point out that both parties share the value of ensuring children have access to good schools. The disagreement lies in how to achieve this goal. By highlighting shared values, we can reduce

An example of a culture war tactic is the issue of trans women participating in women's sports. A politician could argue this impinges on the rights of cis women to have fair competitions and that they will work to pass a law against trans women in the hopes of gaining votes.

THINKING ETHICALLY

hostility and foster constructive conversations. And maybe, if we're lucky, we can develop enriching relationships with those we previously demonized. Surely, there are good people on both sides.

This approach could extend to other disagreements between those labeled woke and anti-woke. Are there areas where we agree on the underlying value or goal but disagree on the methods to achieve them? Might eliminating polarizing labels like "woke" in favor of more descriptive, value-driven language encourage productive, respectful, caring dialogue? When people feel respected and cared for and not boxed into ideologically charged categories, they may be more willing to engage in meaningful discussions. This may make a family Thanksgiving dinner not just tolerable but joyful and interesting.

Perhaps it would be helpful to go further and drop both the labels "politically correct" and "woke" altogether. Doing so would allow us to focus on real disagreements rather than demonize those on the other side.

Final Thoughts

In this chapter we explored the difference between political correctness and wokeness and examined the question: Have these movements gone too far?

As I've tried to show throughout this chapter, most of us, if we are being honest with ourselves, are both attracted to and repelled away from both political correctness and wokeness. And even those who strongly identify as pro- or anti-woke often share common values with people on the other side: fairness, respect, freedom of expression, and justice.

Understanding this complexity doesn't mean we aren't divided, but it might help us disagree more thoughtfully and live with each other more peacefully.

In the following chapter, we'll explore another divisive issue: abortion. Then, in the final chapter, we'll step back and ask a more personal question: What sort of person do you want to be?

13: Is Abortion Morally Wrong?

The Issue: Should women have a legally protected right to abortions? Does the woman's right to control her own body take precedent over the rights of an unborn child?

More than a decade ago, I stumbled on an article discussing an emerging technology—the *artificial* womb. This technology, which some say will be available within a decade, would make it possible to remove a fetus from a woman's uterus and place it in a womb-like device, where it can develop until it is ready to be "delivered" or "born." Even more striking, an embryo created outside the body through in vitro fertilization could be put into an artificial womb for the full gestational period. Thus, we may soon live in a world in which women will no longer have to carry embryos or fetuses in their bodies.

Upon reading this, it struck me how profoundly artificial wombs could reshape the abortion debate. If pregnant women do not wish to remain pregnant, they'll be able to transfer their fetuses into artificial wombs, thereby preserving the life of the fetus. This scenario has the potential to render irrelevant the most common argument supporting a woman's right to abortion. This argument holds that women have a right to decide what happens in and to their bodies, and this includes removing a fetus (or anything else, such as an organ) from their bodies.

If and when artificial wombs are available, pregnant women who don't want to be pregnant, who want an abortion, may be able to have a fetus removed from their body, and then the fetus can be placed in an ar-

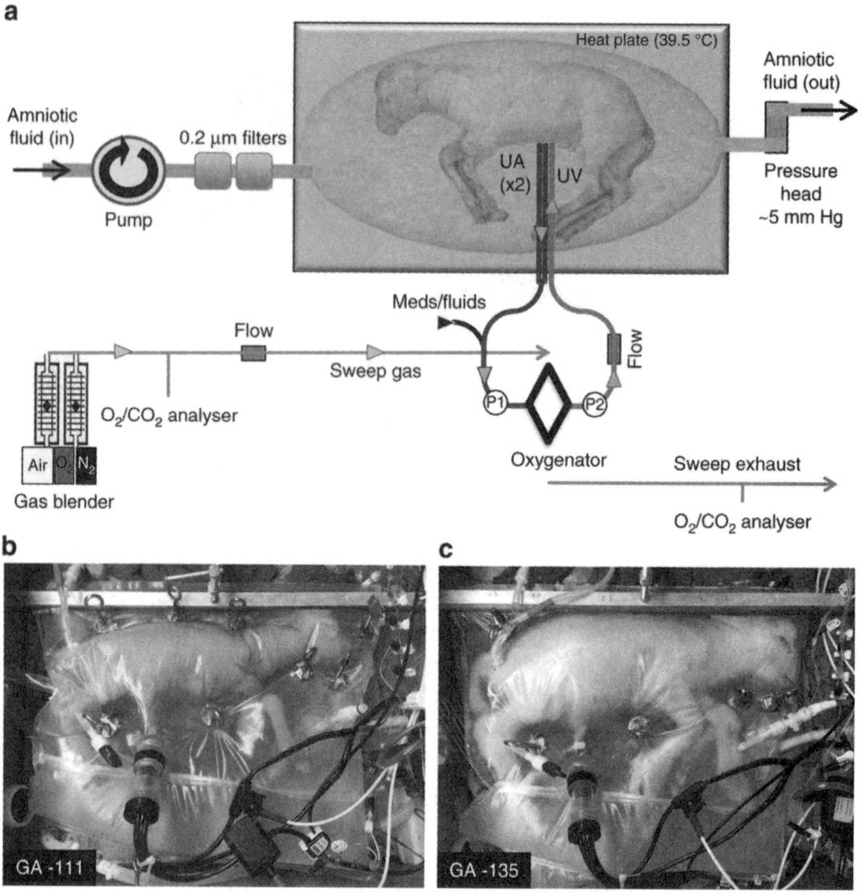

An effective artificial womb has already been developed to gestate lamb fetuses, and one might be available within the next decade to help with human births.

---

tificial womb until the nine-month gestational period is completed. Thus, the woman's right to decide what happens in and to her body is respected, and the fetus's life is preserved. Presumably, this outcome should satisfy many pro-choicers and pro-lifers.

I found this argument so intriguing that I decided to write an article about the artificial womb and explain its impact on the abortion debate. I submitted the article to a conference, and a reviewer suggested that I avoid using the term "pro-life" to refer to those opposed to abortion rights. Instead, they recommended the term "anti-choice." This reviewer knew words have power,

and given their suggestion, I am confident they were pro-choice and believed the term "anti-choice" had connotations that were more negative than "pro-life."

I briefly considered taking the reviewers advice. I'd use the term anti-choice for pro-lifers, but I'd use the term anti-life for pro-choicers. "That'll teach him," I thought. Ultimately, I chose to stick with the terms pro-choice and pro-life. Even back then, I was committed to fostering respectful, productive dialogue about moral and political issues, and retaliating wouldn't help my cause.

Before we proceed, let me remind you—*again*—that I have absolutely no intention or desire to persuade you to adopt a particular position on abortion or any other moral/political issue. My goal is to help you reflect on your own viewpoints and, perhaps, better understand the perspectives and viewpoints of those who disagree with you. As I've already suggested, I believe Americans are far less divided over the issue of abortion than we're led to believe.

That said, I recognize that abortion remains one of the most divisive and emotionally charged issues confronting Americans today. Political contests, from local

The debate over the morality of abortion is still ongoing with both sides presenting their arguments passionately and with great conviction.

mayoral races to presidential elections, are frequently decided by the candidates' stances on abortion. This isn't surprising. Many of those who oppose the legalization of abortion, pro-lifers, believe embryos and fetuses have the same moral status as any other human being. Thus, they believe abortion is no different from killing an innocent child or adult. They equate it with murder. Understandably, then, many pro-lifers find it difficult to support pro-choice candidates or even maintain close relationships with those who support abortion rights or even worse someone who's had an abortion.

On the other side, many pro-choicers find it equally difficult to support politicians or have close friendships with those who oppose abortion rights. To many pro-choicers, laws denying women the right to abortion reinforce their status as second-class citizens. Additionally, some pro-choicers perceive abortion restrictions as religiously motivated infringements on individual religious freedom and pluralism. If a pro-choicer believes pro-lifers want to force their religion on others and see women as second-class citizens, it's understandable they find it difficult to support politicians or maintain close friendships with those opposed to abortion rights.

Given these disagreements, you might be thinking: Why or how can this author believe Americans are far less divided over the issue of abortion than we think?

To address this question, we'll carefully examine the most common arguments made on both sides of the abortion debate. As we explore these arguments, you may come to see your own views in a new light and better understand why others see things differently. You might even find that some of the divisions over the abortion debate aren't as deep as they might first appear.

Discussion

A fair warning: What follows is a bit more technical than the rest of this book. As always, I'll be speaking in generalities. When I say "pro-lifers believe X" or "pro-choicers believe Y," I'm not claiming to represent the views of every person in that camp. Instead, I'm aiming to represent the most popular or frequently articulated viewpoints. Think of this as a CliffsNotes version of the abortion debate.

**Life Before Science:
Ancient Guesswork and Hoaxes**

Throughout history, humanity has grappled with the mystery of where babies come from, creating imaginative explanations. The ancient Greek philosopher Aristotle, one of the most important Western philosophers and an early biologist, theorized that male semen contained the "soul" or the form of a human being—the semen was the force that shaped a child's characteristics. Women, he believed, provided the raw material—menstrual blood that would be formed into a little human. A good analogy is a sculptor crafting a bowl: the woman provides the clay, while the man shapes it into its final form.

Centuries later, medieval Europe saw the rise of an unusual legend: The Vegetable Lamb of Tartary. From the twelfth to the seventeenth century, many believed that in Tartary—a vast, somewhat undefined region in Asia—plants could produce living lambs. Some versions described a fruit that ripened to reveal a baby lamb, while others depicted baby lambs tethered to plant stalks, unable to move beyond their stems. By the sixteenth century, as the scientific revolution dawned, the legend was debunked.

Around the same time, alchemists pursued their own bizarre theories. Paracelsus, a prominent sixteenth century Swiss alchemist, physician, and philosopher, outlined a recipe for creating a human. The recipe involved fermenting human semen in horse manure for 40 days, at which time a tiny transparent little person—a homunculus—emerged. This little person, Paracelsus instructed, must then be nourished with human blood for 40 weeks, and it would grow into a living infant.

Not all theories arose from genuine curiosity; some were intentional deceptions. In the early eighteenth century, Mary Toft, a 24-year-old English woman, claimed she gave birth to animal parts during labor. A local surgeon, observing her for days, was convinced she was birthing rabbit legs, bones, and fur. He informed London physicians.

(cont. p. 244)

(cont. from p. 243)

Later, a Swiss surgeon got involved and also declared Toft's story to be true. But skepticism grew. After about two years, English physicians uncovered the ruse when they caught a porter sneaking a rabbit into Toft's room. Toft knew the hoax was over and confessed to inserting the rabbit pieces into her vagina.

These stories reflect the humanity's amazing curiosity and capacity for imagination.

The Morality and Legality of Abortion

When considering the issue of abortion, it's important to distinguish two different issues or questions. (1) Is abortion *morally* right or wrong? (2) Should women have a legal right to obtain an abortion? The pro-life and pro-choice labels primary refer to the second issue/question.

Most pro-lifers believe abortion is seriously morally wrong, and, therefore, women shouldn't have the freedom or a legal right to have an abortion.

Pro-choicers don't take a unified position on the issue of whether abortion is morally wrong. Some claim abortion is morally permissible, and therefore women should have a legal right to obtain an abortion. Others claim abortion is morally wrong, but unlike pro-lifers, they still believe that women should have the legal right or freedom to have an abortion.

The Right to Do What's Wrong

At first glance, it may seem confused or even contradictory to assert abortion is immoral but should still be legal. However, this distinction—between morality and law—isn't unusual or indefensible. We believe many behaviors are immoral, but at the same time we believe we ought to have a legal right to engage in these behaviors.

For example, most of us would agree it's morally wrong to tell a stranger they're stupid just to feel better about ourselves. Yet few would argue such behavior should be illegal. Similarly, many of us believe adultery

The Supreme Court of the United States (shown here in 2020) ruled in *Dobbs v. Jackson Women's Health Organization* (2022) that the U.S. Constitution does not guarantee a right to an abortion, reversing nearly 50 years of the opposite ruling in the famous *Roe v. Wade* (1973) case.

is deeply immoral and can grievously harm the spouse and children of the adulterer (see Chapter 4), yet we don't believe adulterers should be sent to prison. In both these cases, we distinguish between what is morally wrong and what should be legally forbidden. So, it's not necessarily confusing or inconsistent to claim abortion is seriously immoral and at the same time believe women ought to have a legal right to abortion.

The Pro-Life Position

Now let's take a closer look at the pro-life position. Let's imagine Mavis, who's pro-life, and Darryl, who's pro-choice, are discussing the issue of abortion. Mavis explains: "I believe all innocent human beings have a right to life, and embryos and fetuses are innocent human beings. Therefore, embryos and fetuses have a right to life." She continues, "Since abortion denies embryos and fetuses the right to life, it should be outlawed."

If Darryl were to ask Mavis why she believes embryo/fetuses have a right to life, she might respond that their

moral status (perhaps from the moment of conception onward) is no different from the moral status of a newborn baby or an adult human being. And if babies and adult human beings have a right to life, embryos and fetuses should have this same right.

Mavis may believe embryos and fetuses have the same moral status and right to life as babies and adult human beings for a variety of reasons, including: (1) From the moment of conception an embryo has a full complement of DNA, and this gives it the same intrinsic or special value as a newborn baby or adult human being; (2) There is no morally significant dividing line between an embryo, fetus, newborn baby, and adult human being; therefore, if adult human beings have a right to life, embryos and fetuses also have a right to life; or (3) Religious belief—God grants embryos/fetuses the same moral status as born humans.

The Pro-Choice Position

After listening, Darryl responds, "Here's what I believe. Women, in fact all people, have a right to bodily autonomy. That means women have the right to control or decide what happens with, in, and to their own bod-

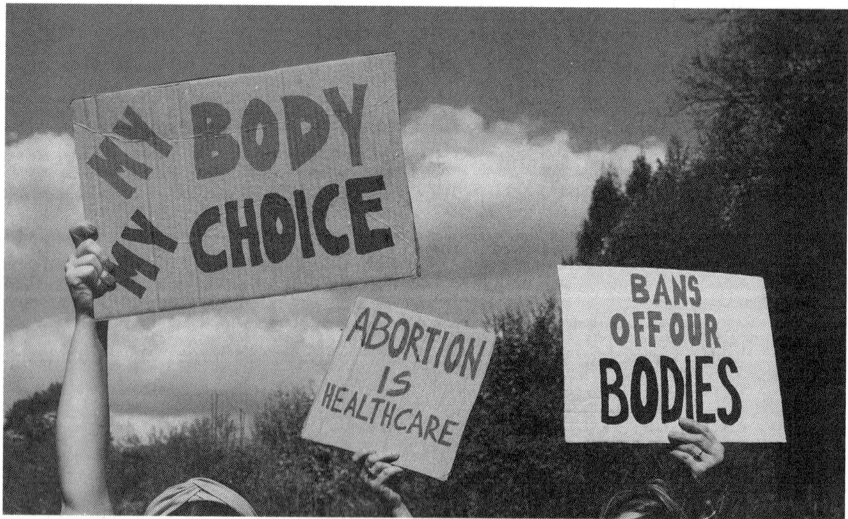

Those on the pro-choice side of the abortion argument believe that women have a right to control their own bodies, which includes when they are carrying an unborn child.

ies. Since embryos and fetuses are in a woman's body, she has the right to have them removed."

Let's take a closer look at the formal structure of Mavis and Darryl's arguments. We'll start with Darryl's pro-choice argument:

1. Women (or human beings more generally) have a right to bodily autonomy—the right to control what happens with, in, and to their own bodies.
2. An embryo or fetus is in a woman's body.
3. Therefore, women have the right to remove an embryo or fetus from their bodies.
4. Abortion is the removal of an embryo or fetus from the body.
5. Therefore, women ought to have a legal right to abortion.

Bodily Autonomy as the Moral Foundation

Notice something important: like most moral arguments, this argument depends on a foundational moral principle. In this argument, the foundational principle is found in Premise 1: Women (or human beings more generally) have a right to bodily autonomy—the right to control what happens with, in, or to their own bodies.

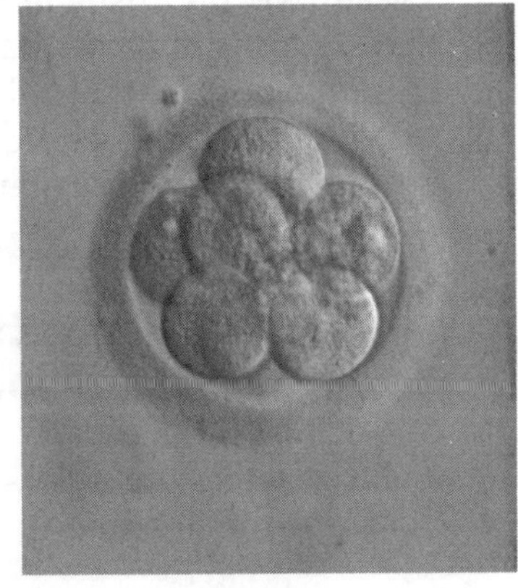

This photo of a human embryo in the earliest stages of development shows it having only eight cells. Do these eight cells have rights? Should the embryo develop a brain or heart first before it is considered a human being? Is it immoral to abort a freshly fertilized egg? These decisions might be considered subjective.

I suggest that almost all of us, regardless of whether we're pro-life or pro-choice, embrace this principle. (As we'll see below, the same is true of the moral principle that serves as the foundation for the pro-life argument.)

To test this claim, imagine a law requiring every

21-year-old to register for mandatory kidney donation. If someone's life depends on a transplant and your name is drawn in a lottery, you're legally obligated to donate a kidney.

Would you consider this law fair or just? Would you support it? Why or why not?

I've posed this hypothetical to hundreds of people, both pro-lifers and pro-choicers, and all but one said such a law is unjust or unfair. When I asked *why*, the usual answer was: "Because a kidney is part of a person's body. It's inside of them, and they should have the right or freedom to decide what to do with their own body parts."

This response is revealing. It shows that pro-lifers, like pro-choicers, embrace the foundational moral principle that motivates the pro-choice argument—the idea that humans should have a legally protected right to bodily autonomy.

The other premises that make up the pro-choice argument are straightforward and non-moral in nature: "An embryo/fetus is in a woman's body" and "Abortion is the removal of a fetus from a woman's body." These two premises are factual claims and are uncontroversial. I imagine that all of us, including pro-lifers, embrace both of them. If this is correct, almost all of us, pro-lifers and pro-choicers alike, accept all three premises contained in the standard pro-choice argument.

The Right to Life as the Moral Foundation

Now let's take a look at the formal structure of Mavis's pro-life argument:

1. Killing a being with a right to life is seriously morally wrong and should be legally prohibited.
2. Embryos/fetuses have a right to life, just like adult human beings.
3. Therefore, killing an embryo/fetus is seriously morally wrong and should be legally prohibited.
4. Abortion is the killing of an embryo/fetus.

5. Therefore, abortion is seriously morally wrong and should be legally prohibited.

As is the case with the pro-choice argument, the moral principle that serves as the foundation for the pro-life argument is articulated in Premise 1: Killing a being with a right to life is seriously morally wrong and should be legally prohibited.

Surely, most of us, regardless of whether we're pro-life or pro-choice, agree with this principle and consider premise 1 to be true.

The pro-life argument also contains two other premises: Premise 2—"Embryos/fetuses have a right to life, just like adult human beings" and Premise 3—"Abortion is the killing of an embryo/fetus."

Pro-choicers, as a group, don't universally accept or reject these premises. That said, although I'm unaware of any surveys focused on the issue of what percentage of pro-choicers believe Premise 2 is true, I think it's reasonable to assume that many—perhaps a majority—disagree with it. Premise 3 is less contentious, as most pro-choicers and pro-lifers believe abortion is the killing of an embryo/fetus. (Some pro-choicers believe abortion is analogous to removing someone from life support and, therefore, abortion is more like letting die than killing.)

We Aren't So Divided over This Issue

As we've seen, almost all of us, regardless of whether we're pro-choice or pro-life, embrace the *foundational moral* principles that lend support to both the pro-choice and pro-life arguments. The real disagreement lies in which of these principles we prioritize when they are in conflict.

The Scale of Morality

The Scale of Morality can help us better understand the disagreement between pro-choicers and pro-lifers. It's not about settling the issue. Instead, it's about visualizing our own beliefs and the beliefs of others.

On the left side, we can place blocks representing the moral claims or values that support the pro-choice argument, such as the value of bodily autonomy. On the right side, we can place blocks representing the moral claims or values that support the pro-life argument, such as the wrongness of killing a being with a right to life.

Since both the pro-life and pro-choice arguments contain one foundational moral claim, there will be one block on each side of the scale.

The tension between these principles helps explain why the debate continues. Pro-choicers tend to attach more weight to the bodily autonomy block, while pro-lifers tend to give weight to the wrongness of killing block. However—and this is worth emphasizing—those on both sides of the issue embrace the values represented by the blocks on both sides of the scale.

In addition to disagreeing over which foundational moral principle takes priority, pro-choicers and pro-lifers frequently argue about Premise 2 of the pro-life argument: Embryos and fetuses have a right to life, just like adult human beings. Pro-lifers embrace this premise, while many pro-choicers reject it.

Can We Disagree and Respect Each Other?

The short answer is: Of course. In the 1970s and even into the 1980s, some pro-choice philosophers (and others) claimed that an embryo/fetus held no greater moral status than a wart or excess hair, and they equated the

moral quality of abortion to having a wart removed or getting a haircut. Such a claim, of course, created a profound divide between these pro-choicers and pro-lifers who view embryo/fetuses as possessing the same right to life as newborn babies or adult human beings. Fortunately, these extreme comparisons have largely faded from contemporary discourse, as most people now acknowledge these comparisons fail to capture the complexity of the issue.

Imagine how conversations might change if people openly acknowledged that they support the moral principles underlying both the pro-life and pro-choice arguments but simply prioritize one of the principles or the other. Recognizing our shared moral foundations helps us see that even though we disagree over the issue of abortion, we might not be as different from one another as we're often portrayed to be. This in turn makes room for more respectful, less polarized dialogue.

Before moving to the next section, I want to reiterate that the preceding discussion only scratches the surface of the abortion debate. There are many more arguments and objections on both sides. My primary goal was to provide a sketch of the different positions and demonstrate that pro-lifers and pro-choicers aren't as different morally as we might believe.

Are We Really So Divided?

In the previous section, I attempted to explain that despite all the hostility, Americans are far less divided over the issue of abortion than most of us believe. That said, we're all too familiar with how some politicians and media outlets portray the debate.

Pro-lifers are often labeled as enemies of women's rights or misogynists who don't take seriously people's right to choose or practice their own religions. Pro-choicers, in turn, are often labeled "baby-killers" who disregard the sanctity of human life. These inflammatory labels, of course, divide us, making it difficult to recognize there's common ground or to engage in constructive dialogue.

It's an increasingly common occurrence in the United States for festive Thanksgiving dinners to turn acrimonious when family members start debating political or social issues at the table.

If, like the vast majority of Americans, we believe that division is a serious problem, perhaps we should strive to reduce the hostility and foster understanding when we have the opportunity to do so. Imagine a heated Thanksgiving dinner conversation in which a pro-lifer refers to a pro-choicer as a "baby-killer," or a pro-choicer accuses a pro-lifer of being misogynistic. In such moments, we can remind everyone that both sides often share a commitment to the same foundational moral values or principles, even though they may weigh them differently. That is, pro-choicers, like pro-lifers, embrace the idea that it's wrong to kill human beings because they have a right to life, while pro-lifers, like pro-choicers, believe humans should have the right to control and decide what happens with, to, and in their own bodies. That is, our moral beliefs or commitments aren't radically different.

It's also crucial to remember that politicians, media figures, and advocacy groups often profit from division. They amplify our fears, prejudices, and biases by creating sensationalist content designed to generate clicks and donations. They know we're far more likely to click on a story about an extreme, fanatical pro-lifer

or pro-choicer than a story highlighting how most of us hold nuanced views when it comes to abortion and other issues.

But we don't have to play along. We don't have to click. And we don't have to let the most extreme voices shape how we talk or think about each other.

When we frame our disagreements as a fight between good and evil, we shut down opportunities to recognize that most of our conflicts are between good people who disagree about what is the best or most just policy.

A Conversation with Dennis

Recently I organized a number of ethics discussion groups. During one session, I was sharing my thoughts about abortion and shared values, and I asked a pro-lifer, whom I'll call Dennis, whether he thought a law requiring someone to donate a kidney to a stranger would be acceptable. Dennis responded, "I know what you're trying to do. You think if you can get me to agree the law is bad, you'll get me to agree that abortion is okay."

His reaction drew laughs from those familiar with my approach, but it highlighted an important point: Dennis was hesitant to share his true thoughts and acknowledge he embraced the foundational moral principle that supports the pro-choice argument—the right to bodily autonomy—because he feared that admitting this would undercut his commitment to the pro-life position or his ability to defend the pro-life position. And Dennis thought my goal was to try to "trick" or "manipulate" him into supporting the pro-choice side.

I assured him that my goal wasn't to trick him but to show that we all embrace many of the same mor-

Media outlets in the United States are seen as leaning left or right instead of being "fair and balanced." Fox News, for example, has been called a tool of the Trump presidency, while networks such as CNN or MSNBC have been accused of being too far on the left. Both sides seem to present slanted information in a bid to gain audiences and advertisers.

Baby Farmers:
Merchants of Mercy and Murder

In 1198, Pope Innocent III ordered all churches in Italy to install what was later called a "foundling wheel." These wheels were like little boxes that could hold a newborn baby. The pope was hoping that offering mothers (or others) the opportunity to anonymously leave newborns in one of these boxes would decrease the number of unwanted babies that were drowned in rivers and creeks.

By the seventeenth century, foundling wheels were present in a number of European cities, and these wheels offered unwed mothers (among others), who were shunned by society, the opportunity to relieve themselves of the responsibility and expense of raising a child. For many, this was the only way to obtain a job and sustain themselves.

But many new mothers lived in areas where foundling wheels weren't an option. Enter "baby farming." This practice consisted of women who took in unwanted babies for a fee, and in return the baby farmer or wet nurse would care for the baby or find a family to adopt it. Oversight of this practice was lax, and too often babies were neglected, starved, or even murdered.

One notorious baby farmer was Amelia Dyer, a trained nurse from Bristol, England. In the 1870s, Dyer became a baby farmer and offered to raise unwanted children until they could be adopted. Of course, like other baby farmers, Dyer charged for this service. So far, so good.

At some point in time, Dyer decided that instead of using the fee she charged to support or find adoptive parents for babies in her charge, she would murder babies and keep the money. In 1879, police discovered what Dyer was doing. She was convicted of negligence and sentenced to six months hard labor. Yet over the next two decades, Dyer continued her baby-farming business and the murder of babies of unsuspecting parents. During this time, she moved frequently to avoid detection. She was also in and out of mental institutions.

(cont. p. 255)

(cont. from p. 254)

Her crimes ended in 1896 when a bargeman working on the River Thames pulled a parcel out of the water. He unwrapped the parcel and discovered the body of a baby girl with white edging tape wrapped around her neck. Police traced the parcel to Dyer, and at her home they found more corpses. Though accused of a single murder, she was believed to be responsible for between 200 and 400 deaths. She pleaded insanity, but the jury didn't buy this defense, and in less than five minutes found her guilty. She was sentenced to death and was hanged on June 10, 1896.

al principles or rules of thumb. I then pointed out to Dennis and others in the group that even though most pro-choicers believe that a woman's right to do what she wants with her own body justifies a woman's right to abortion, most don't see it as absolute. Most of us oppose a policy allowing people to sell their kidneys, even though such a policy is supported by the right to bodily autonomy. Most pro-choicers would claim that even though we have a right to bodily autonomy, this right is not their only moral concern. Allowing people to sell kidneys might result in a world in which those in poverty are exploited and pressured to sell their kidneys to those who are better off financially. They might also worry that such a policy might result in governments cutting off support to vulnerable populations under the assumption they could obtain money by selling their organs. Thus, we see that even though pro-choicers believe a women ought to have the right to bodily autonomy, this right is not absolute and may be overridden by other concerns.

After hearing this, Dennis admitted he believed a law requiring kidney donation was unjust. Later, when I asked pro-choicers if they believed killing innocent people should be legally prohibited—the foundational moral principle of the pro-life argument—I looked at Dennis. He seemed pleased, and I gave him a subtle nod.

When the session was over, Dennis and I chatted for almost 30 minutes, and for the next few months we reg-

ularly communicated. Experiences like these show that fostering mutual understanding and recognizing shared values can pave the way for productive conversations and new relationships.

Final Thoughts

In this chapter, we explored a prominent pro-life argument and pro-choice argument. I explained that these arguments, like most other moral arguments, hinge on a premise that articulates a foundational moral principle. I then isolated these moral principles and suggested that almost all of us embrace both of them. Specifically, we embrace the foundational moral principle articulated in Premise 1 of the pro-life argument: "Killing a being with a right to life is seriously morally wrong and should be legally prohibited." Likewise, we embrace the foundational moral principle articulated in Premise 1 of the pro-choice argument: "Women (or human beings more generally) ought to have a legal right to control or decide what happens with, in, and to their own bodies—the right to bodily autonomy."

I suggested that if we recognize our shared commitment to both of these moral principles but weigh them differently, we might not be as divided over the issue of abortion as we are frequently led to believe. This realization could foster more constructive and empathic discussions about the topic of abortion.

We also briefly examined how politicians, media figures, and advocacy organizations contribute to polarizing pro-lifers and pro-choicers. I suggested that if, like 90% of Americans, we view division as a threat to our country, we might want to strive to remember that pro-lifers and pro-choicers embrace the same moral values. We might further strive to avoid using disparaging terms for those whose beliefs are different from our own. For instance, refraining from labeling pro-choicers as "baby killers" or pro-lifers as "misogynists" can pave the way for more respectful and productive dialogue. Surely, this can't harm our relationships with others. Perhaps we can, in fact, build deep meaningful relationships with those on the other side because we recognize we're all trying to live by the values we care deeply about.

14: What Sort of Person Do You Want to Be?

About a year ago, my close friend Ben and I met up for happy hour. Ben knew I was writing this book, so after saying hello and asking how my family was doing, he said, "I have a moral question for your book."

"I'm listening," I replied.

"Last night I was reviewing my bank statement and noticed I received two paychecks instead of one last month. I know I should probably tell my boss, but I could use the extra money. Sandra and I just moved into a new apartment and bought some furniture, and you know I hate being in debt. If I keep the money, I can pay off my credit card."

Several thoughts ran through my mind, but I bit my tongue. I thought it was important to give Ben the space to share his own thoughts and feelings. I genuinely wanted to listen, hoping that by talking it through, he might answer the question for himself.

After a few seconds, Ben said, "Part of me knows I should tell my boss what happened, but if I keep the money, it won't hurt anyone. My company probably spends more money on coffee each week than what they mistakenly gave me."

Again, I fought my inclination to share my own thoughts. When Ben didn't say anything, I said, "You know I rarely have simple or straight answers to ethical questions. And I'm not entirely sure what your real question is."

"Would it be wrong to keep the money?" Ben replied.

"Are you really asking whether it would be wrong, or are you trying to find a way to rationalize keeping it, even if deep down you suspect it's wrong? I get the feeling you've already decided to keep the money and just

If you knew you could get away with pocketing extra cash from your employer and they would never know, would you do it? Would you justify the act by saying your employer doesn't pay you very much and can afford the loss?

want to feel okay about your choice. Maybe you're looking for a way to keep it and still go to sleep at night without feeling bad. If so, it might be better to just stop thinking about it."

Ben denied that he wanted to rationalize keeping the money but then did just that. He again told me how keeping the money wouldn't hurt anyone, and then for several minutes he tried to convince me he was underpaid.

"I have a question," I responded. "What sort of person do you want to be? Do you want to be the sort of person who keeps money that someone erroneously gives them or the type of person that gives it back? Which choice would make you feel proud or good about yourself?"

Discussion

Throughout this book, we've explored how we make moral decisions and judgments. As you know, we usually start by appealing to rules of thumb when attempting to determine what's the right thing to do. For example, when we hear Patrice stole money from her roommate, Sally, we might initially think: Stealing is wrong (a rule of thumb); Patrice stole money from Sally; therefore, Patrice did something wrong.

But sometimes we believe these rules of thumb should be overridden, and then we frequently, albeit sometimes unknowingly, appeal to ethical theories. Suppose we learn Patrice's mother is diabetic and neither she nor her mother had enough money to buy insulin. Knowing this might lead us to reconsider whether Patrice's actions were morally good or at least less bad than normal theft.

If we further learn that Patrice's mother's life would be in danger if she didn't get the insulin; Sally was out of town and couldn't be reached; and Patrice was going to repay Sally when she got paid the following week, our perspective might shift even further. We might think or say to ourselves: "Even though stealing is usually wrong, in this case it might have been the right thing to do. Stealing the money was the only way to save her mother's life, and Sally didn't need the money to pay rent or buy food. So, stealing the money had much better consequences than not stealing it." Essentially, we're appealing to utilitarianism to justify rejecting the rule of thumb "Stealing is wrong" and claiming stealing was right because it brought about better consequences—more happiness—than not stealing it.

Alternatively, we might appeal to the ethics of care and focus on Patrice's motives and relationships. We'd recognize that Patrice was driven by care, compassion, and love for her mother. Not only that, but her commitment to repay Sally reveals her care or concern for her roommate. Since actions that flow from care, compassion, or love are morally right or praiseworthy, according to the ethics of care, we might conclude Patrice did the right thing or what she did wasn't so wrong. We might contrast stealing the money to save one's own mother's life and stealing it to buy a new smartphone. The former, according to the ethics of care, is morally better because it was motivated by care and love, whereas the latter was likely motivated by a lack of care or love—maybe selfishness.

While it might be more efficient to allow drivers to go as fast as they want on a road, speed limits are established to enhance public safety. What's more important? Getting to your job on time or preventing a car crash?

Similarly, we've explored how we make judgments about public policy. We frequently appeal to the different ethical theories. We might appeal to utilitarianism and say it would be morally wrong to support a policy raising the speed limit to

90 miles per hour because even if higher speeds might save commuters some time, the increased accidents and fatalities would outweigh these benefits.

Becoming the Person You Want to Be

In this chapter, rather than focusing on what's the right thing to do or what makes an action or public policy morally right, wrong, just, or unjust, I'd like you to think about what sort of person you'd like to be and how you might become this person.

Do you want to be someone who actively helps those in need of assistance? Or would you prefer to be a person who ignores people in need of assistance and instead focuses on your own well-being? Do you want to say or do something when you hear someone use hateful words that hurt another person, or would you prefer to be the person who sits back and says nothing? Do you want to be the sort of person who breaks the law or doesn't abide by basic rules of morality if no one will find out? How would you like to respond if your boss unintentionally pays you extra? If you do act immorally or hurt someone, do you want to be the sort of person who convinces yourself you didn't do anything wrong, or would you prefer to be the person who confronts yourself about your wrongdoing?

Ultimately, do you want to be proud of the person you are?

Interestingly, research reveals that a large majority of Americans believe they're above average morally. Of course, a majority can't be above average. Perhaps we believe that we're above average because we want to be good people.

I suspect that almost all of us, if we're honest with ourselves, will say we want to be the sort of person who does the right thing. We want to go to sleep at night and not toss and turn as we wrestle with moral guilt and try to justify a wrong action we performed earlier that day. We strive for moral integrity, consistently trying to live up to our moral ideals. Even so, we know we aren't there yet. We know we can do better.

Do You Really Want to Be a Good Person?

Many psychologists and ethicists believe human beings have a natural and strong desire to do the right thing or be morally good people. I remember during the first week of my first philosophy class, the professor told us that Plato, one of the greats, believed people never did wrong willingly.

When I heard this, my initial thought was that Plato was incorrect. Surely, people do wrong willingly. The person who steals something they don't need—say a new pair of sunglasses or the latest athletic shoes—is doing wrong willingly. And the driver who recently backed into my car, dented it, and left without leaving contact information must have known they did the wrong thing. How could Plato have been so naïve?

I raised my hand, hoping to share my thoughts with the class. Lucky for me, the professor anticipated what I was going to say and explained Plato's reasoning before I had a chance to embarrass myself.

Essentially, Plato believed human beings are motivated by self-interest. Given this motivation, none of us will willingly do something that harms us or is against our own interest. The next part is crucial. Plato believed that living a virtuous life is always in our self-interest. Hence, since we strive to act in our own best interest and living a virtuous life is in our own best interest, we'll try to live a virtuous life. Put differently, we never do wrong willingly.

While Plato believed we do things in our own self-interest, he also felt that being virtuous was in our self-interest.

For me, whether Plato was correct or not is still an open question, and I'll leave it to you to explore whether you believe he was right or wrong. That said, for the purposes of this chapter I'm assuming that most of us want to live an authentic, moral life. We want to have moral integrity.

Moral Exemplars

How can we decide what sort of person we want to be? And once we've made that decision, how should we make moral choices or judgments that align with this vision?

Throughout the history of ethics, philosophers have emphasized the importance of moral exemplars. Moral exemplars are real or fictional individuals whose moral character and behavior we admire. They usually have the right intentions or motives, do the right thing, and have the correct beliefs concerning moral or political questions. We find exemplars to be admirable and can use our pictures of different possible moral exemplars when trying to figure out what sort of person we want to be and what actions we want to perform.

Moral exemplars are real or fictional individuals whose moral character and behavior we admire. They usually have the right intentions or motives, do the right thing, and have the correct beliefs concerning moral or political questions.

I imagine that many of you have read or heard someone say: "What would Jesus do?" This common question is an injunction to use Jesus as a moral exemplar. We should imagine that Jesus is in the same situation we're in and then try to figure out what we believe Jesus would do in this situation. We should then perform that action.

What might the pictures of different exemplars look like? I could fill a book describing detailed portraits of different types of moral exemplars, but for the sake of brevity, I'll focus on caring or loving exemplars. You can, of course, expand on these pictures if any of them resonate with you or construct your own pictures.

Caring Exemplars

As we explore the question "What sort of person do you want to be?" I'm going to focus on the ethics of care.

Why did I select this particular theory? There are two reasons.

First, most (if not all) of us believe that care (compassion, love, or charity) is a virtue, maybe even the highest or best virtue. In fact, I can't think of any religious or ethical tradition that doesn't value care, compassion, love, or charity.

Second, we want to be morally good or virtuous people, and since we believe care (compassion, love, or charity) is a virtue, we want to be caring (compassionate, loving, or charitable) people.

(Note: If you do, in fact, reject the ethics of care and embrace one of the other ethical theories—utilitarianism, deontology, and virtue ethics—there is no need to fret. Almost everything that follows can be adapted to each of these theories.)

Charity as Caring

Before proceeding, I'd like to briefly discuss a term I'll be using throughout this chapter: "charity." When I use the term "charity" in this chapter, I'm using it as a synonym of care or love. Recall, in Chapter 9, when I discuss charitableness, I define it as behavior that contributes to the well-being of others. Thus, in that chapter, helping others without being motivated by a true desire to *help* others, is considered charity. If, for example, I donated money to Save the Children in order to impress my boss or someone I wanted to date, the action was considered charitable. In this chapter, I'm going to adopt a different definition or understanding of charity.

I include charity in the following discussion because of its prominent role in Christianity, Judaism, and Islam, the three religions in the Abrahamic tradition, the first being the dominant religion in the United States. These religions permeate and deeply influence our culture, and I believe bringing them into the conversation will make what I have to say more comprehensible to many of you.

I want to emphasize that I have absolutely no intention to even suggest that one religion is better than another (or that atheism/agnosticism is best). Whether we identify as Christian, Jewish, Muslim, Buddhist, Hindu, agnostic, or anything else, I believe all of us can find value in the sacred texts of many different religions and

traditions. Christians and non-Christians alike can find value and wisdom in the Hebrew Bible and the New Testament. And Muslims and non-Muslims can find value in the Qur'an, just as Hindus and non-Hindus, Buddhists and non-Buddhists can find value in the Vedas and the Tripitaka.

Since Christianity heavily influences American culture, describing care in terms of charity can help illuminate the ethics of care. Sometimes I wonder if we ought to call the ethics of care the ethics of love or charity.

I hope you'll discover that the terms "care," "love," and "charity" are effectively interchangeable in this context.

Paul and Charity

In his First Letter to the Corinthians, Paul famously states: "So faith, hope, charity abide, these three. But the greatest of these is charity."

Paul elaborates, emphasizing charity's inner dimensions:

> *The fruits of charity are joy, peace, and mercy; charity demands beneficence and fraternal correction; it is benevolence; it fosters reciprocity and remains disinterested and generous; it is friendship and communion: Love is itself the fulfillment of all our works. There is the goal; that is why we run: we run toward it, and once we reach it, in it we shall find rest.*

When St. Paul wrote that charity was the greatest of virtues, he often meant it in the sense of doing things with love in one's heart, not just the act of giving.

When Paul discusses charity, he makes it clear that charity involves the correct inner states, emotions, motives, or mindset. Charity, according to Paul, isn't merely giving things to others or doing things that will improve others' well-being. Paul says that even if we have all the knowl-

edge of God, this doesn't make us good. In order to be good, we must have love in our heart. He's talking about love for other humans (and for God within the Christian framework). Again, if you embrace a religion other than Christianity or are an atheist or agnostic, you might interpret Paul's teaching simply as advocating love and compassion toward other human beings.

The Importance of Good Inner States, Intentions, or Motives

Notice that Paul's claim, that we must have the correct inner states or the right motivation in order for an act to have value, is the same as what proponents of the ethics of care claim. In Chapter 6, I provided the example of Kevin, a person who donated all his family's savings to a charity that provides support to malnourished children. Initially, we might have thought that Kevin's behavior was praiseworthy or admirable, to say the least. But, once we learn Kevin's true intention—he donated the money in order to anger or hurt his spouse during a divorce—our admiration wanes. Although the action itself produces good outcomes, many of us sense that his morally problematic motives diminish its value.

Why is that?

I suggested that many of us recognize the importance of having the right motives. Actions performed with self-serving or malicious motives, even if they bring about good consequences, are morally questionable. Of course, our attraction to utilitarian thinking might still lead us to see positive aspects of Kevin's act. As we've seen throughout this book, morality is complex and this sort of confusion or the feeling of being pulled in different directions is something we needn't run from. We might conclude that an act is simultaneously good and bad, right and wrong, or admirable and deplorable.

What might Paul have said about Kevin's behavior? I imagine he might have concluded that Kevin's donation to a charitable organization wasn't truly an act of charity. Even though the money would help relieve the suffering of others, Paul would claim it only counts as charity if it flowed from the right motives or inner states. More specifically, for an act to count as charity, one must be motivated by love or the true concern for the well-being of another.

If Paul's view resonates with you, regardless of your religious commitments, you may see the caring or charitable person as a moral exemplar. You might recognize that you want to live a life inspired by care or charity—that this is the sort of person you want to be. You want to be aware of and open to people's pain and suffering as well as their joy or happiness. You want to perform actions that improve their lives, and this includes alleviating their pain and suffering and increasing their well-being and happiness.

Picking or Building Your Own Moral Exemplars

If our goal is to become caring, loving, or charitable individuals, we might try to picture a caring or loving person, real or fictional, as we conceive of a moral exemplar. Perhaps you see Jesus of Nazareth, Dr. Martin Luther King Jr., or Mohandas Gandhi as your exemplar. Or your model might be a caring or loving friend or family member, priest or religious leader, or a character from a novel, movie, or television show.

Mohandas Gandhi led India to independence from Britain in 1947, and he did so through nonviolent means. Considered a highly moral hero, he was given the honorific of Mahatma, which means "venerable" or "great-souled." Surely someone like Gandhi would not hesitate to come to a stranger's aid.

When confronting a moral question, we can try to imagine how our exemplar might try to determine what to do when confronting a similar moral situation or choice. Suppose it's raining, and you're driving home from work, anticipating a dinner engagement scheduled two weeks earlier. At a stoplight, you notice an adult and two children stranded by a car that has obviously broken down. You might pause and ask yourself: Would Jesus or Dr. King pull over in a rainstorm and help two kids and their parent or caregiver, even if this might cause him

to be late for his own dinner plans? What might my caring friend do in the same situation?

Moral Exemplars and Automatic Action

One of the interesting aspects of the ethics of care (and virtue ethics more generally) is that in many situations moral exemplars don't ask themselves what is the right thing to do. Rather, their actions flow naturally from their character.

Imagine a caring, charitable exemplar who sees another person—call him Quirk—falling or dropping his groceries. The exemplar, at least my picture of the caring exemplar, wouldn't deliberate over whether offering assistance to Quirk would maximize happiness or satisfy some moral rule. Rather, he'd feel, intuit, or understand what Quirk is experiencing. My exemplar empathizes with Quirk and then naturally steps forward and offers assistance.

You probably noticed that my caring, loving exemplar is an empathic person. Empathy drives many of his decisions and actions. My caring exemplar loves his parents, children, and other relatives. And he cares deeply for his close friends, and, while his empathy for strangers is less intense, it remains genuine and motivates his compassionate responses.

When my exemplar sees someone accidently fall into the water from a boat, he doesn't think about what the right thing to do is. Instead, he instinctively recognizes someone is suffering and has a natural desire to alleviate her suffering. He might look for a life-saving ring and throw it toward the person in the water. This is the case regardless of whether it's a family member or a stranger. In fact, my exemplar wants to alleviate this person's suffering, even if he doesn't like her.

Different Motivations: Utilitarianism vs. Care

When I picture a charitable or empathic exemplar, I don't envision someone primarily committed to maximizing (or bringing about enough) happiness, as a utilitarian exemplar might be. Sure, when this exemplar has

time, he may think about the consequences of different actions or social policies. After all, he doesn't want others to suffer or experience unnecessary pain and he wants people to experience happiness. This mindset may sometimes motivate him to think like a utilitarian and focus on the consequences of his actions. But the caring exemplar's motivation is different from the motivation of a utilitarian exemplar. Whereas the latter tries to minimize pain and suffering and maximize happiness because that's the right thing to do, my caring, empathic exemplar isn't focused on doing the right thing. His compassion and empathy naturally guide him toward reducing suffering and increasing (but not necessarily maximizing) happiness.

If we ask my exemplar why he is motivated to help others and protect them from hurt or harm, he might respond: "When I see or think about someone in pain or suffering, my heart goes out to them."

If we ask my exemplar why he is motivated to help others and protect them from hurt or harm, he might respond: "When I see or think about someone in pain or suffering, my heart goes out to them. All I want to do is alleviate their pain. Similarly, when I can bring someone happiness, my instinctive desire is to do exactly that. I don't stop and calculate outcomes or try to determine what's the morally right thing to do."

In contrast, a utilitarian exemplar might explain his behavior differently: "I know maximizing happiness is the right thing to do, so I choose my actions based on possible outcomes."

Both exemplars might produce similar actions, but their motivations differ significantly. For the caring exemplar, actions flow naturally from empathy, charity, and/or compassion. For the utilitarian exemplar, actions rise from a principled commitment to maximizing (or bringing about enough) overall happiness.

A Beautiful Result

Perhaps the most beautiful aspect of using moral exemplars is that, over time, we begin to have the same thoughts, feelings, and desires as those of the exem-

plar. At first, we ask ourselves what we would do if we were a caring, charitable individual, like our exemplar. Eventually, if we're vigilant and lucky, we're no longer mimicking. Rather, we become more caring, loving, and charitable.

This transformation, I have to say, is indeed a beautiful result.

Caring, Charitable Exemplars and Hateful Speech

How might a caring, charitable exemplar respond to someone who uses hateful, harmful speech or a racial slur? Or how might we, aspiring to be more caring or charitable ourselves, respond in such a situation? (In Chapter 7, we explored hate speech and racial slurs.)

I suggest such an exemplar wouldn't approach this situation primarily in terms of political correctness or wokeness. Rather, her first response would be empathy, feeling the pain or discomfort of the individuals targeted by the hateful words as well as the pain or discomfort experienced by others present. This might motivate the exemplar to try to comfort those hurt by the speech.

However, offering comfort isn't always straightforward. My caring exemplary isn't going to downplay or dismiss the pain by saying something like, "They didn't mean what they said. Don't feel bad." Rather, as she empathizes with this individual, she'll respond in a way that genuinely takes his feelings seriously. Perhaps just communicating that she's trying to understand is all that she can or should do.

A caring exemplar might also consider saying something to the person who uttered the hurtful words, but she'd carefully avoid causing unnecessary embarrassment or additional suffering. Perhaps she'd discreetly ask the person to speak privately or approach him later when others aren't around. The goal might be helping the person understand the impact of his words, possibly leading him toward genuine remorse or apology, which might make the object of the words feel better. Or maybe, if the speaker already seems to be remorseful or ashamed, the exemplar might talk to him about human fallibility and the impossibility of being perfect, while at the same time not excusing or justifying his words.

The Ethics of Care and Doing the Right Thing

Significantly, as we become more like our exemplars, as we become more empathic or charitable, we're reminded that in many situations what matters most to us (and the ethics of care) is not what we do but what we think or feel before, during, and after our actions. We might recognize that two empathic people might act in ways that are almost the opposite of each other, yet both believe they did the right thing. Perhaps we'll conclude that talking to the person who uttered the hateful words that evening or waiting until the following day are both right. Why? Because both choices might flow from care, charitableness, and empathy.

Let's return to the example of being at a stoplight during a rainstorm and seeing an adult and two children stranded in the rain on the side of the road. Three vehicles pull up, and the three drivers roll down their windows and ask: "Are you okay?"

The adult responds, "We're fine."

When the light turns green, Driver 1 drives away and never thinks about whether he could or should have done something to help the stranded people.

Driver 2 also drives away when the light turns green, but as she is driving, she asks herself whether she did the morally right thing.

Like the first two, Driver 3 also drives away, but as he is driving, he thinks about how it might feel to be stranded in the rain. He recognizes how difficult it might be for an adult, probably a parent, to be in that situation, and wonders whether he, like the stranded adult, might have said they would be fine, even though in reality they might have been cold and scared and didn't know what to do. Upon recognizing this, Driver 3 had an immediate desire to help the stranded people. But now they're a few miles behind, and he decides not to go back because he believes the

We help strangers in trouble not because we feel we will be rewarded but because in our hearts we know it is the right thing to do. There is a charitable instinct inside of us.

stranded people probably have a cellphone and already called for help. He also thinks that it's likely someone else already saw them and pulled over to provide assistance.

All three drivers did essentially the same thing—drove away instead of pulling over and seeing if they could help. Yet, I suggest that many or most of us believe there's a moral difference among these three responses.

If we had to rank from worst to best the behavior of the three drivers, I think it would be uncontroversial to rank Driver 1's response as the least admirable. What about Drivers 2 and 3?

The ethics of care would likely rank Driver 3's behavior higher than Driver 2's behavior.

Do you have any idea why the ethics of care might justify this ranking?

Notice that Driver 2 isn't directly focused on or concerned with the well-being of the stranded people. Rather, she is concerned with morality and doing the right thing. Whether she is just committed to being a good person or is motivated by self-love and a desire to see herself as a good person is something we may never find out.

If we try to understand or feel what others are thinking and feeling before, during, and after our actions—if we empathize—we're acting out of the right motives or virtue.

Driver 3 isn't focused on doing the right thing. Morality never enters his thoughts. Rather, he's thinking about the well-being of the people in the rain. His empathy is engaged, and he has a desire to alleviate the fear and discomfort of others.

Would your exemplar be more like Driver 2 or 3?

If you choose Driver 3, it's likely because you believe that what we think about or feel before, during, and after our actions may play a greater role in moral evaluations than does what we actually do. If we try to understand or feel what others are thinking and feeling before, during, and after our actions—if we empathize—we're acting out of the right motives or virtue. Since the ethics of care puts primary emphasis on our inner life of care, love, charitableness, and empathy, this theory frequently emphasizes how we make moral decisions and what we think and feel before, during, and after our actions as opposed to our actions themselves.

Moral Exemplars and Social Policy

We can also use moral exemplars when thinking about complex social policies or laws. When considering issues like capital punishment or same-sex marriage, for example, we might ask ourselves: "How would my exemplar think about this issue?"

When contemplating same-sex marriage, I might turn to my exemplar and be reminded that he would consider the ways in which different policies or laws might affect or impact others and try to empathize with these others.

My exemplar might recognize that a law permitting same-sex marriage could distress some people who sincerely believe same-sex marriage is wrong because it violates their religious precepts or might undermine traditional family structures. At the same time, my exemplar would consider or try to understand how members of the LGBTQ+ community and their loved ones might feel if same-sex couples don't have the right to get married. After all, my exemplar believes that members of this community are people and feel pain and suffer just like everyone else.

Empathizing with everyone affected by controversial policies can be complicated and emotionally taxing. Often this doesn't lead to easy or clear answers. Initially, my exemplar might feel conflicted, concerned about how a policy has the potential to cause pain on both sides. Eventually, through thoughtful reflection, my exemplar might decide to support one policy over another. But he would still be disturbed that his chosen stance will likely cause some to experience pain or even suffer. Thus, he would likely be motivated to seek ways to alleviate unnecessary suffering and promote understanding among those with different views.

When the law was passed legalizing same-sex marriage in the USA, it made a lot of LGBTQ+ couples happy, but it also caused many of those against it to experience pain.

If the above is correct, then grappling honestly and com-

passionately with difficult questions in our private lives might be more important than what we actually decide to do. That is, struggling honestly and compassionately with difficult social and political decisions might be what's most important or what really matters.

Are Famous Politicians, Athletes, Musicians, or Actors Good Moral Exemplars?

When choosing moral exemplars, it's important to be cautious about selecting famous people, e.g., politicians, athletes, or actors. Often, we have limited knowledge about who these people really are. Sure, we know how they act in public, but we don't know what they think or feel throughout the day as they make decisions or judgments. We don't know how they treat their children, parents, friends, colleagues, and strangers they encounter. And we don't know if they act differently when no one is looking. We also don't know what motivates their behavior. According to the ethics of care or charity, that's what's most important.

I might believe, for example, that Trump would be a good exemplar because he's a good president—he's strong, he's a good negotiator, and he gets things done. Or I might think Biden would be a good exemplar—during his career he was compassionate and committed to justice and fairness.

But being a good leader, politician, or athlete is different from being a good *moral* exemplar. I repeat, we don't know how they treat others—loved ones, friends, strangers, people in need of assistance—on a day-to-day basis, especially when no one is looking. And we don't know what they think about when they go to sleep or reflect on what happened that day. Do they feel regret or pride? Do they ask themselves whether they lived up to their ideals? Do they recognize that they could have done things differently and maybe better, that they might have unnecessarily hurt others? Or do they focus on how people perceive them, without ever considering whether they truly live up to their ideals?

I remember telling a friend that Gandhi was one of my moral exemplars, and she told me about Gandhi's views of World War II and the Holocaust. Gandhi, she

informed me, believed that the Jews should have raised their arms and calmly given themselves up to Hitler and the Nazis. He believed that they should have opened the doors to their houses and offered "themselves to the butcher's knife." Just to be clear, as far as I know, Gandhi wasn't motivated by anti-Semitism; rather, this was part of his commitment to nonviolent resistance.

Gandhi, she informed me, believed that the Jews should have raised their arms and calmly given themselves up to Hitler and the Nazis. He believed that they should have opened the doors to their houses and offered "themselves to the butcher's knife."

Later that day, I confirmed that what my friend said was true. I understood Gandhi's commitment to nonviolence, but at the same time I couldn't reconcile this with my conception of what it means to be a loving parent, spouse, partner, or friend. This is just my opinion, but I believe that part of what it means to be in love with my partner or to love my children and/or friends is to do what I can to ensure that they don't suffer unnecessarily. I can't imagine offering my loved ones, or anyone else for that matter, to the butcher's knife. I can't imagine sitting back and allowing loved ones to be put in concentration camps, raped, and killed.

I'm not suggesting that I'm definitely correct about this. You may, in fact, agree with Gandhi and believe that the morally best people would avoid violence, even if the result would be the violent death of the people closest to them. If you and I were friends or happened to be sitting next to each other in a park or train station, I hope we'd talk about this and try to get a better idea of what sort of people we want to be and who or what might make a good exemplar.

The Collage Approach to Moral Exemplars

Given that famous people, close friends, and relatives aren't perfect, it might make sense to create our own moral exemplars. We can think of this process as the creation of a collage.

For me, creating this collage entails thinking of a handful of people who have different traits that I ad-

mire and would like to possess. I imagine a large piece of cardboard shaped like the profile of a head, and I am pasting pictures of different people onto it.

One person who's part of my collage is a distant relative, Yolanda. In social situations, people just want to be around Yolanda. She's emotionally open and tolerant, and when you're talking with her, she makes you feel heard. I think her greatest quality is a true desire to understand people, and this involves listening.

While some of us must force ourselves to listen to others, Yolanda seems to want to listen. She isn't actively forcing herself to listen or faking interest. She's truly interested in what others have to say, what others think and feel. She asks questions as she tries to gain a deeper understanding, and her interpretations or judgments of others are charitable. As a result, those she's talking with feel special.

But, for some reason, Yolanda has a poor relationship with her father, her only living parent. She can't forgive some of his mistakes and isn't characteristically charitable when thinking about him or describing him. At times I've wondered if she realizes she's more charitable to strangers than she is to her dad.

Thus, when thinking about how to navigate the complicated parent-child relationship or similar relationships, I don't ask myself how Yolanda would act or what she might think, do, or say if she were in the same position. Instead, I turn to Steve, a friend whose relationships with his children inspire me. Steve, is calm, loving, supportive, and nonjudgmental when interacting with his children. Rather than tell them what to think or do, he truly wants to understand what they're thinking or feeling. His wife once told me that Steve never yelled or seriously raised his voice when interacting with them.

Nobody is perfect, even your mentors and exemplars. But you can pick and choose traits you admire from several people and create a collage of admirable qualities to emulate.

That's not to say that Steve didn't share his wisdom with

his children. He did. But he did so after learning what they were thinking and feeling. He once told me about the conversation he had with one of his children who wanted to quit college during the final year and join a band. His child ended up both finishing college and joining the band.

Even though Steve taught me how I want to interact with my children, I have no idea how he interacted with his aging parents or other relatives outside of his immediate family. Because of this, I have a different exemplar I look to when deciding how to interact with close family members, especially during times of conflict or stress. Here, I look to my wife, Avi, who consistently withholds judgment when someone seems irritable, moody, or uncaring. Instinctively, she wonders whether they've had a difficult day or if past experiences make it harder for them to respond with patience or kindness. Similarly, I have a different exemplar—two, in fact—for workplace interactions.

I think it's also essential to remember that each of us is a work in progress. If I decide to become an Uber driver, teacher, bartender, or attorney, I'm not going to do the job well at first. Over time, I'll see others who do things that I praise or admire. I learn from them how to do the job better. These others are my role models and can be seen as nonmoral exemplars. Even after I locate my work exemplars, I still make mistakes. I can't immediately take on the qualities they possess. In addition, I might discover, as time passes, that one or more of my work exemplars isn't, in fact, someone I want to be like or emulate. Perhaps our personalities are too different for their methods to work for me. This is par for the course.

Morality is the same. It takes time and effort to discover or create our exemplars. It takes time to build our own collage. And when we finally build our collage, it takes time to become the person we want to be. And over time our collage might change as we come to value different traits or aspects of character.

Returning to the Ethics of Care

If, as I'm assuming, most of us aspire to become caring, charitable, empathic individuals, we might not know how to achieve this. Fortunately, research on compassion and empathy provides practical strategies

Instead of arguing your position so hard, try listening to the other person's story, including their background and views. You might learn something that makes you understand their perspective.

that can help us become the sort of person we want to be.

First—and this may be obvious—we might want to develop our listening skills and try to become nonjudgmental, active listeners. This involves trying to understand others or where they're coming from. Someone may tell me, for example, that they believe Gandhi was correct, and victims of aggression should lay down their arms and not resist violence, even if this will likely result in death.

Because I disagree, my immediate desire might be to jump in and tell them my opinion. Notice that my desire to understand the other is now displaced by my desire to explain to them why I disagree or believe they're incorrect. It takes a lot of effort to resist this desire and instead try to understand why they believe what they believe or where they're coming from.

Over time, I may discover that listening and trying to understand others is pleasurable. I enjoy listening as someone tells me parts of their life story and what led them to believe or feel what they're believing or feeling. And there's another bonus: listening and trying to understand frequently results in closer relationships with other human beings.

If we're truly committed to understanding others, we might try to develop our active listening skills and remember to ask follow-up questions when we don't understand someone. I'm not just talking about understanding someone's words. I understand that the person sitting next to me at a wedding believes Gandhi was correct about nonviolence. What I might not understand, however, is why or how someone could believe that allowing our loved ones to die without a violent response to an aggressor is better than trying to save their lives, even if this involves violence. By asking more questions, I'll hopefully be better able to empathize with the Gandhi supporter.

Closely related to asking follow-up questions is reflecting back to the speaker what we think they're telling us. We want to do our best to understand others, and when we reflect back to them what we believe they're thinking or feeling, we provide them the opportunity to correct us if we're wrong or are missing something. I might say to the Gandhi admirer, "It seems like nonviolence is the most important thing to you. I imagine that when you think of violence it makes you sad or anxious."

The Gandhi admirer can agree or disagree. Regardless, this provides them the opportunity to try to make sure I understand what they believe and how they feel about nonviolence. Not only that, but when we reflect back to others, they recognize or discover we are listening to them, we care. This truly is a gift.

Another important step is to practice perspective-taking. This involves trying to see something from another's perspective and trying to imagine how we might feel or what we might think if we were in their shoes. This is what Steve did so well and is, I think, the heart of developing empathy.

Paying attention to our own emotional responses is another crucial step. After listening to someone whose views I challenge, like the Gandhi supporter, I might experience strong emotional reactions that affect my response. When I think back on my response (or while I'm responding), I might listen to myself and wonder why I was so emotional or came on so strongly. Am I insecure about my own views? Is there something about the other person that I don't like? If so, am I proud or happy about this? I might think about my exemplar and how he would express himself if he were thinking and feeling what I was thinking or feeling.

When I think back on my response (or while I'm responding), I might listen to myself and wonder why I was so emotional or came on so strongly. Am I insecure about my own views? Is there something about the other person that I don't like? If so, am I proud or happy about this?

We should also try to recognize and acknowledge our own biases and stereotypes. I might, for example, distrust Democrats. When I hear a Democrat say that

she supports gender-neutral bathrooms, I might immediately say to myself: "Here we go again. Another Democrat going off the deep-end."

I may disagree with much of what Democrats support, but this doesn't necessarily mean they are bad or immoral people. As we've explored throughout this book, most of us embrace the same rules of thumb and ethical theories. Our disagreements frequently stem from how much weight we put on these theories. Remembering this might allow me to listen to what this Democrat has to say or to try to understand her.

The Democrat may explain that her neighbors have a trans child, and the child is home-schooled because of the teasing they undergo on the playground. She may also explain that the child and their classmates are especially uncomfortable when the child uses a bathroom, regardless of which bathroom they use. As I listen and try to understand, I realize that this Democrat feels pain as she empathizes with her neighbor.

I'm not suggesting that we should agree with those whose views are different from our own. I'm not saying we should agree with the Democrat who supports gender-neutral bathrooms. Each of us should decide what we think is best. But discovering that this Democrat is a compassionate, empathic individual may prompt us to think about whether our own views or beliefs are correct. I know there are times that I have to push myself to understand others whose viewpoints are different from my own in order to truly examine my own beliefs. And, as stated throughout this book, deep, honest, respectful conversations frequently bring us closer together. If we want to be caring, empathic people, presumably this involves building connections with a variety of people, not just those whose views are the same as our own. These "others" are likely good people, just like our friends and family members.

Of course, as I practice these steps, I try to remember to ask myself how my exemplar might act if he was in a situation similar to mine.

Obstacles to Making the Right Choices or Doing the Right Thing

As our exploration is coming to an end, I think it's important to be aware of obstacles or impediments to

making the right choices and doing what we believe is the right thing to do.

Even if we've discovered or constructed moral exemplars, there will be times when we make the wrong choice. We make wrong choices at work, when driving, or when trying to find the best recipe for chocolate chip chewies. It shouldn't be surprising that we'll make the wrong choice or do something we regret when interacting with our friends and loved ones, colleagues, or strangers.

It's important not to be too hard on ourselves or beat ourselves up when we make the wrong choices. To state the obvious, we're only human, and humans make mistakes. (Some ethicists believe we shouldn't even aspire to be perfect or to be moral saints, as that would require us to disregard other aspects of our lives—like being humorous, enjoying a day in the woods, or developing other talents, such as becoming a good football player or learning to play the guitar.)

Knowing that we'll make mistakes, it's helpful to be aware of some of the obstacles to being the sort of person we want to be.

Fear

Fear often prevents us from making the right choice or following through with what we believe is the right choice. Imagine walking on the beach and seeing someone physically strike what appears to be their spouse or partner—let's say we see a man hit a woman (but it could be the other way around). The man is screaming at the woman, and it appears he's going to strike her again.

Sometimes people fear others because their background or views feel alien to them. Ignorance of others can lead to people questioning others' motives, which leads to distrust and fear.

My immediate reaction might be a desire to try to stop him. Although at the time I don't analyze why I want to stop him, if later in the day I'm asked why I thought that was the right thing to do, if I'm a caring, charitable person, I'd likely explain that I didn't want anyone to suffer un-

necessarily. "I suppose when I saw what was going on, the caring part of my personality was automatically engaged. My primary concern was protecting the victim from getting hurt."

Let's suppose, however, that even though I wanted to do what I could to stop the man, I didn't do much at all. I tried to make my presence known, without getting too close, hoping he'd see me and stop.

Later in the day, when I think about my behavior, I might feel embarrassed or ashamed. I believe the right thing to do was to step in and try to calm the man down or somehow get him to stop hitting the woman. At the same time, I was fearful, believing that if I got involved, the man would strike me. Fear trumped or overpowered my desire to do what I believed was the right thing.

Just to be clear, I'm not suggesting that in this sort of situation the right thing is to intervene and get beaten up. But there might be other options. Knowing fear might affect what I think or do, when I'm fearful I might remember that my moral exemplar is creative. With this in mind, I might discover a safe way to stop the man from hitting the woman. Perhaps I can scream to get others' attention or look for a group of people who might be willing to help me.

Of course, fear isn't limited to physical pain. I may learn that someone who has power over me—say, my boss—pays women less than men for the same work. Even though I believe this is wrong and want to discuss it with my boss, fear may stop me. I'm scared that if I say anything, I may lose my job. Remembering my exemplar, I may ask myself if there's a creative way I can live up to my own moral commitments and at the same time not risk losing my job.

Cognitive Dissonance

Another common obstacle is *cognitive dissonance*—the mental discomfort we feel when our beliefs conflict or when our actions contradict what we believe. For example, I may believe I'm a good person, and I also believe a good person would speak with their boss when they learn women are paid less than men for the same work. But when I learned this was happening, I stayed silent. That silence created cognitive dissonance. It became difficult to hold both beliefs at once: that I'm a good per-

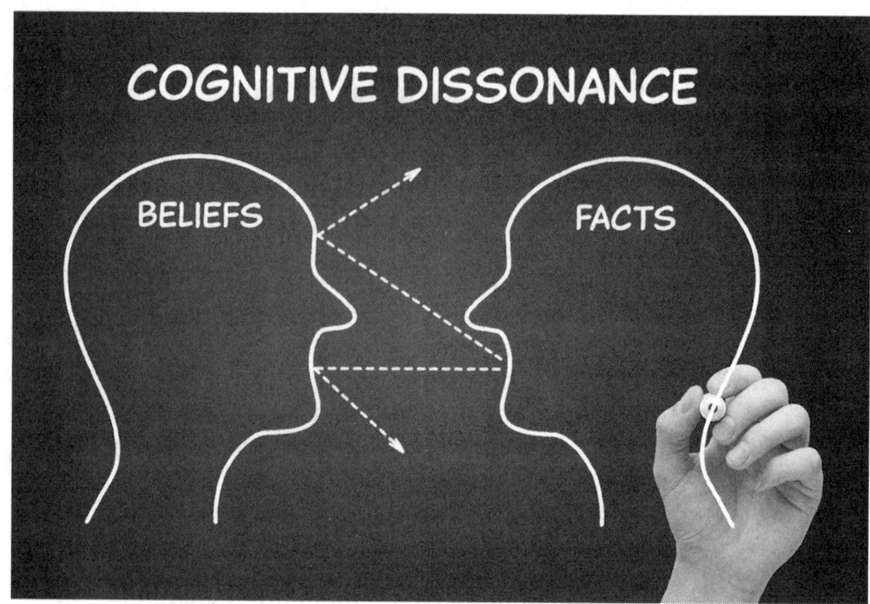

Cognitive dissonance occurs when your beliefs do not match up with the facts of the real world. The result is a feeling of anxiety or guilt or even fear. People resolve the situation by either changing their belief system or simply denying the facts or making up new "facts."

son, and that a good person wouldn't remain silent in the face of injustice.

According to cognitive dissonance theory, when we experience this internal conflict, we experience discomfort and have a natural desire to resolve the dissonance and thereby alleviate the discomfort. Crucially, we're often not aware that this is happening. The dissonance and the urge to resolve it can operate unconsciously.

A relatively easy way to resolve cognitive dissonance is to change one of our beliefs. I might convince myself, for example, that men and women doing the same job shouldn't necessarily be paid the same salary. Maybe I'll convince myself that men get more done in eight hours than do women; thus, the salary discrepancy is justified, and I have no reason to talk with my boss. Again, I may not realize that this belief shift was driven by my discomfort. I may never see that my new belief was shaped by an unconscious desire to ease the tension I felt.

As we'll see when we explore the other reasons why we might not be the sort of person we want to be, cognitive dissonance or a similar psychological process might play a role.

The Allure of Gratification

A third obstacle to doing what we believe is the right thing is the allure of gratification. We might lie, break a promise, or steal something because we believe doing so will lead to good consequences for us.

For example, on Halloween night when we're driving to a Halloween party, we see a pile of pumpkins in front of a roadside farmer's market. We pull over, hoping to buy a pumpkin that we can give to the hosts of the party when we arrive, but unfortunately the market is closed until the following day.

Now that we've thought about it, we really want a pumpkin. We look around and nobody is present. We realize we can steal the pumpkin and not get caught. Yet, we believe stealing is wrong.

Our belief that stealing is wrong and our desire to steal the pumpkin are in conflict, and this conflict is uncomfortable. Again, we have a natural desire to reduce the discomfort, according to cognitive dissonance theory.

One way to reduce the discomfort is to change our belief that stealing is wrong. We might, for example, convince ourselves that since it's the night of Halloween, the pumpkin won't be sold in the future and will likely rot in the sun. Thus, stealing the pumpkin won't hurt the owner of the market or anyone else. We might furthermore tell ourselves that if we steal the pumpkin, no one will even notice it's missing. We thereby convince ourselves that stealing isn't wrong in this situation. The result is that we can steal the pumpkin and not experience the discomfort resulting from cognitive dissonance.

The late American businesswoman Leona Helmsley once famously said that only the "little people" pay taxes. She justified the tax fraud she committed by patting herself on the back that she was too smart and rich to have to pay. The justice system disagreed, and she was sent to prison for her crime.

A different way we might alleviate the discomfort is by convincing ourselves we

don't really want the pumpkin. Thus, the cognitive dissonance is resolved, as we no longer have the desire to do something—steal the pumpkin—that we believe is morally wrong.

Can you think of a creative way to deal with this situation, to get the pumpkin and stay true to your moral commitments?

Peer Pressure

A fourth major obstacle to acting morally or living up to our own moral commitments is peer pressure. In an empirical study known as Solomon Asch's Conformity Experiment, a participant was placed in a group with several confederates (individuals who posed as participants but, in reality, were members of the research team). The group was shown two cards. The first had one line and the second had three lines of different lengths. The members of the group were asked which of the three lines on the second card was the same length as the line on the first card. The correct answer was obvious. Confederates provided their answers first, and they intentionally provided the wrong answer. Would the participant agree with the others (who she thought were participants) even though she believed it was the wrong answer?

When we hear the term "peer pressure," we often think of it in terms of young people being pressured to drink alcohol or use drugs, but it can occur in many other business, political, and social situations among people of all ages.

Seventy-five percent of the participants gave the wrong answer at least one time during the experiment. The researchers concluded the participants sometimes gave the wrong answer, believing it was wrong, in order to fit in with the majority. A second interpretation is that the participants sometimes doubted themselves and concluded that the majority were correct.

Regardless of why the participant gave the wrong answer, we can see that if we're surrounded by people whose moral beliefs are different

from our own or people whose empathy isn't being engaged, we might adopt their beliefs or feelings. We might just want to fit in, or perhaps we begin to question our own moral judgment and conclude the majority must be correct.

In my experience, peer pressure is a particularly problematic obstacle when we're with others who share our political beliefs. My friends and I might, for example, support the same presidential candidate, and during a debate, the candidate proposes a policy that would require the government to pay reparations to Black people for slavery. Even if I've thought about the issue and truly believe this would be unjust or wrong, since everyone else is praising this policy, I might say nothing. Or I might go so far as to say things that I don't believe in order to fit in. I might even question my own beliefs and assume I'm wrong given what my friends believe. Of course, the opposite could be true. I could believe reparations are justified and not say anything because the majority believe they're wrong.

Obedience to Authority

A fifth obstacle to doing the right thing is obedience to authority. If you haven't read about Stanley Milgram's experiments, which showed that many of us would give people dangerous, life-threatening electrical shocks if someone in authority tells us to do so, you might want to look it up.

Necessity or Need

Sometimes necessity pushes us to compromise our moral principles. For example, I might feel justified stealing food from a grocery store if I believe it's the only way to feed strangers in need.

Situations like this can easily give rise to cognitive dissonance. I may believe stealing is wrong, yet I also believe I should steal food to help an unhoused family with young children whom I regularly see in my neighborhood. I might believe that everyone deserves enough food, regardless of their financial situation, and that stealing is the only way to meet this urgent need. As a result, I find myself torn between two moral convictions: stealing is wrong, but allowing people to go hungry is also wrong.

Because we naturally seek to ease cognitive dissonance, I might resolve the tension by convincing myself that feeding the hungry isn't my responsibility, even if the need is right in front of me. Once I adopt this belief, my urge to steal food weakens or even disappears.

If a young child steals food to keep from starving, is that an immoral act? What about stealing a car to take a dying person to a hospital? There could indeed be certain situations in which defying authority is necessary in order to do the right thing.

Notice that in this example, I wasn't consciously thinking about what my moral exemplar might do. Nor was I appealing to the ethics of care, love, or charity. Perhaps if I had tried to truly empathize with both the store owner and the hungry parents and children, I could have thought of a creative or thoughtful way to respond. Perhaps talking to the store owner would be a good first option.

Living with Moral Integrity

Living up to our moral ideals, living a life of moral integrity, is challenging, to say the least. It's natural, even inevitable, that we'll occasionally fail. Yet recognizing these obstacles and practicing the techniques for building empathy and compassion can help us move closer to the person we wish to become.

Ultimately, morality isn't about perfection. Rather, it's about sincerely striving to be caring, compassionate, charitable, and empathic, especially when doing so is difficult.

Final Thoughts

Before signing off, I'd like to indulge myself and share something I've been thinking about for several years. Throughout this book, we've explored what it means to be a moral person, to do the morally right thing, and

to have morally good or praiseworthy character traits. Might there be a different way to talk about morality?

Perhaps, rather than focus on morality, we should instead focus on beauty. Let me explain.

Imagine receiving a text or email from the teacher of your child, your niece, or the child of a close friend. Let's call her Barbara.

Barbara's teacher writes: "Two of Barbara's 6th grade classmates were picking on a third child, calling her ugly and even threatening violence. I started to run over to the three children, but before I could get there, Barbara stepped in. She told them to knock it off. When they asked why they should stop, Barbara asked them to imagine how they would feel if they were the ones being teased and threatened. I was so proud of her and thought you'd be proud too."

An hour later, Barbara comes to your house. You want to hug her and say something. What would be the best, most accurate way to describe what Barbara did?

Would you want to tell Barbara that she did something morally good or praiseworthy? Or would you want to tell her she did something beautiful?

I'm not sure, but I think I'd want to describe Barbara's actions as beautiful. It's something that fills my heart with warmth and joy, in the same way that I feel warmth and joy when I see an excellent movie, read a moving short story, or hear a great song.

I don't know how many times I've said that the moral life is beautiful, perhaps because of its complexity. And more than once I've said that I'm amazed humans have the capacity or desire to try to figure out what's morally right and then strive to do it. I've said that this desire or capacity is beautiful.

Maybe, just maybe, living a life of moral integrity is better described as living a beautiful life. It's a life we can appreciate when we step back and contemplate it. It's the life of an artist. Think of Pablo Picasso, Drake, Anton Chekhov, or John Steinbeck. They can't consult a book or manual that will tell them how to finish their songs, paintings, or novels. They wrestle with the materials of their craft, trying to create a special work of art.

The same is true of ethics. We wrestle with the moral materials of our lives. In the past, I fantasized about creating an app that could tell people what's the right thing to do. By now, you probably know that I've come to see

that as a fool's errand. There are no reliable calculators or moral algorithms. There are no easy answers.

Instead, we think carefully about the situation and its context. We turn to our moral exemplars, strive to be empathic, and talk things through with trusted friends. Even after all of that, we sometimes don't have clear answers and may be left wondering.

Perhaps we should approach ethical decision making in the same way that we'd approach painting a picture or writing a short story, play, or song. We should learn from the past, accept that we and others make mistakes, strive to be empathic and compassionate, and finally be creative and ask ourselves: What would be the most beautiful way to act?

For Further Research

Aristotle. *Nicomachean Ethics,* 3rd ed., translated by Terence Irwin. Indianapolis: Hackett, 2019.

Beckwith, Francis. *Defending Life: A Moral and Legal Case Against Abortion Choice.* Cambridge, England: Cambridge University Press, 2007.

Bentham, Jeremy. *An Introduction to the Principles of Morals and Legislation.* London: Clarendon Press, 1996.

Blustein, Jeffrey. *Care and Commitment: Taking the Personal Point of View.* Oxford, England: Oxford University Press, 1991.

Bush, George H. W. "Commencement Address at University of Michigan," Ann Arbor, MI, May 4, 1991.

Chekhov, Anton. "The Lady with the Dog." In *Selected Stories of Anton Chekhov,* translated by Richard Pevear and Larissa Volokhonsky. New York: Modern Library, 2000.

Festinger, Leon. *A Theory of Cognitive Dissonance.* Stanford, CA: Stanford University Press, 1957.

Foot, Philippa. *Virtues and Vices and Other Essays in Moral Philosophy.* Berkeley, CA: University of California Press, 2002.

Gilligan, Carol. *In a Different Voice: Psychological Theory and Women's Development.* Cambridge, MA: Harvard University Press, 1982.

Greene, Joshua. *Moral Tribes: Emotion, Reason, and the Gap Between Us and Them.* New York: Penguin, 2014.

Haidt, Jonathan. *The Righteous Mind: Why Good People Are Divided by Politics and Religion.* Visalia, CA: Vintage, 2012.

Hobbes, Thomas. *Leviathan,* edited by Christopher Brooke. New York: Penguin Classics, 2017.

Kant, Immanuel. *Groundwork for the Metaphysics of Morals,* edited and translated by Mary Gregor and Jens Timmermann. Cambridge, England: Cambridge University Press, 2012.

Kant, Immanuel. *The Metaphysics of Morals,* edited by Lara Denis and translated by Mary Gregor. Cambridge, England: Cambridge University Press, 2017.

Lakoff, George. *Don't Think of an Elephant! Know Your Values and Frame the Debate.* Junction, VT: Chelsea Green, 2004.

Milgram, Stanley. *Obedience to Authority: An Experimental View*. New York: Harper & Row, 1974.

Mill, John Stuart. *Utilitarianism*, 2nd ed., edited by George Sher. Indianapolis: Hackett Publishing, 2001.

Noddings, Nel. *Caring: A Feminine Approach to Ethics and Moral Education*, 2nd ed. Berkeley, CA: University of California Press, 2013.

Paul the Apostle. First Letter to the Corinthians, especially 1 Cor. 13:1–13.

Pluckrose, Helen, and James Lindsay. *Cynical Theories: How Activist Scholarship Made Everything about Race, Gender, and Identity—and Why This Harms Everybody*. Durham, NC: Pitchstone, 2020.

Rachels, James. *The Elements of Moral Philosophy*. New York: McGraw-Hill, 2018.

Rawls, John. *A Theory of Justice*, revised ed. Cambrdige, MA: Harvard University Press, 1999.

Singer, Peter. "Famine, Affluence, and Morality." *Philosophy & Public Affairs* 1, no. 3 (1972): 229–243.

Thomson, Judith Jarvis. "The Trolley Problem." *The Yale Law Journal* 94 (1985): 1395–1415.

Thomson, Judith Jarvis. "A Defense of Abortion." *Philosophy & Public Affairs* 1, no. 1 (1971): 47–66.

Williams, Bernard. *Moral Luck*. Cambridge, England: Cambridge University Press, 1981.

Philip Zimbardo. *The Lucifer Effect: Understanding How Good People Turn Evil*. New York: Random House, 2007.

Podcasts

Carol Gilligan (Ethics of Care) https://www.youtube.com/watch?v=sxfbWdShtSo.

Immanuel Kant (Duty and Categorical Imperative): https://hotelbarpodcast.com/podcast/episode-165-kants-categorical-imperative/.

Jeremy Bentham (Utilitarianism) https://podcasts.apple.com/nz/podcast/utilitarianism/id463701671.

John Rawls (A Theory of Justice) https://www.youtube.com/watch?v=KOjykdXDhJs.

Jonathan Haidt (Moral Psychology and Political Division) "The Moral Roots of Liberals and Conservatives," TED — Haidt discusses how different moral values shape political divisions. https://www.ted.com/talks/jonathan_haidt_on_the_moral_mind.